T0319905

Modelling European Mergers

Theory, Competition Policy and Case Studies

Edited by

Peter A.G. van Bergeijk
Erik Kloosterhuis
NMa (The Netherlands Competition Authority),
The Hague, The Netherlands

(With the assistance of Simon Bremer)

Edward Elgar
Cheltenham, UK • Northampton, MA, USA

Published by
Edward Elgar Publishing Limited
Glensanda House
Montpellier Parade
Cheltenham
Glos GL50 1UA
UK

Edward Elgar Publishing, Inc.
136 West Street
Suite 202
Northampton
Massachusetts 01060
USA

A catalogue record for this book
is available from the British Library

Library of Congress Cataloguing in Publication Data
Modelling European Mergers : theory, competition policy and case studies / edited by Peter A.G. van Bergeijk, Erik Kloosterhuis ; with the assistance of Simon Bremer.
    p. cm.
    This book reports on the economic content of the conference "Simulation Models for Merger Cases: Theory and Practice."
    Includes bibliographical references and index.
    1. Consolidation and merger of corporations—European Economic Community countries—Congresses.. I. Bergeijk, Peter A. G. van, 1959– II. Kloosterhuis, Erik, 1951–

HD2746.55.E86M63 2006
338.8'3'094—dc22   2005051893

ISBN 1 84542 318 6

Printed and bound in Great Britain by MPG Books Ltd, Bodmin, Cornwall

Contents

Figures and Tables

FIGURES

TABLES

Contributors[1]

Claes Bengtsson, European Commission (EC), DG Competition, Chief Economist Team

Peter A.G. van Bergeijk, The Netherlands Competition Authority (NMa), Economic Council

Patrick van Cayseele, Chairman, Department of Economics, KULeuven; Professor of Industrial Organization, UvA

Eric van Damme, Professor at CentER for Economic Research and Tilburg Law and Economics Center (TILEC), Tilburg University

Fabio Massimo Esposito, Italian Competition Authority (Autorità Garante della Concorrenza e del Mercato), Market Analysis Office

Marie Goppelsröder, University of Geneva

Marc Ivaldi, IDEI Researcher; Professor, École des Hautes Études en Sciences Sociales, CEPR, Toulouse

Pieter Kalbfleisch, The Netherlands Competition Authority (NMa), Director-General

Erik Kloosterhuis, The Netherlands Competition Authority (NMa), Deputy Director of the Merger Control Department

Neelie Kroes, European Commissioner responsible for Competition Policy

Jan de Maa, Merger Control Department, The Netherlands Competition Authority (NMa)

Arvid Nilsson, Swedish Competition Authority (KKV)

Joris Pinkse, Department of Economics, The Pennsylvania State University

Lars-Hendrik Röller, European Commission, Directorate-General for Competition, Chief Economist

Maarten Pieter Schinkel is Associate Professor of Economics, Department of Economics, University of Amsterdam. He is co-director of the Amsterdam Centre for Law & Economics (ACLE) and Deputy Economic Counsel to the Board with The Netherlands Competition Authority (NMa).

Carsten Smidt, Danish Competition Authority (KS), Chef Special Advisor, Infrastructure and Sector Analysis

Niklas Strand, Swedish Competition Authority (KKV)

Gregory J. Werden, US Department of Justice, Antitrust Division, Senior Economic Counsel

Gijsbert Zwart, Netherlands Bureau for Economic Policy Analysis (CPB)

1. All of the contributions reflect the views of the authors and do not necessarily claim to be those of the respective affiliations.

Preface

Neelie Kroes

European economic policy makers have achieved a great deal since the mid 1980s. The European internal market was created in 1992, and the euro was introduced in 1999. More recently further member states joined the European Union in May 2004. The Union presently encompasses 445 million consumers and has a Gross Domestic Product in excess of ten thousand billion euro. The modernization of European competition law and the decentralized implementation by the Commission and the national competition authorities is a centrepiece in this process to further strengthen the internal market.

The achievements of the past cannot be an excuse for neglecting the challenges of the present. Further strengthening and constant vigilance are needed to improve on what has been achieved so far. This is why peer review and exchange of information on, for example, detection, evidence gathering, legal procedures and economic analysis all play an important role within the European Competition Network. Indeed, we all know that the consistent application of competition policy in a decentralized structure is at the heart of the proper functioning of the internal market.

The origins of this book stem from a conference. On November 23, 2004 the Dutch merger control department of the Netherlands Competition authority organized an international conference on empirical methods in merger control. The topic of the conference "Simulation Models for Merger Cases: Theory and Practice" was well chosen and reflected the increasing weight that competition policy attaches to economic analysis.

Participants from twenty member states, Switzerland and the United States agreed on the relevance of discussing the practice of economic analysis, in particular how empirical analysis is performed to strengthen competition policy enforcement in Europe.

Accordingly, it is foreseen that this commendable initiative will be followed up through a series of annual conferences to be organized under the umbrella of the ECN. In that sense this book is the starting point for a series of conferences, designed to share best practice in economic analysis across the ECN.

Modelling European Mergers: Theory, Competition and Case Studies is an important work because it reports on a discussion among competition policy experts about the strengths and weaknesses of economic methods that have been and will be increasingly used in merger cases. It shows the potential of the decentralized European enforcement structure at its best. Economists at the European competition authorities learn from each other's experiences and discuss their approach with colleagues and academic experts from other jurisdictions. In addition the transparency offered by this book allows firms, consultants, economists and legal experts (lawyers and judges) to assess the pros and cons of the empirical economic approach to merger analysis. I am sure that the debate will continue to be fruitful and interesting.

Acknowledgements

This book is an unexpected result of the decision in mid 2001 to install two economic counsels at the Netherlands Competition Authority NMa. The economic intuition of Anne Willem Kist, the first Director-General of the NMa, was essentially to reduce the risk of errors of type I (false convictions) and of type II (false clearances) by getting a better understanding of the respective economic effects of violations and enforcement, both at a general macro level and in individual cases.

At the start of the research project, desk research by, amongst others, Michiel Verkoulen and Bas Postema made it clear that most problems regarding the implicit mandate of the two economic counsels were to be expected in the analysis of merger control. Here the tools required for the analysis were not available in the Dutch research market (this was in contrast to, for example, regulation and cartels where both *ex ante* and *ex post* analysis appeared to be quite possible and had actually been done before by academics and policy makers). We were fortunate because around this time Kasper Roszbach could participate in a workshop on this issue that was organized by our colleagues at the Swedish competition authority. His enthusiastic report on the workshop by Gregory J. Werden and Luke Froeb helped us to structure the research agenda on the use of simulation models from which this book is the direct spin-off. As the director of the Dutch merger control department, Hans Schönau provided guidance and the financial support to actually use merger simulation models in house in order to investigate past decisions empirically and to estimate the direct economic effects of merger control. This part of the research project was undertaken by Bas Postema. His master's thesis at Tilburg University (supervised by Eric van Damme) was honoured by third prize in the ENCORE MA thesis competition 2004.

Pieter Kalbfleisch, the new Dutch Director General, refocused the project emphasizing the need to reduce in particular the errors of type I in competition policy. During 2004 we were assisted by Marie Goppelsröder and her academic supervisor Maarten Pieter Schinkel. The results of the research project were presented in Paris at the Economic Modelling Conference 2004 and in Brussels where we met with the Chief Economist Team and discussed for the first time the idea of an international conference on this topic aimed at providing a platform for the economists working at the European competition authorities. This conference was organized in November 2004 by Gerard la Bastide and Marloes de Boer. It became a great success, not only from the perspective of the sophistication of the economic analysis of merger control in Europe as this book shows, but also because of the positive reactions of all participants to the idea of the creation of an economist working group within the European Competition Network.

This the project continues alongside others by Simon Bremer, who skilfully helped us editing the present volume.

Without implication we thank Anne Willem, Michiel, Bas, Kasper, Hans, Eric, Pieter, Marie, Maarten Pieter, Gerard, Marloes and Simon for their support and input into this project.

Peter van Bergeijk
Erik Kloosterhuis

1. How to Merge with Law and Economics?

Peter A.G. van Bergeijk and Erik Kloosterhuis

One of the challenges that competition policy makers in Europe presently face is the question of how to ensure that advances in modern economics take their proper role in antitrust and merger control. On the one hand, many recognize by now that empirical economics can offer a big step forward in rational decision making. Applied economics offers the possibility to test often implicit legal reasoning on the basis of actual data and explicit and consistent models. Economics puts outcome first. It answers the question "Does it matter (and why)?", thus helping authorities to detect and set priorities on a rational and empirical basis. Of course increasing the weight of economic analysis in competition policy is not a panacea (it is an antidote at best) and it clearly carries a price tag. Arguably *ex ante* legal certainty may decrease as decisions can be contested on new grounds, procedures may take longer since an economic investigation can be time consuming (it can, incidentally, also be quite time saving) and scarce resources including management time are drawn upon when economists get more intensely involved. Economists are and will be involved in all phases of the enforcement cycle, either to deliver or to judge the evidence. Economists will analyse smoking guns, legal documents, raw data and the results of advanced methodologies like those discussed in this book.

Importantly, the proponents of the economic method often suggest a manner of exactness that does not do justice to measurement issues and theoretical ambiguities that plague the dismal science. Accordingly, one needs to recognize that the advantage of being able to say something exact will be lost if one pretends to be exact when one cannot sensibly be. The solution to this problem is by no means self evident and is rightly a recurrent theme in this book. This is the more true since this is an issue that needs to be solved by interdisciplinary means, i.e. between the economic and the legal professions.

The story of merger modelling told in this book is in a sense a metaphor for the role and advent of economic analysis as a decisive tool of competition policy. European economists and mathematicians in the nineteenth century pioneered many concepts that are key in the competition policy practitioner's tool kit today. Indeed, it is impossible to find a textbook in industrial economics without proper reference to Cournot, Bertrand, Pareto and Stackelberg.

Europe, however, lost the lead mainly because policy makers in the United States moved early and thus the United States has a much longer history in antitrust. American authorities have been pioneers of economic applications even though the key economic insights were developed at the European continent. Accordingly, much is to be learned from the US. Indeed (as is the case with many empirical techniques in industrial organization) the US was first in using applied simulation models in a competition case setting. This book in a sense is thus a reflection of the European learning process in industrial economics. It shows the speed with which new concepts can be absorbed and applied in actual case settings.

The speed of the economist may, however, prove to be his Achilles heel if the courts are not yet up to the proposed and implemented changes in the approach to merger analysis. Thus we now face the difficult task of integrating economic and legal analyses. This book aims to provide a stepping stone to bridge the "gap" between legal and economic professionals that are involved with competition policy. We firmly believe that transparency about the strengths and weaknesses of economic tools will provide both an antidote against too ambitious claims and a sound basis to judge what can indeed be achieved by established economic methods.

1. PLAN OF THE BOOK

This book reports on the economic content of the conference "Simulation Models for Merger Cases: Theory and Practice" that was organized in November 2004 by the merger control department of Netherlands Competition Authority NMa. The conference formed part of the informal activities during the six months that The Netherlands held the chair of the European Union.

The book consists of the seven edited papers that were presented at this conference. To these chapters we added six invited papers that are based on the reflections by the referees and panellists. The venue of the conference was well chosen. In the inspiring Paulus Church in the centre of The Hague the contributors both preached the gospel of simulation modelling and were able to admit that one needs faith before one can recognize doubt. The contributions have been organized in three parts: on policy, analysis and application (in actual cases), respectively.

Policy Perspectives

The first part of the book sets out the European policy perspective against the background of an increasing weight of economic analysis in competition policy. Lars-Hendrik Röller, sets the stage by discussing the benefits of using high quality empirical economic analysis as a tool of decision making in competition policy. Analysing the trend towards economics and the integration of economists at DG COMP, Lars-Hendrik identifies three areas where economics will be very valuable: in identifying theories of harm, in developing guidelines and block exemptions and in providing economic evaluation both *ex ante* (as in merger cases) and *ex post* (as in evaluations of competition policy). While the case for more and better economics is clear, Lars-Hendrik also warns against the dangers of abuse by non specialists and is very clear in his advice on communication. If an economist cannot communicate his results to the legal profession and convince the court, then his efforts are a waste of time. Given the need to assure business confidentiality and for strategic reasons he proposes the creation of a working group of economists within the European Competition Network. In this manner peer review within the ECN gets a practical and convincing footing.

Pieter Kalbfleisch offers a more personal perspective on this manner of evidence, both from the point of view of a (former) judge and as Director-General of the Netherlands Competition Authority NMa. He points out that the decentralized decision making structure in Europe may actually provide a comparative policy advantage as the different experiences of different jurisdictions offer a great many opportunities to learn (in addition to cross fertilization between the authorities this may actually provide scientists with a unique testing ground for competing theories on the optimal competition policy). Moreover, being "second movers" in the market for market supervision, the European competition authorities can use the experiences of other jurisdictions such as the United States to their benefit as these experiences are a useful practical guide to the implementation of new legal and economic concepts. Pieter stresses that models can be used to investigate errors of type I and type II in merger control and he discusses some of the main findings for The Netherlands. He also foresees a good market for simulation models as a tool to estimate outcome.

Analytical Perspectives

The second part of the book offers scientific reflection on the method of simulation models discussing the strengths and weaknesses of simulation models in merger analysis. The first chapter in this part is by Gregory J. Werden. Gregory is one of the "founding fathers" of the simulation models that invaded European merger control and he has actively helped to export the methods that he developed with Luke Froeb, giving many workshops. Many chapters in this book are indirect spin-offs of the Werden–Froeb lectures that were held in the European continent around the turn of the millennium. Gregory suggests that unlike the present situation in most European jurisdictions, modelling could start in the first phase of the investigation as the modelling process gives structure to data collection and helps to identify the important economic issues. Gregory provides a useful overview of game-theoretic concepts illustrating the spread of economic theories about unilateral effects to agencies and courtrooms.

Next comes a contribution by Marie Goppelsröder and Maarten Pieter Schinkel. Marie and Maarten Pieter argue that any sound economic approach to merger control should allow for possible efficiency increases. They welcome Europe's new horizontal merger guidelines that offer openings to take merger-specific improvements into account. Starting from an exposition of the basic Bertrand and Cournot model, they investigate the span of applied modelling analysis in terms of construction and empirical calibration in order to show where the measurement problems of these models in actual competition policy making may arise. They offer a new measurement tool to address these problems.

Eric van Damme and Joris Pinkse discuss the benefits and limitations of modern merger analysis from the academic econometrician's perspective. They deal both with game–theoretical issues and insights from experimental economics and explore choices to be made in the empirical implementation. Thus their chapter offers the reader a useful guide on the issues of the appropriate assumptions in applied work and the tradeoff between accuracy, speed and relevance.

Marie, Maarten Pieter, Eric and Joris caution against too much faith and against mechanically applied economic models, essentially because the world is too complex to expect accurate prediction. Still decision makers need indications of the (order of) magnitude of the potential effects since in theory almost anything goes. This means that they need numbers even if these numbers are rough estimates. Yes, we agree with the critics of simulation models that it is impossible to be exact. However, explicitly modelling mergers provides at least a consistent, transparent and traceable means to get at the order of magnitude of the economic impact of contemplated mergers.

Based on a statistical analysis of the notifications and decisions by the European Commission, Marc Ivaldi argues that further investigation is needed of the errors of prediction in allowed, remedied and prohibited mergers.

Anyhow, no competition authority or economic policy maker is willing to put all her cards on one method as they will always try to use all available information to evaluate as many relevant aspects of a case as possible. Thus the cases in this book offer a menu of empirical instruments that can be used as part of the tool kit of a merger control department.

An Important Caveat

The third part of this book consists of detailed discussions of seven European cases in which simulation models have been used. Each case is discussed by economists that have actually been involved in the case either as a modeller or as a decision maker. It is important to note that the views expressed by the authors are not necessarily those of the competition authority concerned, since a case is not decided on the merits of the economic evidence alone. Since for the sake of readability and conciseness the chapters focus on economics per se, other relevant factors that were not included in the econometric exercises may be left out of the picture, or at least are not given the weight that they deserve in making actual decisions on mergers. We refer the reader who is interested in the actual decision and the multitude of arguments that played a role in the actual case to the decisions in which the modelling has been done (see Table 1.1)

Table 1.1 Decisions regarding the discussed cases

Chapter	Decision
7	M. 2978 Lagardère/Natexis/VUP (EC)
8	C 6353 Davide Campari/Milano Barbero 1891 (AGCM)
9	M. 3216 Oracle/PeopleSoft (EC) and C 04 – 0807 (DoJ)
10	3386/182 (NMa)
11	Elsam/NESA (2004) (KS)
12	107/2003 (KKV)
13	2001 – C/C – 34 and 2001 – C/C – 41 (Raad van Mededinging)

Note: European Commission (EC), Autorità Garante della Concorrenza e del Mercato (AGCM), Department of Justice (DoJ), Nederlandse Mededingingsautoriteit (NMa), Konkurrencestyrelsen (KS), Konkurrensverkets (KKV)

Seven Case Studies

The cases provide a good overview of the state of the art of European merger simulation modelling in an applied economics setting. Moreover, the seven cases offer a wide range of experiences, both regarding the decisive impact of the model in the decision making process with respect to the modelling techniques.[1] The seven cases cover six different areas. Our sample includes basic goods (bread), luxury goods (aperitifs), essential goods (electricity), essential facilities (port activities) and intellectual property goods (literature, software). The seven cases illustrate the six key modelling approaches currently in use including (antitrust) logit models, an auction model, Bertrand and Cournot models, an econometric model and supply function models (that are typical for the antitrust analysis of energy markets).

Table 1.2 provides a snapshot of the chapters and the cases that are discussed, giving details on products, country coverage and modelling techniques that were applied in the case. The table testifies to the substantial progress that has recently been made in the empirical analysis of mergers in Europe. The modelling exercises in this book cover 11 geographical markets.[2]

Table 1.2 Characteristics of case studies in this book

Ch.	Year	Product	Country	Authority	Model
7	2003	Literature	F, B, CH	EC	Econometric
8	2004	Aperitifs	I	AGCM	Antitrust logit
9*	2004	Software	EU, USA	EC	Auction
10**	2003	Electricity	NL, UK, G	NMa	Cournot, supply function
11	2004	Electricity	D	KS	Supply function
12	2003	Bread	SW	KKV	Antitrust logit
13	2001	Port activities	B	RvM	Betrandt

Notes:
B Belgium, CH Switzerland, D Denmark, EU European Union, F France, G Germany, I Italy, NL Netherlands, SW Sweden, UK United Kingdom, USA United States of America.
* See also Chapter 4 by Gregory Werden
** See also Chapter 3 by Pieter Kalfleisch

2. LESSONS FROM THE CASE STUDIES

Three questions can put the case studies into perspective:

- Have the models been useful tools to discriminate between anti-competitive mergers and harmless mergers?
- Do the benefits of modelling exercises outweigh the costs of detailed empirical analysis?
- What lessons (i.e. best practices) can be deduced from these experiences?

Discriminatory Power and Errors

As to the decisive impact of the models, it is interesting to note that the range of "verdicts" runs from cases that led to a clear "no, unless" as in the case of the Nuon Reliant merger that is discussed by Gijsbert de Zwart and Jan de Maa to cases with a clear "yes" as in the Hessenatie–Noord Natie case discussed by Patrick van Cayseele. Moreover, intermediate cases are covered as in the case of Campari–Barbero discussed by Fabio Massimo Esposito where the model predicted problems but the merger was consumed because the market shares were below the legal threshold. The empirical analysis of Oracle PeopleSoft offers another interesting intermediate case where, as Claes Bengtsson discusses, the simulation model in the first phase identified potential problems that could be clarified during the second phase and thus the model acted both as a "no" factor and a "yes" factor. It is thus clear from the seven case studies that the technique of simulation modelling provides for a discriminating tool with a potentially decisive impact on the judgement in actual merger cases.

Several cases provide a useful and sophisticated perspective on the errors of type I and type II of the simulation models. Arvid Nilsson and Niklas Strand analyse the Cerealia Schulstad merger case that was cleared and where the model predicted price changes in the range of 1.5 to 2.7 percentage points whereas the actual price increase amounted to 4.7 percentage points. The model thus was not very accurate (with the realization almost 50 per cent outside the confidence interval). Indeed actual price increases could appear to be sufficiently large to invalidate the original decision. In the Italian Campari Barbero case (that was eventually cleared because the operation was below the thresholds) predicted price increases were in the range of 11 to 15 percentage points.

Future market developments will provide useful perspectives on the errors of type II. The European Commission's Oracle PeopleSoft case shows how an initial "no" may change in a final "yes", thus emphasizing one of the sources of the errors of type I: bad or insufficient data.

Costs of Merger Simulation

One of the reasons to use simulation models is that calibrated models appear to require less data and thus less time to produce an answer. To a large extent this time-saving characteristic may be superficial. For one thing, a well organized data collection procedure started early may yield the data necessary for advanced and detailed econometric analysis quickly, as the discussion of the Hachette–Editis case by Marc Ivaldi illustrates. Moreover, once merger control proceeds beyond the first phase in which screening takes place, the collection of good and sufficient data is important although time-consuming even for relative simple calibrated models. The organization of the data collection is thus key. Any how, all contributors to this book stress that the starting point of any modelling exercise must be a thorough knowledge of the industry in order to be able to select the appropriate modelling strategy. This implies that merger simulation will not result in cost reductions in terms of required man-, woman- and brainpower and that external scientific advisors may be essential in building up analytic capacity at the competition authorities. Since scale effects can be expected in the use of models the formation of a relatively small group of specialists within each competition authority (along the lines of DG COMP's Chief Economist Team) as well as a close cooperation between them may be advisable.

Best Practice

We think that the most important "best practice" that is to be distilled from the contributions to this volume is "be modest, realistic and critical". Case handlers, academics and policy makers agree that this "best practice" is key to the future role of applied models in antitrust and they act accordingly as the case studies make clear. We summarize this advice in four principles:

- Do not opt for the perfect method. A large negative bias can be acceptable if the reduction of errors of type I is an independent restriction of competition policy making.
- Report confidence intervals based on alternative methods and parameter constellations (especially a sensitivity analysis for the key elasticities is in order).
- Check the results against alternative sources and methods. An essential feature of a model is to be able to reproduce the strength of competition, i.e. price–cost margins.

- Communicate with an audience of legal professionals in mind *and* according to the Einstein Principle: "Everything should be made as simple as possible, but not simpler".

NOTES

1. In addition Appendix I of Chapter 8 gives an overview of the Campari Bols merger.
2. Note that this is only a subset of the cases where simulation models have actually been used (see, for example Table 11.1 for the case of Denmark).

PART ONE

European Policy Perspectives

2. Economic Analysis and Competition Policy Enforcement in Europe

Lars-Hendrik Röller[*]

The role and scope of modern economic analysis in competition policy in Europe has been changing. Characterizing this change as one towards a "more economic approach" could be misleading. Indeed, antitrust and merger analysis has been based on economics for a long time. The question for effective enforcement is not one of "more" or "less" economics, but rather what kind of economics and especially *how* the economic analysis is used – or indeed sometimes may be abused – in the context of guidelines or cases. The change in the practice of European competition policy is all about the way in which economic principles and economic evidence are brought to bear in the context of decision making. The assessment of decision making in light of modern economic principles that are robust and empirically tested, as well as the reliance on a number of empirical methodologies that help identify a theory of harm, is at the core of this trend. However, there are also non-significant dangers and there is a clear potential to abuse economics, not least by various special interests. As a result, the proper and professional interpretation and generation of economic evidence is essential for the credibility of the process to work towards better decision making.

In this context it is interesting to recall that there seems to be a substantial increase in the use of economics in antitrust. However, the market share of economists in antitrust has not increased accordingly.[1] This is somewhat troubling, not only from the point of view of economics as a profession, but also for the overall quality of decision making (for instance in terms of type I and II errors). Without entering into the debate of what constitutes an "economist", which the previous observation unavoidably triggers, I believe it is fair to say that an increase reliance on economic analysis implies a need for stronger economic expertise.[2]

The purpose of this chapter is to provide some input into the debate on the proper contribution of economics and economists in EU competition policy. The chapter starts by summarizing the reasons for the trend towards the increased significance of economics (and economists). It then discusses

13

various applications for economics, emphasizing the different roles of economics in guidelines and cases. The chapter then argues that these developments raise a number of challenges, and suggests that an effective enforcement needs to address these potential dangers and pitfalls in order to reduce the potential for abuse of economics. In the end, the increased reliance on economics and economists will only be successful if it is able to contribute towards better decision making. And that is exactly the way it ought to be.

1. THE TREND TOWARDS ECONOMICS

The emphasis on economic analysis in the decision making at DG COMP has been a steady process, which has been reinforced in the last few years.[3] The introduction of the non-horizontal merger guidelines has been a recent indication of this process. Earlier examples include guidelines on horizontal and vertical agreements. Moreover this trend is continuing today. For instance, there is an internal review process – with the intent to publish guidelines – on the policy regarding the abuse of a dominant position, where recent advances in economics play an important factor. There are plans for guidelines in the area of non-horizontal mergers, pending the outcome of some recent cases in court. Finally, and perhaps most challengingly, is the area of state aid, where a reform process is being planned for the coming years. Again, one of the main principles will be to base decision making in the area of state aid control on a sound economic assessment, both in terms of operationalizing a more explicit analysis of the distortions of competition, as well as the use of the concept of market failures.

What are the reasons for this trend? Former Commissioner Mario Monti, an economist himself, has emphasized the importance of economic analysis and soundness during his tenure. Together with Director-General Philip Lowe, who is also an economist, a number of reforms have already taken place. As far as future developments are concerned, Commissioner Neelie Kroes has made it clear that economic reforms, and the contribution of competition policy towards these goals, are at the top of her agenda.[4]

More broadly even, the Barroso Commission is committed to improve Europe's economic performance. An important goal of the revamped Lisbon agenda is to increase European competitiveness. Competition policy – including the upcoming reforms in the area of state aid control – is at the heart of making Europe more competitive. Perhaps even more importantly, competition policy is one of the policy fields where the European Commission has significant legal powers. It is therefore essential to use the instruments of competition policy (including sector inquiries into financial and energy markets) to the benefit of the European consumer and the European economy. This can only be done by ensuring that the rules and practices of competition policy enforcement are in line with sound economic thinking. Without going into the substance of the debate surrounding the goals set out in the proposed revamped Lisbon agenda, let me just submit that a firm grounding of competition policy and state aid control in sound economic principles not only makes sense for the European economy, its welfare and its citizens, but it will also be necessary in order to preserve its significant role. A primarily legal defence of competition decisions is ultimately unlikely to leave the considerable enforcement powers of the Competition Commissioner in tact.

Another crucial factor is the Community Courts. For example, in its conclusion on *Airtours vs. Commission*,[5] the Court of First Instance concluded that the decision of the Commission "far from basing its prospective analysis on cogent evidence, is vitiated by a series of errors of assessment as to factors fundamental to any assessment of whether a collective dominant position might be created". The judgment indicated that the Courts are in favour of better economic evidence when reviewing the Commission's decision. The Court also addressed the required standard of evidence, arguing that it was the Commission who had to produce convincing economic evidence of a situation of collective dominance. On February 15th, 2005, the European Court of Justice ruled on the appeal against the judgement of the Court of First Instance annulling the decision of the European Commission prohibiting the merger of *Tetra Laval/Sidal*.[6] In its press release the European Court of Justice stated that "The fact that the Commission enjoys discretion in economic matters does not mean that the Community Courts must refrain from reviewing the Commission's interpretation of information of an economic nature, especially in the context of a prospective analysis".[7]

Finally, the use of economic analysis is useful when working closely and on a consistent basis with other jurisdictions. This is the case for DG COMP and its US sister institutions, i.e. the FTC and DoJ. More generally, reliance on economics – rather than other policy considerations – has the potential to reduce conflict between jurisdictions.[8] Increased emphasis on economics will not, however, lead to complete convergence, in the sense of one-to-one decision making. Important differences and asymmetries exist and will continue to exist.

In sum there are a number of factors for the trend toward the use of economic analysis in EU competition policy. Moreover, there are reasons to believe that this trend will continue, even though this raises a number of challenges that need to be addressed. We will return to this point below.

2.   THE INTEGRATION OF ECONOMISTS AT DG COMP

There are a large and increasing number of economists at DG COMP. Approximately 200 out of the over 700 officials working at DG COMP have an economics background, where "economics" relates to all areas of economics (including macroeconomics), as well as other related business disciplines (such as accounting). The number of officials that hold a PhD in economics is about 20, 10 of which are currently working in the office of the Chief Competition Economist.

2.1   The Office of the Chief Competition Economist ("CCE")

The office of the CCE consists of 10 specialized economists, the Chief Economist Team ("CET"), all of which hold PhDs in Industrial Organization. Approximately, half of the members are permanent EU officials, while the others are temporary agents. The CCE gets involved in selected cases and guidelines. There are two basic functions that the CCE performs[9]:

1.   "Support function": one member of the CET gets assigned to the case team, reporting to the CCE. In this way, the CET is closely involved with the day-to-day work of case teams, getting involved early on in the investigation, giving economic guidance and methodological assistance.
2.   "Checks-and-balances function": the CCE provides the Commissioner and the Director-General with an independent opinion on all cases and guidelines that the CET was involved in, in particular before a final decision to the College of Commissioners.

Given this dual function, it appears reasonable to keep the position of the Chief Economist separate from the other Directorates and attach it directly to the Director-General.

One of the primary objectives of the CET is to work closely with others economists across DG COMP. The integration of economists at DG COMP is different from its US sister institutions – the DoJ and FTC – in the sense that case teams are put together in an interdisciplinary way. In other words, case teams are put together early on with both economists and lawyers. This EU model may have advantages, as it facilitates the coordination between legal and economic lines early on in cases, yet it may also have disadvantages. In particular, it is sometimes argued that the line of reporting needs to be to an economic hierarchy in order to have the proper quality controls as to facilitate high-quality economic analysis. To the extent that the case team as a whole does not report to the CCE, this may be a concern. However, the EU model partially addresses this concern: the case team member that is also a member of the CET does report back to the CCE on the economic direction and analysis. Overall, the institutional set-up of the CCE and CET constitutes somewhat of a hybrid model in this regard, where members of the CET are full member of the case team, yet also report back to the CCE.

2.2 Economic Capacity Building

The mandate of the CCE states that "he shall act as a focus for economic debate within DG COMP, in liaison with other Commission services and in association with the academic world". The CCE is thus responsible to help capacity building with regard to economic expertise. The investment in economic expertise and capacities is central in ensuring that the full value of economics can be realized in the decision making process.

In order to contribute towards capacity building, the CET has initiated the following activities.

1   Economic Advisory Group on Competition Policy ("EAGCP")
     The EAGCP is a group of around 15 leading academic economists in the area of industrial organization. They advise DG COMP and the Commissioner on selected important policy issues.
2   Annual FORUM
     An annual internal one day event where DG COMP discuss past cases with EAGCP, in particular with regard to the appropriate usage of economic analysis.
3   Economic Seminar Series on Competition Policy
     A monthly public seminar, where external academic speakers are presenting their latest work in the field of competition policy.
4   Brown Bag Lunch
     An internal luncheon, where DG COMP case handlers discuss economic analysis of cases in an informal setting.
5   EU–US bilateral meetings of economists
     Economists from DG COMP, the FTC and DoJ meet to discuss past case work, in particular economic methodology.

There are also a number of external links that the CET maintains and develops through speeches, participation in conferences and events. For example, there are close links to the Association of Competition Economists ("ACE") and the Centre for Economic Policy Research ("CEPR").

There are plans to further strengthen the capacity building in economics, which is essential for the timely and proper employment of economic and econometric applications to competition policy and the decision process by antitrust agencies. One possibility is to create closer links between economists within the European Competition Network ("ECN").

3.   ON THE ROLE OF ECONOMICS

The use (as well as abuse) of economic principles and analysis may vary substantially across the particular policy context. In my view, one can broadly differentiate between three areas – depending on the time horizon – where economics and economists can potentially strengthen anti-trust enforcement.

3.1 Cases – Identifying Theories of Harm

The first area is case work, which is frequently of a rather short-term nature, in particular in merger cases. Economists are used to provide analysis into an otherwise fundamentally legal process. Both theoretical and empirical approaches are typically brought to bear in the context of cases. Nevertheless, the roles of theory and empirical testing are rather different.

Economic theory is necessary to "frame" a case, which in turn is fundamental to arrive at a particular theory of harm. This typically involves information about the structure of the industry, the firms, the structure of demand and the technology, as well as a preliminary understanding of possible strategies. It will always be the first step in an economic analysis in the context of a competition case (including, in principle, a state aid case).

The extent to which economic theories are useful in this context may be called economic principles.[10] The development of new theories (such as de novo models, which are based on alternative assumptions, leading to radically different results) are likely to be less influential in the context of case proceedings for a number of reasons,[11] including the difficulty of communicating a new theory in a rather short period of time. As a result, one is tempted to conclude that the analysis of the merit of new theories is best left to the academic journals, where a long and rigorous peer review will ensure consistency and ultimately empirical relevance.

The goal of a plausible theoretical framework in the context of a particular case is to come up with testable hypothesis concerning the theory harm. In this sense, competition policy decisions need to be based on empirical evidence. Economic theory is not meant to provide the answer by itself. There is nothing that can be true in a general. As a result, every theory needs assumptions. In the end, the effects of a merger or a pricing practice will depend on the circumstances, that is the assumptions and implications of models have to be checked against observable facts and data. Checking which theoretical framework is consistent with which pieces of observable and available evidence, is fundamental to decision making and is known in social sciences as the *identification* problem.

An effective economic analysis in the context of a case has to be based on empirical analysis, which in turn needs to be rooted in solid economic principles. The key challenge is to identify a particular theory (or behaviour) from other alternatives. Identification thus involves the uncovering of empirical evidence that is only consistent with the claimed theory, and is inconsistent with other theories.

There are numerous ways to achieve identification. The most common approach is to check the assumptions that have gone into the theoretical framework. However, this is not always the best way to achieve identification. For example, certain assumptions may be necessary, but not sufficient, for an alleged anti-competitive practice. Another way of identifying is through the *comparative statics* of a theoretical framework. The basic idea is to use the prediction of economic models and compare these to observable data.[12] There are a number of well-developed methodologies available in empirical industrial organization, such as simple correlations over time and/or markets, other types of reduced form evidence, as well as more structural and semi-structural empirical evidence. Finally, there are natural experiments, which are – as the name suggests – situations where an exogenous events has happened, such as a particular regulation. The reaction by the market can then be attributed solely to this exogenous event, under the assumption that nothing else did change. In such circumstances, the reaction by the market might then be used to reject certain theories in favour of others.

Clearly, the practicality of all the methods for identification depends on the theoretical framework employed as well as on data availability and/or other political and institutional developments.

3.2 Guidelines and Block Exemptions

The second area where economic reasoning is important is guidelines, and similarly block exemptions. In contrast to cases, which are by definition rather context specific and as a result do not lend themselves easily to generalizations, guidelines give general rules that describe the frameworks that will be used under various circumstances. In this sense, guidelines are more general and more long-term.[13]

The challenge for economists in developing guidelines is to be able to provide relatively simple rules that are yet economically sound in a large set of circumstances. Guidelines cannot spell out the entire economic analysis that would take place in the context of a case. Yet they are useful in providing guidance as to the kind of theoretical and empirical analysis to be undertaken, and thus raise predictability and legal certainty.[14]

There are a number of guidelines and block exemptions that are currently either up for review – such as in the area of state aid – or are being considered for the first time – such as the guidelines for non-horizontal mergers or abuse of a dominant position. The above mentioned challenge – i.e. simple, yet economically sound – is apparent in all these policy areas. To be clear, and we will return to this point again below, introducing more sound economic reasoning in these areas of policy should not be seen as a trade-off between rules vs. discretion. Basing policy on solid economic principles does not imply that guidelines can not be simple and predictable.

3.3 *Ex Post* and *Ex Ante* Analysis

The third area is yet even more long term in nature. There are two contributions from economics: *ex post* and *ex ante* analysis.

Ex post analysis is undertaken in order to understand how antitrust, state aid, and merger decisions have effected markets. A prominent example is the *ex post* studies that attempt to categorize antitrust and merger decisions in terms of a type I and II error framework. The main difficulty in this line of research is to establish the relevant counterfactual, i.e. what would have happened if some relevant alternate decision had been taken instead. This is of course a very well-known problem in social sciences, and particular in policy evaluations: just because nothing changes after the policy intervention does not mean that there is no effect, or vice versa.

Economics and econometrics can be useful to establish the relevant counterfactual. Counterfactuals can be derived from theoretical models and/or econometric analysis. The central empirical challenge is to control for other factors that might have had an influence on market outcome, in order to identify the impact of the policy decision itself. Industry and market knowledge is crucial at this point in order to understand the precise factors involved (i.e. to design the experiment: timing, factors, causality). In the end the proper empirical methodology to answer the relevant question of impact boils down to a multivariate analysis – i.e. an econometric analysis.

Another problem occurs when the policy decision is *endogenous*. By endogenous we mean that the market outcome and the policy decision are linked, which can easily happen in practice. If so, the *ex post* evidence may be biased. For example, if a policy maker subsidizes only competitive firms, then an *ex post* study that compares the performance of subsidized firms to non-subsidized firms would find that the subsidy program was indeed very successful. The example shows that the way the subsidy is allocated is important to understand the correct effectiveness of the subsidy as measured through an *ex post* study. This is yet another important empirical issue that *ex post* studies need to address.[15]

Despite its inherent empirical difficulty, the importance of *ex post* evidence can not be underestimated. The know-how obtained from *ex post* evidence helps to justify or refine policies and practices. It is the only logical justification for the effectiveness of an agency's decisions, which is evermore important in times where the impact of competition policy actions is increasingly scrutinized.

The second area where economics is important is *ex ante* analysis, such as in market monitoring.[16] Market monitoring is the analysis of whether or not markets function well, in principle prior to possible antitrust action. *Ex ante* analysis, such as market monitoring, is important, since whenever an agency relies exclusively on complains, firms' incentives may be negatively effected. The challenge for market monitoring is to identify instances when markets do not function, such as anticompetitive conduct or the existence of entry barriers. One contribution of economics is to help define a set of indicators that signal a high likelihood of a particular competition problem.

A related issue is that of priority setting. While market monitoring is primarily about the *likelihood* of a competition problem, priority setting is about the *magnitude* of the competition problem. Economics can be used to identify situations where the likely impact of the alleged anticompetitive conduct or barrier is small. Given scarce resources, however, an agency needs to allocate its priorities such that the expected return is highest. In other words, assuming a consumer standard, resources should be devoted to cases and activities where the expected loss to consumers is highest. Priority setting is thus about both the likelihood of an infringement and the magnitude of the loss to consumers.

The same principle applies to the instrument of sector inquiries. For example, Commissioner Kroes has recently announced[17] to launch sector inquiries into energy and financial markets.

4. CHALLENGES FOR ECONOMICS AND ECONOMISTS

As was argued above, there appears to be an increased role of economics in competition policy. In this section, I would like to mention some challenges that economics and economists need to face in order to ensure that the full value added from using economics in antitrust decision making is realized.

4.1 Effective Enforcement

The first challenge is to ensure that the increased use of economic reasoning and analysis does not erode effective enforcement. Clearly, if the economic analysis is not done in a proper and professional way, it can be misused in the sense of introducing type I and II errors. Take, for example, the employment of econometric evidence. As discussed above, econometric evidence is a methodology to disentangle the individual impact of an event, when other factors are also at work. In a sense, it is the logical extension of a simple correlation, and thus in principle essential information for establishing evidence in favour or against a theory of harm.

On the other hand, econometric evidence can also be misused in a number of ways. As anyone knows who has "played" with econometric estimation, robustness is always an issue.[18] In other words, the estimated effects depend on the specification and assumptions. This is, of course, neither surprising nor could anyone fundamentally object to it. Indeed, if the results would not depend on the assumptions, one should be worried! Nevertheless, a careful understanding on how the assumptions link to the results needs a certain understanding of the underlying methodology. Without such expertise, one is at the mercy of some "defunct economist's" econometric estimates.[19]

A related issue is that there is often a substantial asymmetry in resources between outside parties and an antitrust agency. Resources do matter, in particular in providing labour-intensive empirical evidence. If the asymmetry is too large, relying extensively on economic analysis has the potential for distortions, resulting in a reduction of effective enforcement.

The proper and professional usage of economics is also relevant in the context of the so-called revamped Lisbon agenda, which is focussed on more economic growth and competitiveness. In this context, it is argued that competition policy enforcement should be closely linked to generate economic benefits. As the objective of antitrust and merger control is to ensure the proper functioning of the market to the benefit of the consumer, increased reliance on economic analysis is essential to contribute towards the Lisbon agenda.

In the area of state aid control, Commissioner Kroes has recently announced[20] that more weight should be given to market failures. This is the correct emphasis if the Lisbon agenda is taken seriously, as it focuses state aid in areas where such aid contributes towards economic growth.[21] Only when market failures exist, is there a potential for state aid to increase the "economic cake". An important aspect of this "more economic approach" in the arena of state aid, is to ensure that market failures actually exist. In theory there are many market failures and the likely existence of market failures is an empirical issue. As with econometric evidence, reliance on market failures as a rationale for state aid requires a proper and careful analysis of the economics and economic evidence. Merely paying lip service to some vague market failure argument will not lead to effective enforcement.

4.2 Legal Certainty

The second challenge to economics and economists in competition policy is legal certainty. Predictability and legal certainty are important aspects of competition policy law. There is real economic value to transparency and predictable procedures. Running a successful businesses is all about the ability to be forward looking. Management decisions about technology, markets, competitors are complex and determine the success or failure of companies. Increased regulatory uncertainty raises costs, threatens survival and potentially reduces economic growth.

More generally, clarity and credibility are likely to increase the effectiveness of a policy. The effectiveness of an antitrust agency is not solely determined by the decisions that it takes. To a large extent, the impact of an antitrust agency can be attributed to the decisions that it does not have to take. Indeed, if competition rules were well understood, and the consequences of breaking these rules are reasonably unattractive, less antitrust action would indeed be needed. In this sense, the credibility of the antitrust agency is a significant determinant of its effectiveness.

The challenge to economics is to ensure that economic analysis does not come at the expense of legal certainty and predictability. As John Vickers recently pointed out,[22] legal certainty and economic principles are not substitutes but complements. In other words, given the current state of affairs, we can get more of both, in particular in the context of guidelines. By enhancing predictability and legal certainty guidelines contribute towards the effectiveness of competition policy.

A related challenge – or criticism – is that economic analysis delays proceedings, thereby raising the costs of enforcement. Notwithstanding whether the value from additional economic evidence justifies additional delay, it is debatable whether economic analysis necessarily delays things. Besides, one may seriously wonder whether legal analysis and argumentation is often less prone to "unnecessary" delay, in the sense of helping to reducing the likelihood of type I or II errors. In any case, the production time of economic evidence and analysis – including more sophisticated evidence – needs to be kept within reason.

4.3   Communication

The third challenge to economists is communication. To a certain extent this is largely responsible for the lack of market share by economists. An effective economist in antitrust needs to be able to communicate with non-economists, in particular lawyers. This point cannot be overstated. For example, the effectiveness of the members of the CET at DG COMP depends crucially on their ability to communicate their views to others, possible with less or little training in formal economic modelling. The bottom line is communicate or be ignored, which takes on added value in the institutional set-up in Europe, and perhaps even more so under modernization.

The importance of communication goes beyond interactions between antitrust agencies and/or parties. Most importantly, economists need to be able to communicate their economic reasoning and empirical evidence to the courts. Independent of whether the courts decide to facilitate the process by which economic arguments and analysis can be exchanged – for example through court appointed experts, training of judges, or more specialized courts – it is incumbent to economists wanting to have an impact in competition policy law that they are able to explain their economic reasoning clearly to non-experts in economic modelling. The challenge to economists is thus to be understood, yet not to trivialize or even abuse.

In sum, there are a number of challenges facing economics and especially economists in order to ensure effective enforcement and minimize potential abuses. Many of these challenges can only be met through a process of economic capacity building, which is a challenge in itself.

4.4   Capacity Building – ECN

A final challenge is economic capacity building. By economic capacity building I mean the process of investing in analytical understanding of how to analyze markets in order to identify theories of harm. In order to properly use economic analysis, a certain stock of expertise is necessary.

DG COMP has invested considerable resources in economic capacity building. Besides the new position of the CCE, there are a number of complementary internal and external investments that have been undertaken. Some of these have been discussed above, such as seminars, luncheons, training, the EAGCP, external links (ACE, outside experts, consultants), as well as bilateral meetings between enforcers.

More generally, but perhaps even more significantly, the challenge of building economic capacities applies to all members of the ECN. Many of the ECN members have themselves invested in economic capacity – indeed several members have recently appointed Chief Economists. This is a welcome development and will undoubtedly help to improve the decision making, provided that the above challenges are met. Moreover, modernization requires not only that the same legal and procedural rules apply, but it also implies that the economic analysis is performed in a consistent and transparent way all across the ECN.

As economic analysis becomes more prominent across the ECN, it is essential that economists across the ECN keep in touch and learn from each other. This is why a conference like the present one is a valuable contribution toward capacity building across the ECN.

5.   CONCLUSIONS

This chapter has provided some thoughts on the various contributions for economists and economic analysis in competition policy. The implications of relying more heavily on economic principles and their empirical support are not automatically positive. To ensure the full benefits of modern economic analysis, a number of complementary factors are needed.

One of these factors is economic capacity building. This conference is a welcome initiative in economic capacity building within the ECN network. I hope we can build on this in the future.

NOTES

*   The views expressed are those of the author and do not necessarily reflect those of the European Commission.
1.   Bobby Willig recalled this point at an OECD working party Panel on the "Use of Economic Evidence in Merger Control", June 10th, 2004.
2.   The reasons for a presumably lower market share of economists, when it comes to economic arguments and evidence, are due to several factors. Some of these factors are legal and institutional and vary across member states. Others are more under the control of economists – both empirical and theoretical, such as the way economic analysis is conducted, the type of analysis employed, and perhaps most importantly the way the analysis is communicated to non-experts of economic science.
3.   For a more detailed discussion of this see Röller and Buigues (2005).
4.   See, for instance, the Speeches by Commissioner Kroes "Effective Competition Policy – a key Tool for Delivering the Lisbon Strategy", Brussels, 3rd February 2005, and "Building a Competitive Europe – Competition Policy and the Relaunch of the Lisbon Strategy", Milan, 7th February, 2005.
5.   Case T-342/99, *Airtours plc v. Commission*, [2002] ECR II-2585.

6. Decision 2004/124/EC (OJ 2004 L 43, p. 13). Judgments of the Court of Justice in Cases C-12/03 P and C-13/03 P, *Commission of the European Communities v Tetra Laval BV*, 15 February 2005.

7. It should be noted that the courts emphasis on more and better economic analysis in DG COMP decision making has been largely in the field of merger control. So far, this can not be equally said for other areas of antitrust or state aid control.

8. For a formal analysis of this argument see Neven and Röller (2003).

9. For a more detailed discussion see Röller and Buigues (2005) for excerpts from the mandate of the Chief Competition Economist.

10. Speech by John Vickers "Law and Economics: the Case for Bundling", IBA conference, Brussels, March 10th 2005.

11. See also the discussion in Vesterdorf (2004).

12. An economic model predicts the outcome of certain *endogenous* variables, such as price, quality, innovation activity, etc. When other variables change (these other variables are not explained by the model and are therefore called *exogenous* variables) the model would of course predict a different outcome. Comparative statics relate to how these *endogenous* variables change in response to changes in *exogenous* variables. An economic model can thus be used to predict how certain (namely *endogenous*) variables change over time or across markets. Or to put it the other way around, one would expect precise changes in the *endogenous* variables whenever the *exogenous* variables change in a market, assuming that the model is correct. This is the basis for identification.

13. To a large extent guidelines are statements of economic principles while cases are empirical applications. In this sense, cases can be used to refine and complement guidelines.

14. The recent Merger Guidelines are a good example of this.

15. For a discussion of this issue see for example Duso and Röller (2003).

16. Note that *ex post* analysis can also be informative for priority setting, i.e. to more effectively allocate scarce resources with an antitrust agency.

17. Speech by Commissioner Kroes "Taking Competition Seriously – Anti-Trust Reform in Europe", Brussels, 10th March, 2005.

18. Robustness is perhaps an even bigger concern in the so-called structural approach, where assumptions (either tested or derived from theory) are explicitly imposed on the econometric specification.

19. Equally worrisome potentially is the pro-active abuse of econometric evidence (or simulation methods for that matter), which might occur when non-specialists are running econometric methods, in particular with the help of user-friendly software packages that are largely black-boxes, thereby hiding the assumptions to the user.

20. See various speeches cited above.

21. Note that market failures are not the only rationale for state aid, as there are other important objectives of state aid such as social cohesions and culture.

22. Speech by John Vickers "Law and Economics: the Case for Bundling", IBA conference, Brussels, March 10th 2005.

3. European Merger Control: A Case of Second Mover Advantage?

Pieter Kalbfleisch

To many lawyers the technical and complicated issues related to the use of simulation models at first sight may seem pretty irrelevant. Such mathematical, numerical techniques are best left to the professional economists. Simulation techniques may look a bit like voodoo maths or number cooking.

Understanding, however, *what* matters economically in merger control and *why* it matters is not only relevant for economists but also for the legal professional. And this is true both for the (business) lawyer and the judge. Moreover, I believe that it is also useful for economists to understand where the law, the lawyer and the judge may have a problem with their products and where the economic approach actually may offer a solution. Thus an intensive exchange of ideas between legal and economic professionals may be very fruitful on the topic of the economic analysis of contemplated mergers.

In this chapter, I would like to offer some personal reflections. I will do so both from the perspective of my present position as Director General of the Netherlands Competition Authority NMa and from the point of view of my former job as Acting President of the Court of The Hague. When I speak as a former judge, my main concern will be with the question of how to distillate the legal evidence from economic analyses. Speaking as a director general I will be dealing with the related questions of how simulation models can be used to estimate outcome and to evaluate and ultimately reduce errors in decision making. Indeed, I am firmly convinced that economic analysis can help to reduce errors in decision making in the related fields of merger control, cartel busting, the fight against the abuse of market power and regulation of specific sectors such as transport, energy and telecom. This is why the NMa is preparing the grounds for a team of economic experts that will directly report to the Board of Directors and will become fully operational as of 2006.

1.   SOME LEGAL ISSUES

Let me start from the legal perspective. First of all, we need to acknowledge the basic problem of insufficient case law. Competition policy is a relatively new topic in commercial law even though antitrust has existed for a good century in the US. Even in the US, however, legal paradigms develop and sometimes shift. An example is the US "high enforcement regime" which lasted from about 1910 to the mid-1960s. In this period enforcement was about twice as high as in the early years of US antitrust (Holliday and Hopper 1996). Whenever a regime shift occurs, established legal assessments need to be reassessed and the analysis of critical issues needs increased attention.

The same is of course true for merger control in the European Union. Actually, the issue of lacking case law is probably more important in Europe. The EEC Treaty did, for example, not specify provisions on the application of competition policy to mergers. It was not until 1989 that a Council Regulation on the control of concentrations was adopted.[1] Indeed, before the turn of the century simulation models had hardly ever been used in actual cases in Europe. In April 2004, the adoption of Regulation 139 enabled merger control to challenge a merger that would significantly impede competition.[2] This implies a shift towards a greater need to understand the effects of a merger and for this purpose economic models may offer an apt tool

With so much change going on, it is fair to assume that European judges have no established way yet to benchmark the evidence that is presented to them by economists and their models. One obvious reason is that confidentiality issues make it difficult to be as transparent about methods and results as one theoretically might want to be. This is a serious problem, that needs to be addressed, but fortunately it can be solved. An intensive dialogue between competition practitioners and economic scientists offers a realistic way to establish best practices that will help courts to understand and value an economic analysis even if it is very complex.

At the international conference from which this book is a direct spin-off Lars Hendrik Röller and Hans Schönau suggested that a working group of economists within the European Competion Network be established. I agree with that proposal, but having a working group is not enough. We need to discuss methods not only with the ins (i.e. the economists at the competition authorities) but also with the outs (i.e. the legal staff, academics and business leaders).

I hope that this book may also serve that purpose and that it may become the starting point for such a fruitful exchange of views, both on legal and economic issues related to the use of merger simulation models and other advanced techniques.

2. EUROPE'S SECOND MOVER ADVANTAGE

The introduction of a new competition policy concept should not retard the application of the law. Fortunately, European policy makers will be able to move quickly as they can "reap" second mover advantages.

Being a second mover means that it is possible indeed to make intelligent use of the knowledge and experience of other jurisdictions, adapting where necessary methods and standards to local needs and issues. The experience of other jurisdictions may help to prevent wrong decisions by the European competition authorities that could otherwise give rise to negative judgements on the economic method. The knowledge of other authorities may thus help us to use data more efficiently and to become more conclusive in the analysis.

Indeed this book gives credence to the hypothesis that substantial second mover advantages can be reaped. It was only in 2002 that Gregory Werden and Luke Froed held their seminars that "exported" the method of merger simulation to the European continent. The case studies reported in this book show how quickly knowledge can spread within the European Competition Network. In addition the example of the application of analytical tools in other jurisdictions will enable second movers to convince politicians, legal and economic professionals and the public at large. All in all, second movers can point out that the proposed or newly introduced standards are actually adhered to in other countries.

Perhaps here the European diversity of 25 national authorities may become a comparative advantage. Diversity provides a multitude of relevant practical experiences. That means there is a lot to be learned from these differing national policies.

3. DUTCH COMPETITION POLICY AS AN EXAMPLE

The special situation in The Netherlands in the early 1990s may provide an example of how second mover advantages can actually be harvested and reaped. (See, for example, van Bergeijk and Haffner 1996, pp. 152–159 for an overview.)

In The Netherlands industrial economics was virtually non existent as an academic field. In the 1970s and 1980s only a handful of empirical scientific publications on the working of Dutch markets had been published (van Gent

1997). This changed dramatically around 1994 when plans to introduce the new competition legislation were voiced by policy makers. Building on international scientific and policy oriented studies, economic analysis of markets became a serious topic involving applied general equilibrium models and aimed at estimating the macroeconomic costs and benefits of the contemplated institutions. The focus was macro-economic, the tools were econometric, and the economic advice was on policy and institutions. The proof of the pudding is available today. The economist's advice was implemented and we can see and measure how this has changed the economy. Internal and independent estimates, for example, show that new competition legislation has significantly helped to reduce inflation since 1998 (see, for example, Nieuwenhuijsen and Nijkamp 2001; Warzynski 2003 and Janssen et al. 2004).

Of course relevant differences do exist between the introduction of competition policy in The Netherlands in 1994 and new modelling methods of merger control in Europe in 2004. Indeed, the conference "Simulation models for merger cases: Theory and practice" from which the present volume is a spin-off, focused on microeconomic issues, dealt with simulation, and delivered advice that is an input in a legal decision regarding a possible market structure.

One typical problem is that the pudding does by definition not exist in this manner of exercise. Patrick van Cayseele once remarked that "competition lawyers want to see the blood of the victim" and this makes *ex ante* investigation of potentially anti competitive behaviour difficult from a legal perspective.[3] The essential justification of merger control, however, is that the consumer is *not* victimized. If a simulation model predicts large price increases *ex ante* then the merger is blocked or modified. Only when the model predicts that the merger is not anti-competitive will we be able to compare prediction and actual result. So here we tread on unknown territory that is unknown for most judges: the victim does not exist if the verdict is right.

4.   THE NEED FOR PEER REVIEW

This problem is the more relevant since academic economists cannot replicate the merger simulations as these analyses are often based on highly confidential information. Of course consultants for the parties involved in the merger can with certain provisions and safeguards be allowed to check the data and its analysis (as has reportedly been the case in some merger investigations in Europe). An objective test of non-involved expert analysts would be difficult to achieve. One promising and viable way may be to establish peer review within the group of National Competition Authorities especially at the level of Chief Economists. A platform for such peer review would be able to bundle the experiences in the many jurisdictions that deal with these issues. Indeed, national competition authorities can learn a lot from one another. It is true that at the national level only a handful of cases exist where simulation models have been used. It is relevant, however, that we now have in Europe as a whole a reasonable large number of merger cases that have been analysed with this economic tool.

Merger simulation models have been used in US merger control for almost a decade now. Early models, developed by amongst others Gregory Werden, led to the use of simulation techniques in the Department of Justice, the Federal Trade Commission, and in cases at court. Indeed the use of these models amongst European competition authorities is growing. Sweden, Denmark, Ireland, Italy, the Netherlands, and the European Commission have reportedly used advanced merger simulation models in actual merger cases (Göppelsröder 2004). Moreover Greece, Hungary, Portugal, Slovenia and the UK plan to do so if a case emerges that requires the use of merger simulation tools. So far these exercises cover some 20 to 30 product markets and eight national markets. The bundled experience of these and future cases will provide a reasonable good basis from which to judge the usefulness of simulation models.

5. OUTCOME AND SIMULATION MODELS

Simulation models are not only useful to make decisions in merger cases. They are also important because they offer a good instrument to assess the outcome of merger control policy. Politics is interested in the net benefits of policy. Thus we have to take a look at costs and benefits of merger control.

Table 3.1 Estimates of annual costs of firms (millions of euro)

Notifications of mergers to SMEs	1.3
Notification of mergers by large firms	12.4 – 19.0
In-depth merger reviews	1.4 – 2.2
Total	15.1 – 22.5

Sources: EIM (2003) and Oxera (2004), based on PwC (2003).

Although revenues are diffuse, the costs of merger control are concrete and easier to estimate. Let me give you a few Dutch numbers. Firstly, the public sector pays personal and related expenses that reportedly have been €2 million per year, on average. Secondly, companies involved in merger proposals obviously bear the costs of compliance (Table 3.1). During the period 1998–2002 notification costs of mergers by small and medium-sized enterprises (SMEs) amounted to an annual €1 million and for the large businesses this was estimated at some €15 million. In-depth review adds about €2 million to the private sector's bill. So the total of private and public and internal and external costs amount to about €20 million a year, on average. These private costs are comparable to the costs of OPTA, the Dutch post and telecom regulator (Oxera 2004). It is relevant, moreover, to note that the public sector's costs are substantially lower for merger control than for the telecom regulator.

These Dutch averages, of course, have been influenced by the fact that the new legislation was introduced at the top of the merger wave. The more you merge the more it costs. Moreover, an upward bias exists in these cost estimates since firms and lawyers, as well as the merger department, had to learn how the new job could best be done. Indeed, firms may have notified cases without prospects in the early phase when the law was new and the legal and economic principles and methods governing Dutch merger decisions were still developing. For me as a director general it remains important to understand whether communication is on the right track. For this reason our merger department has commissioned a large survey into the anticipatory effects of merger case law in the years 2001–2004.

Anyhow, it is useful to confront the estimated annual cost of €20 million a year with a conservatively estimated prevented consumer loss of about of €80 million a year. The estimated benefits are derived from in-house simulations with the kind of model which are used to analyse merger cases. All in all, confronting costs and benefits we can establish the economic gain of the new Dutch merger control regime that appears to have saved the Dutch economy an annual €60 million of added value. Merger simulation models can thus be used to estimate the benefits of a new merger regime.

It is important to note that the order of magnitude of these calculations is independently confirmed by the findings in the Nuon-Reliant merger case that will be discussed by Zwart and De Maa (see Chapter 11). In this case the modelling was done by external advisors and with quite different models and these results have recently been scrutinized by an independent advisor of the Dutch Ministry of Economic Affairs. The studies agree that the prevented consumer loss in this case alone amounts to some €500 million per year and that the annual dead weight loss in addition would have been at least €5 million a year.

My personal taxation is that we will have to be transparent about costs and that we thus should prepare to show the benefits of competition policy as well. In our annual report for the year 2004 the NMa does not only report on our ongoing effort to analyse the costs and benefits of merger control. The NMa is also transparent about welfare gains and consumer savings in our portfolio of cartel cases and abuse of dominance. Concrete evidence of consumer harm was uncovered in 26 cases that led to a sanction in 2002–2004. A conservative quantification would amount to roughly €250 million over this period. (Annual outcome increased from almost €20 million in 2002 to more than €140 million in 2004.) Since we are actually dealing with infringements of the law, the costs for the firms that are convicted should not be seen to constitute part of the administrative burden so that the benefits of the cartel busted need only be netted for the cost of the antitrust department. Clearly then benefits exceed costs by far.

6.   IMPROVING DECISION MAKING

These results may have an alternative interpretation that is extremely relevant to the courts and to economic and competition policy makers. Modelling cases where models have not been used to make decisions offers a very useful perspective on the errors of type I (that is on false convictions). Reducing the errors of type I is high on my agenda. After all, care for competition is in the end the essential economic drive for any competition authority. This care explains why competition authorities are careful, but note that careful application of competition policy does not mean that we want to be perfect in every case and at any costs. One can be careful in an intelligent, selective and economic way. Let me illustrate this point. If the hypothesis is that a specific arrangement violates competition law, then an error of type I (that is: convicting the innocent) would seem to be much more serious than an error of type II (that is: letting a criminal escape his rightful punishment … for the time being). For merger control this means that to rule out a merger that is not anticompetitive in effect is far more serious a mistake, than the related error of type II.

Economic intuition suggests the existence of a trade-off between the errors of type I and type II. Very strict competition policy results in more type I errors. In contrast, a lax or relaxed competition policy stance will increase the amount of type II errors. In the final equation, the art of competition policy requires us to be especially vigilant against the errors of type I when we are deciding on actual cases. The upshot is that errors of type I in this case amount to the prohibition of mergers that were *ex ante* considered to be anti competitive, but are not anti competitive according to the *ex post* simulation analysis. And on this topic merger simulation models shed new light.

Such exercises do not only help us to analyse whether the old decisions were right. They also help legal and economic professionals to evaluate whether the models could have been used in actual cases and what are the strengths and weaknesses of these new tools. In this sense Europe may have a clear second mover advantage. We did not use the tools in the major cases of the past and thus our files provide a natural testing ground for simulation models and other new techniques. The proof of the pudding of the introduction of the new techniques may very well rest on the question of how these techniques would have fared in old and established cases.

NOTES

1. Council Regulation (1989) No. 4064/89, OJ L 395.
2. Commission Regulation (EC) No. 802/2004 of 7 April 2004 implementing Council Regulation (EC) No. 139/2004, OJ L 133, 30 April 2004.
3. Reported and quoted in Chapter 10 ("Discussion"), van Bergeijk et al. 1997, p. 80.

PART TWO

Strengths and Weaknesses of Simulation
Models

4. Merger Simulation: Potentials and Pitfalls

Gregory J. Werden*

Merger simulation quantitatively predicts the competitive effect of a proposed merger through the straightforward application of a well-accepted economic model of competitor interaction. Merger simulation first calibrates such a model to match critical features of the industry, such as prices and outputs. It then uses the calibrated model to compute the post-merger actions of the merging firms and their rivals that incorporate the "unilateral", or "non-coordinated", effects of the merger.

Because merger simulation entails a straightforward application of economic models giving rise to unilateral merger effects, it was introduced into competition policy analysis immediately upon the introduction of unilateral effects theories. Over the past decade economists (e.g. Hausman and Leonard 1997; Werden and Froeb 1994, 1996, 2002; Werden 1997) have advocated merger simulation, especially for mergers involving differentiated consumer products. Merger simulation also can be applied in variety of other settings (Werden and Froeb 2005), and to some extent it has been. Merger simulation can be useful whenever a well-defined formal economic model accurately and uniquely predicts the actions of competitors before a proposed merger and the same model can be relied upon to predict those actions after the merger.

The discussion below begins by explaining what unilateral merger effects are, and how evolution in economic theory and competition policy led to the introduction and widespread use of unilateral effects theories. The potentials of merger simulation are then examined: Agency deliberations and courtroom presentations can both benefit significantly from merger simulation because it provides a concrete analysis predicated on a formal economic model of competitor interaction that is firmly grounded in the facts of the particular case. Finally the pitfalls of merger simulation are addressed, and by far the most important of these is using a model that has not been shown to fit the industry in which the proposed merger occurs.

1. UNILATERAL MERGER EFFECTS AND MODERN OLIGOPOLY THEORY

Basic Game Theory Concepts and the Meaning of Unilateral Effects

For more than a quarter century economists have analysed the behaviour of oligopolies using the tools of game theory. Both unilateral theories of merger effects and the use of merger simulation to quantify those effects are applications of these tools. Appreciating exactly what unilateral effects are, and how they can be quantified in particular cases, therefore, requires a basic understanding of a few game theory concepts.

A game is defined by its players (i.e. the competitors), by rules defining how the players interact and what actions they may take, and by an equilibrium concept that indicates which actions are best and determines the outcome of the game. The key equilibrium concept employed in oligopoly theory is "Nash non-cooperative equilibrium", which defines an equilibrium as a set of actions by players such that no player has an incentive to alter its action in light of the actions being taken by the other players (Nash 1951).

Unilateral effects arise from the implications of Nash equilibrium in "one-shot" oligopoly games in which competitors interact just once. Consider an abstract model of such a game in which n profit-maximizing competitors simultaneously choose actions that can be represented by numbers. To make the model and its analysis clear, it is useful to introduce just a bit of mathematical notation. The action chosen by competitor i is a_i, the list of actions chosen by its rivals is a_{-i} and the profit of competitor i is $\pi^i(a_i, a_{-i})$. Competitor i's profit is written as a function of its own action, as well as the actions of all of its rivals, to highlight the fundamental interdependence that characterizes oligopoly; each competitor's action affects all of its rivals.

If a small change in the action of any competitor would increase its profit, that competitor would have an incentive to make that change. Each competitor therefore maximizes its profit by selecting an action such that a very small change in that action would not increase its profit. In mathematical terms this condition involves the concept of a "partial derivative". The "derivative" of a function at any point is its slope, and the partial derivative of a function of several variables is the slope of a cross-section of that function, holding constant all of the variables except the one with respect to which the derivative is taken. The "first-order condition" for profit maximization by competitor i is that the partial derivative of $\pi^i(a_i, a_{-i})$ with respect to a_i equals zero.

Solving competitor i's first-order condition for a_i as a function of a_{-i} yields its "best-response function". This function defines its best action in view of the actions being taken by all its rivals. The competitors in this oligopoly game find themselves in Nash non-cooperative equilibrium if they all operate on their best-response functions, so no competitor has an incentive to alter its action. The Nash equilibrium actions of all of the competitors can be computed by simultaneously solving the *n* first-order conditions.

In elementary presentations of simple oligopoly models, it may be said that competitors treat rivals' actions as fixed, but this view reflects a misunderstanding of the models and a misinterpretation of their equilibrium concept. The first-order conditions in the abstract oligopoly model just described contain partial derivatives holding rivals' actions constant, but these first-order conditions should not be understood to indicate how competitors are assumed to interact in a dynamic world. Many game theory models, including this abstract oligopoly model, predict a game's outcome – e.g. the equilibrium prices and quantities – while abstracting entirely from the process through which competitors achieve that outcome. When each competitor's first-order conditions are satisfied, each is happy with the action it has chosen, so they all are in Nash equilibrium; how the competitors reach this equilibrium simply is not addressed.

With the foregoing foundation in place, the unilateral effects of a merger are easily understood. The merger of competitors i and j produces a new competitor that chooses both a_i and a_j to maximize the sum of π^i and π^j. The merger alters the choice of a_i because the merged competitor accounts for the effect of a_i on π^j. Similarly the merger alters the choice of a_j because the merged competitor accounts for the effect of a_j on π^i. Unless both effects are negligible, the merger affects the choice of both a_i and a_j and thus gives rise to anticompetitive effects. Changes in a_i and a_j also lead non-merging competitors to alter their actions, and the post-merger equilibrium fully reflects all competitors' responses to others' responses and so forth.

What makes a merger anticompetitive is that it internalizes the rivalry between the merging competitors and thereby causes them to alter their actions. What makes the anticompetitive effect of a merger "unilateral" is that the actions of non-merging competitors are determined by the same, Nash-equilibrium, best-response functions before and after the merger. The term "unilateral" is applied even though the non-merging competitors do not take the same actions after the merger that they took before it, and even if the changes in their actions increase the merged competitor's profit.

Oligopoly Models Giving Rise to Unilateral Effects

Among the oligopoly models giving rise to unilateral merger effects are the two classic models developed in the nineteenth century, each of which is a special case of the abstract model just presented. The first formal model of oligopoly was introduced by Antoine Augustin Cournot (1838). The actions of competitors in the Cournot model are the quantities they produce, so the Cournot-Nash equilibrium is a set of quantities such that each competitor is happy with its quantity, given its rivals' quantities. Werden and Froeb (2005) detail the analysis of unilateral effects in a Cournot model with a homogeneous product, which is the sort of product to which the Cournot model generally is applied.

The second oldest oligopoly model was introduced by Joseph Louis François Bertrand (1883) in a review of Cournot's book. Bertrand argued that it was more realistic for competitors to choose the prices they charge than to choose the quantities they produce. Hence the actions of competitors in the Bertrand model are their prices, and the Bertrand-Nash equilibrium is a set of prices such that each competitor is happy with its price, given its rivals' prices. Werden and Froeb (2005) detail the analysis of unilateral effects in a Bertrand model with differentiated consumer products, which are sort of products to which the model generally is applied.

The Dominant Firm model was proposed by Karl Forchheimer (1908). It posits that all competitors but one in an industry act as a "competitive fringe", producing up to the point at which their marginal costs of production equal the market price. The remaining, dominant, competitor acts as a monopolist with respect the portion of total industry demand that the competitive fringe does not elect to supply. The Dominant Firm model may be used to analyse the unilateral effects of a merger in a homogeneous product industry if the merged competitor would have far greater productive capacity than any of its rivals.

The foregoing models characterize outcomes of a competitive process without indicating exactly what that process is or how it results in those outcomes. Auction models, in contrast, specify the competitive process in detail, and how it is specified may affect its outcome. William Vickery (1961) initially formalized the analysis of competition in an auction setting. Significant elaboration was provided by others, and over the years, the economic literature on auctions grew vast as economists studied every form of auction observed in the real world or conceived by academic theorists. Paul Klemperer (2004, ch. 1) usefully summarizes this literature. An auction model may be used to analyse the unilateral effects of mergers when competitors interact through what may be described as a bidding process, and Werden and Froeb (2005) detail the analysis of unilateral effects in one particular auction model.

Models of bargaining also may be used to analyse the effects of mergers. John F. Nash, Jr. (1950, 1953) developed the theory of bargaining, and Osborne and Rubinstein (1990) usefully present both Nash's contributions and subsequent developments. The economic literature has developed two quite different types of bargaining models. An axiomatic bargaining model characterizes the equilibrium outcome of a competitive process without detailing the process itself, just like the Cournot and Bertrand models. A strategic bargaining model specifies in detail how bargaining proceeds, just like an auction model, and variations in that process are likely to affect the bargain that is struck. Werden and Froeb (2005) sketch the analysis of unilateral effects in bargaining models.

Evolution of Merger Policy and Introduction of Unilateral Effects Theories

A structural approach to merger analysis was crafted by the US Supreme Court in a series of decision beginning in the late 1940s and continuing into the early 1960s. *Columbia Steel* introduced the concept of a "relevant market" and first focused on market shares.[1] *Brown Shoe* emphasized market shares and held that delineation of a relevant market is a "necessary predicate" to competitive the analysis of a merger.[2] *Philadelphia National Bank* further held that a "merger which produces a firm controlling an undue percentage share of the relevant market . . . is so inherently likely to lessen competition substantially that it must be enjoined in the absence of evidence clearly showing that the merger is not likely to have such anticompetitive effects."[3]

Philadelphia National Bank justified presuming anticompetitive effects from only market shares partly on the grounds that doing do was "fully consonant with economic theory". But invoking this presumption meant avoiding economic theory and economic evidence, and the court expressed a clear intention to do so. In retrospect that may have been for the best because the theory of oligopoly in vogue at the time was not based on game theory and did not support unilateral effects. The prevailing view was that of Edward Chamberlin (1933, ch. 3), who maintained that cooperation would tend to emerge spontaneously in oligopolies if the number of competitors was sufficiently small.

Although economists now view the Cournot and Bertrand models merely as applications of the well-accepted concept of Nash non-cooperative equilibrium, this has been true for only about one generation. Several prior generations of economists understood the Cournot model in particular to posit irrational behaviour: As the model was presented verbally and mathematically, each competitor assumed that its rivals would not alter their quantities in response to its own quantity changes (Fisher 1898, pp. 126–127). That assumption, however, made no sense because it was flatly inconsistent with the behaviour of competitors in the model itself. After the concept of Nash equilibrium assumed its current position in the mainstream of economic thought, "Cournot [was] reread and reinterpreted", and Cournot equilibrium came to be viewed as the product of fully rational behaviour (Leonard 1994, p. 505).

Concepts of game theory, especially Nash equilibrium, took considerable time to diffuse, but they eventually led to a revolution in economists' thinking about competitor interaction in oligopolies. By the release of the *Horizontal Merger Guidelines* (HMGs) issued by the US Department of Justice and the Federal Trade Commission (1992), the revolution was over, and the HMGs drew heavily on the teachings of the game theoretic analysis of oligopoly. The HMGs (§ 2) identified two general categories of competitive effects theories, dubbed "coordinated" and "unilateral". The HMGs (§ 2.2) further explained that unilateral effects "can arise in a variety of different settings", which "differ by the primary characteristics that distinguish firms and shape the nature of their competition". The HMGs thereby used abstract and non-technical words to invoke the full panoply of oligopoly models giving rise to unilateral effects. Also drawing on the game theoretic analysis of oligopoly, the European Commission's 2004 guidelines (§ 22) similarly divided the competitive effects of mergers into categories labeled "coordinated" and "non-coordinated".

Since the release of the HMGs, the US competition agencies have challenged many mergers on the basis of unilateral effects theories, and these challenges were contested in six cases. In *Staples*[4] and *Swedish Match*,[5] proposed mergers were enjoined on the basis of unilateral effects theories. In *Gillette*,[6] *Kraft*,[7] *Long Island Jewish Medical Center*[8] and *Oracle*,[9] courts presented with unilateral effects theories found the evidence insufficient to warrant enjoining the challenged mergers.

2.   POTENTIALS OF MERGER SIMULATION

In the Cournot model (Farrell and Shapiro 1990) and in the Bertrand model (Deneckere and Davidson 1985), all mergers of competitors produce unilateral anticompetitive effects, unless there are offsetting efficiencies. Yet the vast majority of mergers produce anticompetitive effects so slight that they are easily offset by efficiencies and in any event do not warrant interference by competition agencies. The agencies therefore require tools that permit them to reliably identify the relatively few mergers likely to produce significant anticompetitive effects, and merger simulation potentially provides such a tool.

Tools are also needed to generate the clear and convincing evidence of likely anticompetitive effects courts increasingly demand. Recent US decisions – most notably *Oracle* – make clear that it can be quite difficult to convince a judge to enjoin a proposed merger. The judgment of the Court of

First Instance in *Airtours*[10] indicates that it is similarly difficult for the European Commission to defend its decisions to prohibit mergers. Merger simulation potentially provides what is required to carry the burden imposed in litigation.

Merger Simulation *versus* Expert Intuition

Merger simulation has important limitations, and to quote Winston Churchill, these limitations make merger simulation "the worst form" of merger analysis "except for all other forms that have been tried from time to time". Merger simulation has been used primarily with differentiated consumer products, and its advantage in that context over other forms of analysis that have been tried are illustrated by the *Kraft* case.

The state of New York challenged Kraft's consummated acquisition of Nabisco, which combined Post Grape-Nuts cereal, owned by Kraft, with Nabisco's Shredded Wheat. To assess the unilateral effects of the merger an economist acting for the merging firms estimated the cross elasticities of demand for these and other brands. He contended that the estimated cross elasticities were sufficiently small that the merger could not be expected to cause significant price increases, and the court accepted his contention.

Several years later Nevo (2000) independently estimated the relevant demand elasticities and used his estimates to simulate the merger. His simulations predicted price increases of 3.1 percent and 1.5 percent for Shredded Wheat and Grape-Nuts. The merging firms' economist and the court may well have believed that smaller price increases were implied by the cross elasticity estimates, but in any event neither of them had the benefit of any systematic analysis of the implications of the elasticity estimates. While possibly true, there was no apparent basis for the contention that the estimated cross elasticities were so small that significant unilateral effects could not arise.

The *Kraft* case typifies the manner in which intuition with some basis in economics has been relied upon in litigated merger cases, and the same sort of intuition has played essentially the same role in agency decision making. Economic intuition has considerable value, but is also tends to be a "black box". When conclusions – particularly on quantitative matters – are derived from intuition alone, they lack a clear factual and logical foundation. As a consequence, there may be no systematic way to probe for errors and inconsistencies. With merger simulation, transparent formal economic modelling substitutes for intuition. Merger simulation thereby replaces subjective and unverifiable surmise with objective and verifiable calculation.

In much the same way the use of merger simulation can also sharpen the focus of a merger investigation or court proceeding. Formal modelling makes all assumptions explicit and allows critical assumptions to be identified and tested. Merger simulation thereby can help to identify the key factors affecting the likely unilateral effects of a proposed merger. When different economists take different views about the likely effects of a particular merger, the use of merger simulation allows the precise identification of the basis for their difference, thereby focusing the debate on the critical facts and modelling choices.

For those mergers that end up in a court proceeding, merger simulation also can enhance the persuasiveness of arguments that the mergers are, or are not, anticompetitive. Properly done, merger simulation is firmly anchored in reality, with model assumption based on the stylized facts of the industry and model parameters based on actual data. Merger simulation also employs standard tools of economic science, both theoretical and empirical, in straightforward ways. This can make a unilateral effects analysis far more convincing to a judge.

Merger Simulation *versus* Structural Analysis

Merger simulation is particularly useful with differentiated consumer products because the traditional structural analysis of mergers is especially problematic in that context. The unilateral effect of merging two differentiated products depends largely on the cross elasticities of demand between the products merged together, and those elasticities are only very roughly suggested by market shares. Werden and Froeb (1996, pp. 73–78) illustrate the point by simulating mergers in randomly generated Bertrand industries. They find a huge variance in the price effects of mergers conditioned only on a given set of market shares.

Werden and Rozanski (1994) also explain that market delineation is likely to obscure more than illuminate when highly differentiated consumer products are involved. Consumers typically have differing and complex preferences, and they chose among alternatives with a broad and fairly continuous range of prices and attributes. Merging firms generally argue that no meaningful boundaries can be drawn within a price and quality continuum, yet shares of a very broadly delineated market may mask an intense competitive interaction between the merging products. If the merging brands are particularly close substitutes, an agency might reasonably delineate a very narrow market, yet shares in such a market ignore the potentially significant competitive impact of products outside the delineated market.

Merger simulation has a significant potential to improve on traditional structural analysis by eliminating the need for market delineation and thereby shifting the focus to the competitive effects of a merger. It is necessary to decide which products to include in a merger simulation, but that requires neither anything like market delineation nor has similar implications. The competitive significance of products are accounted for in the relevant demand elasticities even if those products are excluded from a simulation.

The most enduring contribution of the *Oracle* decision to unilateral effects analysis may come from the doubts it expresses on the application of the traditional structural approach to merger analysis in differentiated products industries. *Oracle* (pp. 1120–1123) discusses at length the "difficulties in defining the relevant market in differentiated product unilateral effects cases". *Oracle* (pp. 1121–1122 and 1172) also explains that market shares may not be good predictors of unilateral competitive effects with differentiated products and faults the government for not presenting "any thorough econometric analysis" quantifying factors suggesting significant unilateral effects. Most significantly, *Oracle* (p. 1122) declares that: "Merger simulation models may allow more precise estimations of likely competitive effects and eliminate the need to, or lessen the impact of, the arbitrariness inherent in defining the relevant market."

Simulation *vs.* Documents, Industry Experience and Historical Evidence

Especially in the United States, competition agencies and courts attempting to assess the competitive effects of mergers rely to a significant extent on documents from the files of the merging firms. However these documents often do not address the key issues directly and may present a highly incomplete picture of competition. Some documents may reflect only the ill-conceived views of single employees. Competition agencies and courts also rely on the experience of industry participants, particularly the merging firms' customers. But only in extraordinary cases can industry experience alone provide a sufficient basis for a reliable evaluation of the likely competitive effects of a proposed merger. Indeed the recent *Arch Coal*[11] and *Oracle* (pp. 1125–1145) decisions in the United States found the testimony of industry participants to be a wholly inadequate basis for concluding that challenged mergers were anticompetitive.

Economics offers two basic approaches to the problem of predicting the competitive effects of proposed mergers. One employs deductive reasoning: Based on axioms about competitor behaviour, assumptions about functional forms, and data reflecting key parameters, this approach logically deduces what the effect of a merger must be. Merger simulation takes this approach. The other approach employs inductive reasoning by generalizing from specific events. This approach predicts the effect of proposed mergers on the basis of historical evidence from "natural experiments" such as prior mergers.

Inductive reasoning has serious limitations in predicting the effects of proposed mergers because useful evidence from past mergers generally is unavailable. For most prior mergers, generating reliable estimates of actual effects proves quite difficult for a variety of reasons, and even if such effects could be determined, the effects of few prior mergers are likely to be useful guides. Active enforcement prevents the consummation of the vast majority of mergers likely to have significant anticompetitive effects. Evidence from natural experiments other than mergers is much more readily available, but it is apt to be highly misleading. Werden and Froeb (2005) explain that the effects of mergers may be quite different from any prediction that would be derived from such evidence.

Some Applications of Merger Simulation

Merger simulation has been used extensively in the analysis of proposed mergers involving differentiated consumer products. In a few cases the simulation analysis was subsequently published. Werden (2000) simulates a merger of leading US bread producers, which the government challenged in 1995. Hausman and Leonard (1997) simulate a merger of US producers of bathroom tissue, which was not challenged.

Only once has merger simulation been used in the courtroom. In *Oracle* (pp. 1069–1070, 1172) one of the government's economic experts used an auction model to simulate the proposed merger. The simulation predicted price increases of 5–11 percent for one product line and 13–30 percent for another. The defendants strenuously objected to the simulation, and in particular to the use of an auction model, but the court did not endorse any of those objections. The court (pp. 1158–1161, 1170) did reject the predictions of the simulation, but it did so on the sole grounds that the simulation was based on "unreliable data" in view of the court's determination that a far greater range of products should have been included.

Merger simulation most often is used after a substantial investigation to provide the best and final estimate of a proposed merger's likely unilateral effect; however merger simulation also can be productively used very early in an investigation. Simulation can be performed with only the sort of data likely to be available during the first week of an investigation, provided that strong assumptions are made. Werden, Froeb and Scheffman (2004, pp. 91–92) illustrate this practice with a proposed merger of US long-distance telecommunications providers (the proposed WorldCom-Sprint merger), and Werden and Froeb (2002, pp. 75–77) illustrate it with a proposed merger of Swedish brewers (the acquisition of Pripps Ringnes by Carlsberg).

For both mergers the simulation results are presented in the form of contour plots with contour lines reflecting various average price increases for all of the products included in the simulation. Both simulations also employ a Bertrand model with differentiated products and are predicated on the strong assumption that substitution away from any product is distributed over the other products in the simulation in proportion to their shares (as is the case with "logit" demand). On the two axes of the plots are the aggregate elasticity of demand for all of the products in the simulation and the elasticity of demand for one of the merging products. Because these elasticities generally are unknown at the outset of the investigation, a broad range of plausible values is considered.

For the Swedish brewing merger the plot indicates likely average price increases of 4–7 percent for Class II beers (including alcohol contents of 2.8 percent and 3.5 percent). This sort of merger simulation could have usefully focused the investigation of that merger on the four possibilities that would have made the merger much less anticompetitive than these price-increase predictions suggest. Contrary to the assumptions of the simulation, the merging brands could have been particularly distant substitutes, all Class II beers could have been viewed by consumers as essentially fungible and beers outside Class II could have been very close substitutes for Class II beers. In addition, the proposed merger could have generated substantial reductions in marginal cost.

Inherent Limitations of Merger Simulation

At best, the predictions of a merger simulation are reasonable, but rough, estimates of the likely effects of a proposed merger. The oligopoly models used in merger simulation never completely capture the complex competitive processes of real-world industries, and statistical error is associated with estimates of some of the inputs into a merger simulation (e.g. demand elasticities). With the current state of the art merger simulation also can predict only the relatively near-term effects of proposed mergers. The models used in merger simulation do not allow for the possibility of entry of new products or repositioning of existing products. Merger simulation also has little to say about the likely long-term evolution of an industry, which may be significantly affected by many factors that cannot be accounted for in a merger simulation.

The foregoing are inherent limitations of merger simulation and must be kept in mind in evaluating the significance of any particular predictions from a merger simulation, but these limitations are not a basis for heavily discounting the predictions of merger simulation or eschewing it altogether. Rough estimates are much better than none at all. Entry and repositioning can be considered outside the context of merger simulation, and Werden and Froeb (1998) find that mergers are not likely to provide much incentive for either. Furthermore the focus of competition policy is on the near-term effects of mergers precisely because the long term is imponderable.

3.   PITFALLS IN MERGER SIMULATION

There are many pitfalls in merger simulation, the most important of which is using a model that does not fit the industry under review. A model should not be employed just because it is handy, and modelling assumptions should not be made just because they are convenient. Rather every modelling choice in a merger simulation apt to matter significantly should be accompanied either by some sort of justification or by a sensitivity analysis exploring its impact. For a few modelling choices an ample justification can be found in an axiom of economics, e.g. that firms maximize profits. For most modelling choices, however, the justification should be that they fit the relevant facts.

Evaluating whether modelling choices fit the facts draws on the full array of qualitative evidence developed in a case, as well as on particular quantitative features of the industry, which may be directly measured or estimated econometrically. Anyone performing a merger simulation on which significant weight may be placed, ultimately should be convinced, and prepared to persuade others, that the model explains the past well enough to provide useful predictions of the future.

Competition policy in the United States is enforced primarily in the courts, and economic analysis therefore is subject to a discipline imposed by rules of evidence. As the court declared in one significant antitrust case, these rules require a "thorough analysis of the expert's economic model", which "should not be admitted if it does not apply to the specific facts of the case".[12] The same discipline should be imposed by a competition agency in its evaluation of the likely competitive effects of a merger, even if that evaluation is unlikely to be tested in court proceedings.

Fit Between the Simulation Model and the Industry

A simulation model must reflect essential features of an industry, including whether the product is differentiated and whether prices are set separately for different customers. A simulation model also must incorporate important asymmetries across firms or their products in a realistic manner. But a simulation model should not be rejected merely because it ignores certain complexities or in some ways is unrealistic.

Economic models are abstractions that never perfectly describe the real world. Nor is a perfect fit between the model and the industry even a goal. If models become too complex, through elaborate attempts to fit every detail of an industry, they are apt to be useless in merger simulation because their calibration is likely to impose unreasonable informational demands and they may yield no clear predictions. The fact that the real world is observed with error also must be acknowledged. On some points a model may paint a realistic view of an industry even though it is at odds with some apparent facts, which have been misperceived.

The predictive – not descriptive – powers of a model are what matters most. The most important tests of fit of an oligopoly model is whether it explains the intensity of competition in the industry as reflected in price-cost margins, i.e. price minus marginal cost, all divided by price. Oligopoly models used in merger simulation make specific predictions about the average level of margins and about differences in margins across firms and products, and these predictions should be compared with the available data.

The relevant price-cost margins for evaluating the fit of an oligopoly model are averages over a substantial period of time. A merger simulation is used to predict the overall price effects of a proposed merger over a period of several years, and not its effect on week-to-week price movements. For that reason it is wholly unnecessary that a simulation model explains short-term price movements, although essential that it explains the average level of prices and margins over a year or two.

The Cournot model predicts that the price-cost margin of each competitor equals its output share divided by the industry elasticity of demand. The fit of the model should be evaluated by comparing the average level of margins in an industry to the level predicted by the Cournot model and by comparing the differences in margins across firms to the differences predicted by the model. In a US non-merger case a court reasonably rejected the application of a Cournot model to an industry with highly unequally sized firms but not the significant differences in margins the Cournot model predicts.[13]

A Cournot model with a homogeneous product clearly does not fit a consumer goods industry in which brands are important. On the other hand, the fact that competitors do not literally set outputs does not imply that the Cournot model cannot be useful in the analysis of mergers. As just noted it is essential that a model accurately predicts but not that it accurately describes.

The Bertrand model may fit a wide variety of industries in which products are differentiated in important ways, particularly consumer goods industries in which brands are important. The model may fit an industry quite well enough even though price is the not only dimension of competition in the industry.

The Bertrand model (with single-product firms) predicts that the price-cost margin of a differentiated product equals the reciprocal of that product's elasticity of demand. The fit of the model should be evaluated by comparing the margins implied by econometric estimates of these elasticities with margins derived from accounting data. The data required for this comparison should be available from the merging firms, and it is important that the model explains their margins reasonably well. The data required for this comparison may not be available from non-merging firms, but it is less important that the model explains their margins. Moreover it is neither unusual nor worrisome that some minor products are not priced as the model predicts.

The Cournot and Bertrand models do not fit an industry in which prices vary significantly across transactions, but an auction or bargaining model can easily reflect price dispersion in an industry. An auction or bargaining model also may fit an industry well enough even though it does not perfectly describe the industry. An auction model may be appropriate when the merging firms compete through a process that resembles either open or sealed bidding, even if there is no formal bidding process, and even if competitors' actions are not limited to the submission of bids. What is most important is the merging firms buy from, or sell to, a firm playing the role of the auctioneer by dictating the rules of the competitive process and by committing to those rules.

In *Oracle* (p. 1172) the defendant objected to the use of an auction model on the grounds that the customers were "extremely powerful at bargaining" and the merging sellers did "not simply 'bid' for business" but rather engaged in "negotiations [that were] extensive and prolonged, with the purchaser having complete control over information disclosure". However an auctioneer has just such this sort of power and exercises this sort of control. Moreover Oracle did not explain why its objections provided a basis for questioning the predictive accuracy of the model, which is what matters.

Just as with the Cournot and Bertrand models, a key test of the fit of an auction model is how well it explains the intensity of competition as reflected in winning bidders' profits. The fit of an auction model also should be evaluated by comparing the predictions of the model to the observed relationship across competitors between winning bids and profit rates.

Pitfalls of Merger Simulation with Differentiated Consumer Products

Merger simulation has particular pitfalls in its most frequent application – differentiated consumer products industries. The most basic, and easiest to avoid, concerns model "calibration". In that process a set of prices and shares is chosen to represent the equilibrium "but for" the proposed merger, i.e. the prices and shares that are expected to prevail in the near future absent the merger. The usual practice is to take the "but for" equilibrium to be the average prices and shares over a substantial recent time period. The predicted price effects of the merger are the differences between the simulated post-merger prices and the prices used in the calibration. A major pitfall in merger simulation is failing to calibrate the model properly or comparing the simulated post-merger prices to a set of pre-merger prices not used to calibrate the model.

Merger simulation with differentiated consumer products tends to be largely concerned with estimating the relevant elasticities of demand governing substitution among competing products, and challenging econometric issues commonly arise in estimating these elasticities. For example the existence of consumer inventories can present a difficult problem when using the usual high-frequency (e.g. weekly) data.

The number of products also can easily be so great that the ability of the data to identify all of the relevant elasticities is seriously taxed. Flexible models of consumer demand, designed to let the data speak for itself, may have so many parameters that they produce very imprecise estimates. This variance problem can be addressed by imposing restrictions on substitution possibilities, but doing so may introduce significant bias in the elasticity estimates. Thus estimation may involve a delicate trade-off between variance and bias.

Conventional models of consumer demand all have inherent "curvature" properties relating to how the demand elasticities change with changes in prices, and these properties substantially affect price-increase predictions from merger simulations. Four functional forms have been used significantly in merger simulation – AIDS, isoelastic, linear, and logit demand. Crooke et al. (1999) show that the former two yield higher price increase predictions than the latter two. Indeed the former two can easily yield predicted price increases several times those of the latter two.

There is unlikely to be a sound empirical basis for favouring one demand model over all others, particularly since the functional-form best fitting of the available data may not be best for predicting outside the range of the data, as merger simulation often entails. Rather an assumption must be made, and a conservative assumption (e.g. logit) generally is best.

The Bertrand model used in simulating mergers involving differentiated consumer products posits competition only in price, while other dimensions of competition often are important in real-world consumer products industries. Over the relatively near term, which is what matters in competition policy toward mergers, it may be reasonable to treat as fixed all dimensions of competition other than price. On the other hand aspects of marketing strategy may interact in important ways with the choice of price or be affected by the merger in ways that would cause the price-increase predictions to be a seriously misleading description of the merger's effects.

Finally, merger simulation using the Bertrand model ignores the fact that differentiated consumer products generally are not sold to the consumers directly by the manufacturers; rather there is an intervening retail sector. That presents no difficulties if retailers apply a constant percentage mark-up to the prices paid to manufacturers, as Werden (2000) found was true in one case. In that event the relevant demand elasticities at the retail level are exactly the same as those at the manufacturing level, so ignoring the retail sector is an unimportant simplification. In other cases the relationship between retailers and manufacturers can have important implications for the effects of manufacturer mergers on consumers, so that relationship must be examined and accounted for. There is only sparse economic literature addressing the impact on merger effects of retailer-manufacturer relationships, and it has considered only the unrealistic case of monopoly retailers. This literature suggests that the merger of manufacturers can have no effect on retail prices, and it can have the same effect as if the manufacturers sold directly to consumers.

NOTES

*   Senior Economic Counsel, Antitrust Division, US Department of Justice. The views expressed herein are not purported to represent those of the US Department of Justice.

1.   *United States v. Columbia Steel Co.*, 334 U.S. 495 (1948).

2.   *Brown Shoe Co. v. United States*, 370 U.S. 294, 335 (1962).

3.   *United States v. Philadelphia National Bank*, 374 U.S. 321, 363 (1963).

4.   *FTC v. Staples, Inc.*, 970 F. Supp. 1066 (D.D.C. 1997).

5.   *FTC v. Swedish Match*, 131 F. Supp. 2d 151 (D.D.C. 2000).

6.   *United States v. Gillette Co.*, 828 F. Supp. 78 (D.D.C. 1993).

7.   *New York v. Kraft General Foods*, Inc., 926 F. Supp. 321 (S.D.N.Y. 1995).

8.   *United States v. Long Island Jewish Medical Center*, 983 F. Supp. 121 (E.D.N.Y. 1997).

9.   *United States v. Oracle, Inc.*, 331 F. Supp. 2d 1098 (N.D. Cal. 2004).

10. *Airtours plc v. EC Commission* (T-342/99), [2002] E.C.R. II-2585; [2002] 5 C.M.L.R. 317.

11. *FTC v. Arch Coal*, Inc., 329 F. Supp. 2d 109, 145–146 (D.D.C. 2004).

12. *Concord Boat v. Brunswick Corp.*, 207 F.3d 1039, 1055–1056 (8th Cir. 2000).

13. *Heary Brothers Lightning Protection Co., Inc. v. Lightning Protection Institute*, 287 F. Supp. 2d 1038, 1066–1068 (D. Ariz. 2003).

5. On the Use of Economic Modelling in Merger Control

**Marie Goppelsröder and
Maarten Pieter Schinkel**[*]

Merger control is both an important and quite an invasive form of government intervention in competitive processes. By requiring notification and approval of firms' intentions to integrate business, with investigation periods in which market developments continue, merger control interferes with business strategies in ways that potentially have significant consequences. Obviously, the power to block mergers or grant exemption conditional on divestiture requirements gives teeth to competition authorities in their role as guardian of the competitive arena. When applied appropriately and with care, these powers are beneficial to consumers and welfare, preventing the build-up or abuse of positions of dominance. But these far-reaching competencies of competition authorities also come with the obligation to exercise restraint and care in where and when to use them.

The dynamics of real markets, of which mergers are often a natural part, are inherently complex and often difficult to understand. It is therefore not an imaginary danger that competition authorities, be it the US Department of Justice, the Directorate General Competition of the European Commission, or the concentration control units of the various national competition authorities (NCAs), occasionally err, either allowing mergers that are in fact predominantly anti-competitive, or blocking some that would have had important potential to generate welfare gains. The full extent of the consequences of such mistakes is difficult to assess. Yet, it has been argued that the error margin is quite substantial.[1] It seems justified to ask, therefore, that adverse findings in a merger investigation be based on a thorough understanding of all aspects of the case at hand. Since the question whether certain concentrations are socially desirable is essentially an economic, rather than a legal one, merger control decisions should be grounded on sound economic analysis and extensive study – something that is increasingly recognized by higher courts in the US and the EU alike.

Basic economic theory predicts quite unambiguously, however, that – apart from the extreme of homogenous goods that post-merger still are supplied by two or more firms in Bertrand competition – mergers always have at least some, although not necessarily substantial, unilateral anticompetitive effect.[2] Hence, when these effects are indeed significant, one should only consider allowing the consummation of a merger if there are sufficiently strong merger-specific benefits, such as efficiency gains, to counter the inevitable anticompetitive effects of the concentration. A call for merger control based on sound economic analysis – and abstracting from regulatory transactions costs – therefore asks for the inclusion of efficiency arguments into the analysis.[3]

Until recently, however, there was little or no regard for weighing any welfare-enhancing effects of large mergers in European Commission policy. Instead, as European merger control developed out of Article 82, the frame of mind has always been that mergers are potentially an abuse of dominance. In line with this, merger analysis thus far concentrated on the question whether the anticompetitive effects would or would not be substantial – that is, whether there is dominance in a given case. For that, the prime economic concept applied was (and still is) that of the Hirschmann–Herfindahl index (HHI). So long as the relevant market in which the merging parties are active measures an HHI below an established threshold value, and if indeed the merger would not increase the HHI by a given number either, no reason for concern would exist. And otherwise there always would.[4]

Static *ex ante* HHI measures, however, are a poor instrument for assessing the *ex post* effects of consolidations. One can easily devise exercises in which mergers that go over the threshold generate welfare increases, and others that remain well within the HHI safe-haven are socially undesirable. Furthermore, the HHI obviously has no relation to the possibility of merger-specific benefits. The new *Horizontal Merger Guidelines* of the European Commission reflect, however, that European merger control – and in its wake undoubtedly NCA enforcement too – is opening up to an assessment of countervailing effects. The effects-based 'Significant Impediment of Effective Competition' test (SIEC test) is more than a mere market share analysis. In addition, the guidelines give an explicit opening for mounting a merger defence based on efficiencies that are specific to the merger and passed on to consumers to a sufficient degree. These will be taken into consideration and balanced against anticompetitive effects in the case:

> The Commission considers any substantiated efficiency claim in the overall assessment of the merger. It may decide that, *as a consequence of the efficiencies that the merger brings about*, there are no grounds for declaring the merger incompatible with the common market pursuant to Article 2(3) of the Merger Regulation. This will be the case when the Commission is in a position to conclude

on the basis of sufficient evidence that the efficiencies generated by the merger are likely to enhance the ability and incentive of the merged entity to act pro-competitively for the benefit of consumers, thereby *counteracting the adverse effects on competition which the merger might otherwise have.*[5]

This new chapter in European merger control clearly promises an improvement over the existing practice, as it allows for a more balanced and complete analysis of economic effects. Fulfilling this promise, however, implies a serious obligation to economics. The question arises, whether economic theory is presently up to the challenge of assisting competition authorities in their new and difficult task to use this widened regulatory space. In this chapter, we assess the state of the art in applied economic models implemented with computer aided modelling techniques, which are advanced by a number of scholars and practitioners as a means to improve proper decision making in merger control.[6]

The remainder of the chapter is organized as follows. In the next section, we provide a survey of the basic models that underlie existing merger simulation techniques, as they have been applied in the US, as well as in a few EU merger cases. Emphasis is on the dimensions of variations of the applied models, both in terms of construction and empirical calibration. After critically evaluating the span of these dimensions, it is concluded to be rather narrow, relative both to what often are highly complicated industries and to existing economic theory. We warn for an over-enthusiastic placing of more faith than is justified into what existing economic modelling can do in terms of predicting the future consequences of mergers. Section 2 focuses on some enforcement issues associated with sophisticated merger simulation analyses. The analyses are typically costly, and there is often considerable sensitivity in their findings to small variations in the underlying assumptions. This, in turn, may result in detrimental legal uncertainty and stimulate rent seeking. Section 3 subsequently introduces a new measurement tool, the Werden–Froeb index (WFI), as a middle way between the limited and rigid use of economics in past merger control and the potential drawbacks of overly sophisticated methods that are presently being developed in the various competition authorities. Section 4 concludes.

1. STATE OF THE ART IN MERGER SIMULATION

The development of merger simulation techniques for merger investigations started some ten years ago in US enforcement agencies and academia. Important early contributors in the field are Gregory Werden and Luke Froeb, who worked on the use of logit models, as well as Jerry Hausman, who was one of the first to use the multi-stage budgeting approach together with the

AIDS model to analyse mergers. Merger simulation analysis today uses as its basis one of two methods. The first, which requires a considerable amount of data, and therefore often time, estimates a demand model using econometric techniques. Examples of this approach are Hausman, Leonard and Zona (1994), Hausman and Leonard (1997) and Pinkse and Slade (2004). The second approach, which is less data intensive, is to calibrate a simulation model using critical features of the industry at hand such as quantities, prices and elasticities. The calibration approach requires quite some structural specification, such as a choice of the appropriate functional form of demand. This methodology has been applied in Werden and Froeb (1994), as well as in Epstein and Rubinfeld (2002).

As markets in which a larger merger is investigated are by definition markets with a limited number of players to begin with, oligopoly models are an appropriate class for understanding the potential effects of the merger. The prime structural choice faced in the implementation of a simulation model then is on the mode of strategic interaction between the firms in the relevant market, that is, which oligopoly model suits the industry under investigation best. The purpose of this section is to briefly and non-technically survey the basic models underlying those merger simulation models currently in use for the novel reader. We start with the classic model of quantity competition, followed by an analysis of mergers in quantity-setting markets. We will then continue with an outline of models of price competition and the effects of mergers therein. Subsequently, we review two more recent methodologies, using auction and bargaining theory, to analyse mergers in markets with more specific forms of price formation. The coverage is basic and included only for completeness of the survey.[7] Those familiar with the literature may want to skip to Section 1.5 on the dimensions of variations that have so far been exploited in actual US and EU merger simulation analyses.

1.1 Mergers in Markets with Quantity Competition

In the classic Cournot model of oligopolistic market interaction, firms simultaneously choose the quantity they produce in order to maximize their profit, well aware that the eventual market price is determined by the total amount supplied by all competitors together. Each firm individually determines the profit maximizing output level it would set in response to any level produced by its competitors – assuming that rival production does not in turn depend on that response. The market equilibrium then is characterized by production levels that are all a best-response to one another, so that all firms produce exactly what they intended to, given the output of all the others. How such a Nash equilibrium can be found is easily seen in a triopoly, homogeneous goods setting with linear demand and constant marginal costs, illustrated in Figure 5.1 below.[8]

Figure 5.1 Best-response functions in Cournot competition between three firms, pre- and post-merger

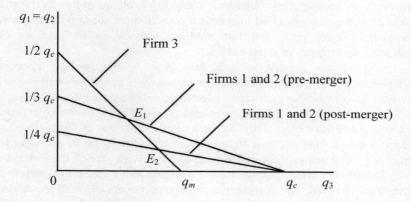

In this basic model version, there are three firms in the market, each producing the exact same good or service at identical production costs, with constant marginal costs. The regular linear best-response curve of each firm is drawn for firm 3. It is downward sloping, because the more its rivals produce, the less firm 3 should produce in reply, in order not to sink the market price – Cournot actions are therefore also classified as strategic substitutes. As the firms are all identical, the individual output levels in equilibrium will have to be equal. Exploiting this symmetry in equilibrium also outside equilibrium allows for a two-dimensional illustration of this three-dimensional problem. In Figure 5.1, the pre-merger reactions curves of firm 1 and firm 2 are added up to return the total output of those two firms in reply to any output level of Firm 3. The intersection of the two best-response functions thus constructed defines the Cournot–Nash equilibrium, E_1 prior to the merger. At this point, neither firm will find it profitable to change its output, given the other firms' output. It is straightforward to extend this basic Cournot triopoly model to include more than three firms which makes the equilibrium quantities, and hence the market price, crucially depend on the number of firms in the market.

Since firms behave non-cooperatively in these models, they do not take into account the negative impact of their own increase in output on their competitors' output levels, and hence not on aggregate output and price. This externality implies that each firm chooses an output that exceeds its optimal output from the viewpoint of the industry as a whole. As a consequence, total output will be higher than it would be if the market were controlled by a single dominant firm. The Cournot market price will be lower than it would be under a monopoly regime. For three firms, although distinctly different, the Cournot equilibrium output is close to that produced by a monopolist that serves the market alone. Only when the number of firms in the market increases to become very large will competition on quantities eventually yield equilibrium prices close to marginal costs. From a social point of view, therefore, market price and total welfare increase in the number of independent competitors in the market.[9]

Analytically, a merger between two firms in the pool of Cournot competitors really is a reduction in the total number of independent players by one. Two firms that previously exerted negative externalities upon each other – with positive effects on consumer welfare – now have these internalized. Post-merger, they act as a single unit, that is. In a duopoly example this is obvious, as a merger would by construction be a merger to monopoly. The analysis applies in general for any number of firms. Figure 5.1 illustrates the effect of firms 1 and 2 merging into a single firm with two integrated divisions. The post-merger reaction curves are closer to the origin, while the best response of the merged firms is still to produce nothing in reply to firm 3 producing the competitive output level. The post-merger Cournot-Nash market equilibrium is E_2, at which total output is lower.

A seminal paper in the early literature on mergers in Cournot markets is Salant, Switzer and Reynolds (1983), which shows that mergers among Cournot competitors will generally be unprofitable for the firms involved.[10] The argument is as follows. First observe that before the merger, firm 1 did not take into account any negative effect its own expansion of output would have on firm 2. Post-merger, however, the united management of both firms will take into account any changes in the revenues of the both divisions that used to be independent firms when it sets the combined output level. Since a reduction in output of division 1 will raise revenues in division 2, and *vice versa*, each division will produce less than it did compared to the situation pre-merger. Irrespective of the output of the third firm in the market, the merged entity will therefore produce less than the sum of the output of the independent firms 1 and 2 pre-merger.

Second, since the merged firm cannot control the output setting of the independent third firm, the latter will take advantage of the reduction in quantity followed by the merger and expand its own output in best-response. As a result, the net output reduction in the overall market is less than the output reduction by former firms 1 and 2. This can be seen directly in Figure 5.1, by comparing the horizontal distance between E_1 and E_2. Therefore, the merged firm earns less than the sum of the profits the independent firms 1 and 2 earned pre-merger. What is more, the firm that stayed out of the merger benefits from the merger of the other firms with an increased profit, compared to the competitive situation with three independent firms. Since this qualitative effect transfers to markets with a larger number of firms, typically all firms would want the others to merge, without being involved themselves. The more firms there are in the market, the more of them would need to be involved in the merger in order to make it profitable – and two is always too few, unless there is a merger to monopoly. Therefore, the prediction is that in classic Cournot markets no mergers materialize, unless the merging divisions believe that substantial efficiency gains will materialize as a result of the merger.

The classic Cournot model has been studied extensively in the literature. Extensions of the model include variations in the cost structures, non-linear demand functions, asymmetry in costs over the firms, differentiated commodities, repeatedly played quantity setting games in both finite and infinite time, the introduction of expectations on rival reactions – so-called conjectural variations – the incorporation of capacity constraints to production and uncertainty in demand and rivals' strategies, for example. Each of these variations has an effect on the qualitative predictions of the Cournot model – ranging from the non-existence of equilibrium to the sustainability of a monopoly equilibrium. When one wants to use the Cournot setting to predict production and price levels, these variations in assumptions are crucial to the outcomes of the models. Yet, Farrell and Shapiro (1990) established in a more general set up that, in the absence of efficiency gains, horizontal mergers always lead to price rises that decrease consumer welfare. In fact, only in the presence of large efficiencies will the anticompetitive effects of a merger be offset. The insight that Cournot mergers are not likely to be consummated for their anticompetitive effects is a robust finding. Yet price competition is the basis of many merger simulation analyses.

1.2 Mergers in Markets with Price Competition

Bertrand proposed in his review of Cournot's work an almost analogous strategic model, which predicts crucially different effects. In the Bertrand model, firms compete on prices rather than quantities.[11] Using a triopoly setting again, the three firms simultaneously and non-co-operatively determine their strategies, with the difference that in this setting, price levels, not quantities, are set as strategic variables. Assume that all firms have full information and identical marginal costs, that there are no constraints on production, and that consumers can easily switch between the producers in response to price differences. Since the products are perceived by the consumers to be perfect substitutes, only the firm offering the lower price will serve positive demand, while the other firms will sell little to nothing at all. Should they each set the same price, firms would share the market more or less equally. As a result, each firm understands that its best reply to any price by its rival is a slightly lower price, as long as the price is not below the constant marginal cost level – since then it would rather sell nothing than serve demand at a loss. Given identical cost structures, in the resulting Bertrand–Nash equilibrium all firms will consequently sell exactly at marginal costs: a higher price would be undercut, a lower one loss-giving.

That price setting with only a few (three, but also two) large suppliers generates an equilibrium that is in its features identical to the equilibrium under perfect competition between many price-taking firms is a very powerful result. It implies, *ceteris paribus*, that the number of firms in the market is irrelevant for the market outcome, which in turn leads to the conclusion that any merger, unless it leads to monopoly, should not raise any concerns. So when two or the three firms merge, given that at least two firms remain post-merger, there is no effect on total output and the market price level. As in the Cournot model, in the homogeneous Bertrand model it is uninteresting for any of the firms to merge. Even though firms do not face a loss from being part of the merger, they will not profit from it and are therefore indifferent towards the transaction, unless there are merger-specific efficiency gains.

Figure 5.2 Best-response functions of three Bertrand competitors selling differentiated goods pre- and post-merger

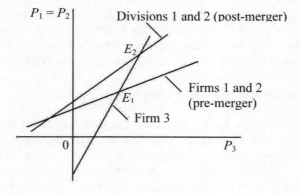

Mergers do generate detrimental concentration effects in a price-setting structure with variations from the basic model, in particular differentiated commodities.[12] When goods are not perfect substitutes, consumers do not immediately switch away from the more expensive to the cheaper firm.

Hence, although prices are still strategic complements – in that one firm decreasing (increasing) the price of a variety is responded to by the other firms with lower (higher) prices as well – these replies are more mellow. That is, the best-response functions slope upwards – their slope being directly related to the measure of product differentiation: the more heterogeneous goods are, the steeper. Figure 5.2 illustrates this, using the same graphical construction as before: product differentiation is assumed to be symmetric, so that the quantities of firm 1 and firm 2 can be taken to be identical in and outside of equilibrium.

In equilibrium (either pre- or post-merger) prices are above costs, so modest profits are made. As in quantity-setting markets, the merged firm will take into account that its price setting policy will have effects on the other division's price level. Since prices are strategic complements, the new merged entity will increase the prices of both its products as a result of the merger. This will, in turn, increase demand of the product manufactured by the outside firm 3, and hence its price – albeit by a smaller amount than by which the prices of the merged firms increase. In the pre-merger equilibrium, E_1, prices and therefore profits of all firms are lower than in the post-merger equilibrium E_2. In contrast to quantity setting markets, a merger in a price setting market can therefore be profitable for both the merging parties as well as the outside firms, for any number of firms initially in the market, even when the merger does not lead to efficiency gains for the merging parties.[13]

Like the Cournot model, the Bertrand model has been studied extensively under different structural and behavioural assumptions. In contrast to the Cournot model, variations in the price setting structure quite generically move the equilibrium away from the nice property that just a small number of firms suffice for efficient pricing. This is true for product differentiation as discussed above, but also when firms are heterogeneous in costs structures prices are above the more efficient firms' costs as well. Likewise, capacity constraints – particularly when they can be *ex ante* chosen by the firms – introduce artificial scarcity and hence higher prices. This also holds for different expected reactions of rivals, and a variety of dynamic extensions of the market game. The strategic price competition model, therefore, has many features to study the effects of mergers in real markets. Note, however, that the choice of model has profound consequences for the conclusions reached.

1.3 Mergers in Auction Markets

Whereas the previous classes of models consider markets in which the equilibrium establishes a single market-clearing price, in many markets pricing works differently. In particular, auctions are increasingly being used to model certain markets, for example those for large development or research projects allocated through a tender system. Auctions have the benefit over ordinary pricing in that they can allocate the goods for sale to the highest bidder, which in the context of unique projects would ideally be the most efficient producer. Hence, tailor-made pricing through auctions has desirable efficiency features. These only materialize, however, when the bidders for such unique commodities compete for winning the project.

There exist four main types of auctions: the ascending-bid (open) auction, the descending-bid auction, the first-price sealed-bid auction and the second-price sealed-bid (or Vickrey) auction.[14] A full analysis of the different auction types is beyond the scope of this chapter. In the following, we will illustrate the potential of auction models in merger simulation analysis by confining ourselves to ascending auctions and second-price sealed-bid auctions concentrating on situations with differing private bidder values.

In ascending-bid auctions, also known as open auctions, the seller of the good announces an incremental sequence of prices, at which the bidders successively indicate their willingness to buy. The price is then raised until only one bidder remains. This highest bidder obtains the item at the final price. Each player's non-cooperative strategy in the ascending auction is to bid up maximally to the individual willingness to pay. Since the next-to-last bidder will stop bidding when his willingness to pay has been reached, when private values differ, the winner of the auction pays (slightly more than) the second highest willingness to pay.

In the sealed-bid second-price auction, each bidder independently submits a bid. These bids are kept unknown to the other bidders during the bidding process. They are collected by the seller, who then sells the item to the bidder that submitted the highest bid. It has been agreed in advance, however, that the price paid by the winner is not his or her own bid, but the bid submitted by the second-highest bidder instead. This aspect of the Vickrey auction assures that each bidder bids up exactly to his or her reservation price, so that the seller is sure to end up with the second-highest evaluation. The reason for this is that, since each bidder knows it will never pay its own bid if it wins, it has no incentive to hide it, for that would only reduce its chances of winning the auction, whereas it does not increase the price when winning.

As said, auctions are competitive events that require a number of players bidding non-cooperatively. If two firms, that initially are independent bidders, decide to merge, it can have important effects on the efficiency of the outcome. It is important to note that in the ascending-bid auction and the Vickrey auction, and when private values differ, a merger would only affect the outcome of the auction if it involved the bidders with the highest and the second-highest valuations. Imagine that there are four bidders 1–4 with respective valuations of $V_1<V_2<V_3<V_4$. Prior to a merger in this market, bidder 4 will win the bid and pay the price of the second-highest bidder,

which is V_3. Let's now assume that bidders 3 and 4 decide to merge. The combined entity will then win the bid at a price of V_2 instead of V_3, the second-highest independent bid. Obviously, any other combination of the above mergers, however, would not affect the outcome of the winning bid, since these bidders are unimportant for the allocation.

It follows directly from this logic that it is only the players with the highest willingness to pay that would want to merge at all to reap the benefits from eliminating a rival bidder that drives up the price in the auction. In the context in which auctions are relevant, this would often be the most efficient firm that could carry out the tendered project. As a result, post-merger the conglomerate that includes the most cost-effective firm is likely to win the bid still, but at a higher tendered sum, for the second-highest independent bidder is now a less efficient one. If efficiency – in the sense of the most cost-effective firm winning the project – is the evaluation criterion, this would not matter much. However, if consumer welfare is central, the post-merger auction may generate purchaser and ultimately consumer detriment. Also, it could be argued that when too much is paid for the project to the winning division in the post-merger conglomerate, it has an incentive to produce less cost-effectively – for example by including its less efficient merger partner in the project.[15]

Finally, note that auctions often are held for a combination of products, or in a sequence of separate biddings over time. In order to assess whether a merger in a certain auction market would affect the market allocation, one has to assess in how many different auctions the merged firms originally placed the highest- and second-highest bids. It is also important to know if there are different winners in the pool of players over the sequential auctions. The frequency at which the merged entity placed the first and second bid prior to the merger multiplied by the difference between the second and third largest bid then yields the expected effect of the merger.[16]

1.4 Mergers and Bargaining

In the single price models and the auction models, the (local) power to establish prices is asymmetrically given to the sellers. In many markets in which the buyers are quite well organized, however, prices are negotiated in a process in which the buyers have an important say as well. A model increasingly used to simulate mergers in such markets is the Nash bargaining model. Nash's axiomatic model of bargaining can be thought of as a bargaining game between two or more parties where there is a (implicit) planner who distributes the gains from co-operation in a way that reflects the bargaining strength of each party.

The solution to the symmetric bargaining game offered by Nash positions a number of axioms, among others that the outcome should not depend on which player makes the first proposal, nor should it change when irrelevant alternatives exist. To see how this works, see the following. Let x be the outcome of a bargaining game, let d denote the payoff each player gets if no bargain is reached – referred to as its threat point. Let U_i be the payoff players get once an agreement has been reached. Nash then showed that any solution satisfying these axioms maximizes the value of:

$$[(U_1(x) - d_1)]^\alpha [(U_2(x) - d_2)]^{1-\alpha} \qquad (5.1)$$

where α measures the bargaining power of player 1 relative to that of player 2 – note that the power factor is unimportant when relative bargaining power is equal, so that $\alpha = 0.5$. This function can be interpreted as the product of incremental surpluses each player gets by reaching an agreement.

Rubinstein (1982) showed that the equilibrium of Nash's axiomatic approach was also the outcome of a non-cooperative game. When two players have to divide a given pie, they alternate in making a take-it-or-leave-it sharing offer, and so long as they do not reach an agreement and time keeps on ticking the total pie shrinks due to discounting. It can be shown that the first to make an offer will do so according to the Nash-bargaining solution and the other players will accept. The bargaining strength of each party depends on the individual discount factors and risk attitude.

Bargaining theory can quite naturally be applied to merger settings. It can be used for mergers in markets in which the players have indeed a shared influence on prices, for example because there are both few suppliers and few purchasers, as often is the case in industrial relationships higher up the production chain. In this setting, the players on each side of the bargaining table frequently pool together their powers to negotiate prices, effects that can become important in the assessment of a merger. Assume that there is an upstream and a downstream industry, each consisting of two firms. Let competition downstream be characterized by Cournot competition. The upstream industry supplies the downstream industry with a single input. Input prices are not unilaterally set by the upstream industry, but are negotiated between the upstream and the downstream firms. The input is supplied to each downstream firm by a single specific supplier, and there is no competition between the suppliers. What is more, the model has two stages: in the first stage, the suppliers and the downstream firms bargain over the price of the input, in the second stage, once the price agreements are fixed, the firms set quantities in the product market.

Assume now that a merger between the two suppliers in the upstream market is notified, and assume also that a supplier bargains with the two downstream firms symmetrically and simultaneously, and that the demand curves are linear. Intuitively one might think that a merger upstream strengthens the suppliers and thus makes a merger profitable. This would be so indeed if suppliers set their price independently without prior bargaining, since post-merger they would then internalize the lost sales due to any price increase in one division – a formerly independent firm. In Horn and Wolinsky (1988), a party strengthens its bargaining position over another party when it can make a credible commitment, which in turn makes concessions more costly. The bargaining position of the upstream industry is strengthened (weakened) by horizontal integration when the sign of the cross effect of a change in the input price of one division on the input demanded from the other division is positive (negative). This implies that if downstream products are substitutes, an integration of the upstream industry strengthens their bargaining power and thus increases their profits. It would weaken their bargaining power, however, if the downstream products are complements. Applying this result to mergers, it implies that when downstream products are substitutes, monopolization of the upstream industry is profitable and suppliers have an incentive to merge. With complementary downstream products, however, monopolization is unprofitable and there is a disincentive to merge – again, absent merger-specific efficiencies.

A similar reasoning holds for mergers of the downstream industry. That is, if the downstream industry is supplied by a single producer and there is symmetric bargaining power, a downstream merger is profitable when the products are substitutes but unprofitable when the products are complements. Inderst and Wey (2003) also present a model of input price determination in a bilateral oligopolistic industry with an upstream and downstream industry and analyse the incentive to merge on both levels. Other than Horn and Wolinsky (1988) however, they do not assume that each buyer is locked-in with a specific supplier. What is more, Inderst and Wey (2003) consider non-linear pricing contracts. They find that suppliers have an (dis-) incentive to merge if the inputs they supply are substitutes (complements). Moreover, they show that the downstream firms will find merging profitable if the upstream industry is characterized by strictly increasing unit costs. In a follow-up paper, Inderst and Wey (2004) further show that in the face of bilateral bargaining, increasing concentration in the downstream industry can in fact be welfare-enhancing as it increases the supplying industry's incentive to innovate and to choose a more efficient technology.

For application purposes, it is important to note that auction and bargaining solutions, as well as the effects of mergers between previously independent parties on them, have first and foremost an effect on distribution, and not necessarily so much on efficiency and total welfare. Nevertheless, these effects can be of considerable concern in merger settings, in particular when a consumer welfare standard is applied – as is explicitly the case in European merger control, and effectively in that in the US as well.[17] Models along these lines could therefore also address issues of sufficient pass-on of merger-specific efficiency gains to consumers. Bargaining models, or elements thereof, can be instrumental in a full weighing of anticompetitive and efficiency effects of intentions to merge.

1.5 Dimensions of Variation in Applied Models

The debate on the use of sophisticated modelling techniques in merger control, despite the involvement of leading protagonists in the enforcement agencies, is to a large extent still academic. Very little use is made of full-blown simulation modelling in published cases – although behind closed doors, apparently these methods are quite widely used to obtain a basic intuition for countervailing effects.[18] The only supra-national case where in-house developed simulation models have explicitly contributed to decision making, simultaneously by FTC in the US and by DG Competition for the EC, has, in fact, been the recent Oracle/Peoplesoft case.[19] The sensitivity of the analysis makes legal counsel cautious about using conclusions based on simulation exercises as evidence, out of fear that the analysis may backfire. After all, slight variations in models may lead to significantly different findings, and might even come to support the opponent's case.

In Europe, the legal climate for experimenting with these new methods has recently become friendlier. Analyses in which strategic interaction was assumed to be of the Cournot type were recently done for the iron ore industry by Lyons and Davies (2003), as well as for the Dutch electricity industry in the Nuon/Reliant case.[20] Extensive merger simulation analyses based on Bertrand competition were carried out by DG Competition, among others, in Hachette/Lagardère and Volvo/Scania.[21] The number of cases to which merger simulation techniques have been applied by national competition authorities in the various Member States is also considerable, given the short time since the implementation of these techniques in Europe (see also the chapters by Van Bergeijk and Kloosterhuis and Kalbfleisch in this volume). The literature on applying auction models in the context of merger simulations is still in development.[22] Finally, merger simulation analysis applying sophisticated bargaining theory has, to the best of our knowledge, not been used in public cases so far.

The modelling techniques that have been used in these recent merger decisions are, although impressive in their own right, still only exploiting few of the many dimensions for sophisticated tailor-made analysis that economic theory has to offer. As a result, this application of microeconomic models of market competition amongst a few in the assessment of mergers is, although a field with some history and in quite rapid development, still rather rudimentary. Many well-understood extensions to the classic models have so far not found application. These include: as non-linear cost structures; capacity constraints and their associated mix of Cournot and Bertrand competition; different conjectural variations of parties on the strategic reactions of their rivals; and full-blown modelling of issues associated with longer, and discounted, planning horizons. Neither has there been much regard for R&D impulses, or the opening up of new markets, instigated by mergers. Instead, the debate is rather top-heavy on the specification of demand functions – possibly because demand analysis also underlies the determination of the relevant market.

Since merger control is, indeed, trying to anticipate future developments, it should ideally assess mergers taking their long-term implications for the relevant market into consideration. This would call for more dynamic modelling, including, for example, the possibilities of preemptive mergers, triggering a merger wave when allowing an in itself presumably innocent merger, or alternative merger strategies in response to a blocked merger.[23] Relative to the potential for this, the present use of the available spectrum in the few cases in which merger simulation techniques were applied is still rather narrow, which has had significant effects on the conclusions reached.[24]

Finally, we note that in the existing models it is relatively straightforward to include assessments of potential merger-specific efficiencies. In fact, several merger simulation packages developed for merger control assessments already include this option. They allow for setting a decrease in costs when a merger is consummated, thus weighing such effects against all the other ones in equilibrium. These possibilities have, however, to our knowledge not been explored very much in the merger simulation cases mentioned above – with the notable exception of Volvo/Scania and Oracle/Peoplesoft, in which, however, only a few efficiency scenarios with exogenously fixed merger-specific gains were considered for their qualitative effect on the model predictions, and no systematic efficiency analyses.

2. ENFORCEMENT ISSUES IN MERGER CONTROL

Merger simulation analysis clearly is an open field for further research that is promising for theorists and practitioners alike. Yet, we would like to point to some limitations of this type of analysis as well. In fact, although they may help to structure arguments and bring out underlying assumptions and logical reasoning for all to see, it remains an open question as to how far the present economic models can be used to predict the future effects of mergers at all. Moreover, it is important to be aware of enforcement issues linked to the use of these techniques. These relate to the actual application of simulation in cases and their role in the final decisions of competition authorities or courts. One crucial point in the implementation procedure in general is a guarantee of an appropriate degree of transparency in the use of these models. It seems a minimum to ask, for example, that the source code of an applied simulation model is open and shared minimally by all parties with a stake in the proceedings —obviously respecting constraints on confidentiality and copyright. In fact, any (competing) model applied should be open to critical scrutiny, just like an economists acting as an expert witness is asked to explain the logic leading to his or her conclusions. If the model applied cannot be critically discussed and questioned, this may introduce unwanted strategic behaviour. In fact, without openness, the key benefit of using merger simulation models forwarded in Werden's contribution, which is that "[m]erger simulation ... replaces subjective and unverifiable surmise with objective and verifiable calculation", will not be reached. An open debate is also likely to ease the acceptance of simulation models in court. If parties and authorities use confidentiality arguments to hold back information used in the model exercises, this could shield and thereby maintain models that are, in fact, ill-suited for the market at hand or out-dated. Transparency is likely to have a positive influence on the progress of simulation techniques, by weeding out false methods and advancing robust ones.[25]

Even when their logic is open for everyone to see, the results of simulation studies or other kinds of empirical analyses are often difficult to interpret and appreciate, even for economic experts. Without an economic background it can be hard to fully understand the link between the empirical analysis and the conclusions drawn from it, or to compare the outcomes of two competing econometric studies. This presents difficulties for all involved: parties, competition authorities, outside counsel and often eventually judges. When used as part of the argument in a case, simulation models could therefore be misinterpreted or disregarded by decision makers lacking the experience and knowledge in the field.[26] In fact, Coleman and Scheffman (2005) note for the US practice that econometric evidence in general is often disregarded by judges in antitrust cases when taking the final decision in a case. More specifically, the authors stress that once there are concurrent empirical analyses with diverging results, there is a danger that the judge might interpret this as a "cancelling out" of the analyses. As a result, courts might not take the analyses into account as a whole.[27] An associated danger is that analyses that were accepted in the past in a given case are relied upon as precedent for later decisions. Since the applicability of sophisticated economic argument to merger control is often idiosyncratic, there should not develop an automatic best-model standard on the basis of past jurisprudence that is not constantly revised in light of progressing economic insight.

In order to prevent these undesirable developments, we stress with Coleman and Scheffman (2005) the need for a proper education of competition practitioners, lawyers and judges in the methodology of scientific theory. Divergent conclusions in different studies are common and often beneficial in finding the right answers. What is more, it obviously is not analytically sound to argue that conflicting results from different studies neutralize each other. Instead, conclusions should be based on an informed balancing of the quality of the analyses, their limitations and appropriateness for admitting findings based on their application in any given case. Again, openness of applied methodologies is key to this.

Furthermore, an efficient procedure in gathering data is essential to properly run the simulation. This also implies that the parties involved supply the requested data in an early stage of the investigation, which ensures that there is sufficient time for the authorities to check their quality and increase it, if necessary. One way to ensure proper and timely data is to make sure that there is a standard format in which the data is to be delivered by the parties involved. This would make it easier to work with the data for the simulation analysis, which speeds up the process. A recommendation could be to standardize Phase I requests along these lines.[28]

In the panoply of implementation scenarios for simulation models, some European Member State authorities have opted to build their own tailor-made simulation model for each case where they believed simulation analysis to be useful.[29] Others have worked with outside experts (academics and specialists in the consultancies) to construct simulation models for specific cases, with varying degrees of own involvement.[30] In order to avoid methods quickly becoming outdated and their application undesirably mechanistic, a firm link with experts in the field seems desirable. A third possible scenario is to only use fairly generic models as a quick screen for cases. Such generic models could be used in Phase I of the investigation to see whether they point towards possible concerns on balance in the case under investigation. In case they do, this information could be used alongside qualitative data to opt for an in-depth Phase II investigation. Should the authority wish to use a simulation model for Phase II, it could then commission a complete tailor-made simulation analysis to academics or outside consultants. Which of these various options is chosen by a given authority very much depends on factors such as the expectations of how often simulation analysis will be used in future cases and how much in-house build-up of expertise is desired. All European authorities, including the European Commission, that are using simulation analysis, presently have a separate economics department that has as one of its responsibilities to build up sustained economic expertise.

Generally, merger simulation analyses that go beyond Phase I screening, irrespective of the mix of outside and in-house expertise, typically consume a considerable amount of resources and time. For competition authorities with limited budgets, it is therefore crucial to weigh the costs and benefits of using such complex techniques. On the benefit side surely, and other things equal, enhanced empirical methods can reduce the error margins in assessing mergers and thereby help to contribute to sound interventions. Real industries, however, are complicated and difficult to understand in detail – particularly for outsiders, which is what competition authorities are. Also, economic theory has developed into a quite sophisticated body of insights. General equilibrium theory, for example, provides a deep understanding of how essential it is that markets are analysed as interrelated.[31] To some extent, this deep dimension has been incorporated in the traditional macroeconomic models used with authority particularly in the 1970s and 80s by national central planning bureaus. Whether or not these multidimensional models can really predict beyond the first digit with much confidence today is questioned. As basic as they are relative to both actual market developments and economic theory, the question how much predictive power the simulation techniques presently available really have remains open.

One way to enlarge the applicability of merger simulation techniques is to establish a feedback learning loop from previous merger decisions back into the state of the art in modelling. Various testing stages can then shed light on how well the models are (or rather were) able to predict. A comparison of past predictions with eventual developments may help to determine the sizes of past errors in enforcement. On top of that, previous cases can be used as a tool to practice the use of simulation models before applying them to actual cases. These analyses can then give insight into the amount of understanding that is lost by the application of basic models to intrinsically complex markets and how much structural effect they nevertheless pick up. So far, and for understandable reasons, authorities have been reluctant to open up their books and allow an evaluation of their past decisions.[32] Self-assessments should become part of an open learning process, however, for this competition policy practice to progress.

In all of this, an essential and fundamental early question to ask is whether the benefits of applying a rule of reason approach to merger control outweigh the costs involved in this. Apart from the obvious outlay of resources for personal and equipment to do the involved merger simulation analyses, these costs include detrimental regulatory effects from allowing efficiency arguments to be weighted in the decision whether or not to block a merger. Fisher (1987) points to the drawbacks of regulatory capture and rent seeking when parties are allowed to argue their case using merger-specific benefits. In a context of asymmetric and costly information these arguments are considered in Lagerloef and Heidhues (2005).

The central question here obviously is what can be gained by applying a rule of reason, rather than a per se rule. In merger control, the stakes are high, which would merit some form of tailored weighing of the pros and cons to reducing the error margins in merger control, that are felt at the firm level as well as by consumers. Nevertheless, surely relatively fixed rules have their benefits for all parties involved: they reduce enforcement costs on both sides and provide legal certainty. Also, per se rules avoid a danger that is always lurking when sophisticated methods are given status, yet their limitations are not fully grasped. This danger is the "crystal ball syndrome", which is the tendency to read with too much confidence too much future in media that are unsuited for that purpose. With all its potential to enhance merger control, when falsely assessed, merger simulation models may give an illusionary objectivity that may do more harm than good to proper merger analysis.

3. THE WERDEN–FROEB INDEX (WFI)

As a safe route to sail between the Skylla of static *ex ante* HHI thresholds and the Charybdis of costly and uncertain merger simulation methods, we propose a new measurement tool that captures merger-specific efficiency gains, yet does not have all of the drawbacks pointed to above: the Werden–Froeb index, or WFI. The WFI is based on the concept of Compensating Marginal Cost Reductions (CMCRs), developed in the late 1990s by Werden and Froeb.[33] CMCRs measure merger-specific relative cost savings that are required to just replicate the *status quo* in terms of prices and quantities that exist prior to the merger, after the merger. As explained in Section 2, given a structural model of an industry, if two formerly competing firms integrate their pricing or production decisions, prices will typically rise and market shares of all the firms in the industry will adjust accordingly. When together with the change in firm structure other variables are also properly adjusted, it would be possible to re-establish the pre-merger market equilibrium in terms of prices, quantities and market shares. The CMCRs are based on the decrease in marginal production cost levels – representing efficiency gains – that just offset the competition-reducing effects of the merger. The CMCR of each commodity in the merger is equal to this required decrease in marginal costs, relative to the original marginal costs level.

If a merger involves a number of differentiated commodities sold prior to the merger by the merging parties – and hence after the merger by the single merged firm – the required efficiency gains typically vary over the goods. That is, for some commodities it may be necessary to generate very large merger-specific efficiencies, whereas for others small cost savings would suffice.[34] The Werden–Froeb index really is only a minor advance over the original CMCR concept, to deal with this. The main innovation is that it is a single statistic: the WFI is the weighted average of the different minimally required merger-specific efficiency gains, in which the weights are the shares in total production of the merged firm. This generalizes the notion of CMCRs to a measure of the total relative decrease in the costs of producing the commodities involved in the merger required to preserve the *status quo*.

Let there be two firms that intend to merge, with the first merger partner producing n_1 commodities and the second n_2. Should the merger indeed be consummated, the merged firm produces $n = n_1 + n_2$ products.[35] The WFI should measure how much more cost efficient this bundle is to produce after the merger. Let the absolute required decrease in the marginal costs of producing commodity j – initially c_j – in the merged firm's production vector be $\Delta c_j \geq 0$. The WFI is then defined as

$$WFI = 100 \frac{\sum_{j=1}^{n} q_j \Delta c_j}{\sum_{j=1}^{n} q_j c_j}$$

(5.2)

The WFI should be thought of as a critical percentage in the assessment of merger-specific efficiencies in merger control. If its critical level of efficiency gains – or more – can confidently be expected to materialize as a result of the merger, competition authorities should be inclined to consider allowing the merger. To determine its value requires a specific choice of competitive model (Cournot or Bertrand with product differentiation), information on sales quantities, demand elasticities and marginal costs. Sales volume data are simply equal to the pre-merger sales by construction. Moreover, marginal costs could – when not directly available, which will often be the case – in theory be recovered from the mark-ups when (pre-merger) prices are known, since a structural model is assumed to underlie the required cost reductions. Hence, for calculating WFI values, no more information is required than for determining the original CMCRs – which admittedly still is a demanding amount.

The WFI can be a useful statistic in merger control for a variety of reasons. First, it is an exact measure. That is, rather than performing an approximate calculation of the price and quantity changes, and possibly product repositioning, that would result from the merger in a full structural model fleshed out with the relevant data, the WFI has an explicit expression. Although it does not escape the problem of model choice specific qualitative findings, a second advantage of having the *status quo* market situation as a base is that the WFI value is independent of the functional form of demand

and costs. As set out above, in the few applied merger simulation models, the functional form of demand significantly affected the predicted post-merger prices and quantities.[36] The issue consequently claims a large share of both discussions and research budgets. Since the WFI is only a local measure, it requires much less specification. Third, the statistic is well-defined and easy to interpret, and it can be published without revealing the underlying data, which is often confidential. It thus avoids some of the drawbacks of undisclosed model approaches, as discussed in Section 3 – although, obviously, a (confidential) specification of underlying elasticities and mark-ups is still required. Fourth, the WFI incorporates the EC competition law requirement that claimed efficiencies are passed on to consumers. After all, it is *minimally* required that the *status quo* in consumer prices and quantities is restored. These and any further efficiency gains, therefore, come to the direct benefit of consumers. Fifth, the WFI can be produced by several of the existing merger simulation packages. It could, therefore, find application relatively straightforwardly. Finally, the measure is practical and decreases legal uncertainty when specific acceptable WFI threshold values are set.

Setting such threshold WFI values for application in merger control is not obvious. One way to substantiate it departs from the following observation. In the past decade-and-a-half of European merger control, in a number of mergers that were initially challenged and led to a Phase II investigation, the competition authority handling the case nevertheless eventually decided to allow the merger – with or without divestitures.[37] Since the mergers that raised such concerns had, if only by construction, at least some anticompetitive effect – typically substantial concentration concerns when a Phase II investigation was entered into – the underlying justification for nevertheless allowing the consummation of the merger must at some level have involved implicit merger-specific benefits.[38] In other words, the history of merger control enforcement in hindsight may well allow for establishing implied threshold values for apparently acceptable WFI values that were expected to materialize after the merger, prior to the merger. These implied safe-haven values of the WFI could be distilled to determine appropriate threshold values below which a notified merger can safely be allowed. Perhaps these thresholds are 5 per cent or 10 per cent, perhaps 15 per cent. Perhaps, also, they do not display a pattern at all. This is an issue for further research –and, of course, only one way to go about this policy matter.

If indeed merger control is to be further enhanced by sophisticated economic modelling, the WFI could serve as a derived criterion that is free from many of the drawbacks of a full merger simulation approach. We suggest it be considered for a next edition of the horizontal merger guidelines. In a Phase I investigation, a merger that surpasses the HHI concentration threshold values, may, for example, nevertheless be cleared without the need to enter Phase II, if its WFI is lower than a set level.[39] Just like with the HHI, firms could then know what is expected of them in terms of required efficiencies for the merger to be allowed. This would extend the application of economic logic and rigor considerably over its present role, without creating a large amount of legal uncertainty or room for lengthy and expensive legal and economic argument. Using the WFI in this manner, the minimum required efficiencies are compared to a fixed target that is *a priori* set by the competition authority. As a result, if the WFI-based efficiency defence were to be allowed as a standard, less rent seeking would be triggered than any general post-merger efficiency claims would. Moreover, the WFI focuses the debate.

5. CONCLUSION

Proper merger control wisely exploits the new openings for the inclusion of merger-specific efficiency arguments in the latest *Horizontal Merger Guidelines* of the European Commission. It should go beyond the static use of pre-merger HHI threshold values, and allow a weighing of anticompetitive effects and merger specific benefits. Merger simulation techniques hold a promise to assist in this. We have reviewed four fundamental models that underlie the merger simulation techniques that are presently in gradual demand in merger control. We found that, although quite sophisticated, these models remain rather basic, in at least two respects. First, they draw from a class of partial oligopoly models that does not include the full wealth of insights economic theory has to offer. Second, within this class, at present the techniques in use explore only a few of the dimensions of variation known in the literature. Given the complexity of real economies, it can be questioned whether the underlying models are suitable as a basis to derive reasonably reliable predictions. These models were never, in fact, intended for that purpose. Only seasoned economists, who combine the various theoretical and empirical insights that have been established over the years in the field of industrial organization, draw on extensive experience, and form opinions only after detailed study of the industry at hand, are sometimes capable of good judgement in given cases. It does not seem possible to replicate such good judgement by explicit modelling mergers in only a few dimensions. Merger simulation techniques are not expert knowledge systems, and it is unlikely that they ever will be. Although they can be a useful tool to focus on particular aspects of a case at hand and complement traditional methods, at best simulations can substantiate parts of the analysis. They should not be mistaken for the full story.

Current developments in both US and EU merger control to embrace complicated and costly, yet inherently partial methods, which may well lead to unwanted legal uncertainty and rent seeking in merger cases, has to be followed critically for a variety of reasons. Moreover, there exist other, more pressing problems perhaps, between which competition authorities should wisely allocate their limited budgets. This risk of a disproportionally strong emphasis on merger control in competition policy is increased when more faith than justified is placed in merger simulation techniques. Rather than running the risk of furthering the "crystal ball syndrome", we suggest in this chapter to first take the careful intermediate step of using the Werden–Froeb Index. The WFI is exact, informationally efficient, and well-defined. It is not as sensitive to model specifics as full-blown merger simulations often are. It can focus the debate on sufficient merger specific efficiencies, is therefore less likely to trigger rent seeking and gives legal guidance. The WFI thus allows for a fair weighing of the pros and cons of mergers, without many of the known drawbacks of doing so, and without pretending that we can predict with very great accuracy what we often really cannot.

NOTES

* This chapter is based in part on a study by Marie Goppelsröder for the Netherlands Competition Authority (NMa), published as Goppelsröder (2004). We benefited from discussions with Wim Driehuis, Patrick van Cayseele, Fabio Massimo Esposito, Luke Froeb, Eric Kloosterhuis, Bruce Lyons, Serge Moresi, Damien Neven, Rainer Nitsche, Torben Thoro Pedersen, Damiaan Persyn, Lars-Hendrik Röller, Carsten Smidt, Jan-Willem Velthuijsen, Frank Verboven, Ludo Visschers and Gregory Werden, as well as members of the Chief Economist Team of the European Commission and the Merger Control Department of the NMa. We thank Simon Bremer, Theresa Carpenter, Tomaso Duso, and Jan Tuinstra for comments to earlier drafts of this chapter. Marie Goppelsröder gratefully acknowledges financial support from the CEPR Research and Training Network project "Competition Policy in International Markets".

1. An extensive seminal empirical analysis of such Type I and Type II errors in European merger control, Duso, Neven and Röller (2003), finds the error margin to be quite symmetrically around 25 per cent.

2. See Section 1.

3. The seminal paper on the weighing of anticompetitive and efficiency effects, consequently also called Williamsonian calculus, is Williamson (1968). The point is well taken that there are detrimental regulatory effects from allowing efficiency arguments to be weighted in the decision whether or not to block a merger. For some observations on this, see Section 3.

4. These threshold static HHI values presently are 2000 in absolute value, and 150 in terms of the change in HHI post-merger – using pre-merger measurements. See OJ C31, p.7.

5. European Commission (2004), para. 77, italics added. See also Walker (2005). The EC Guidelines follow in this respect on the 1997 revised US Guidelines, which allowed for merger-specific efficiencies already, see US DOJ and FTC (1992), as well as the survey in Kolasky and Dick (2003).

6. See in particular Werden and Froeb (2005) and many of the references given therein, as well as Gregory Werden's contribution to the present book. Seminal in the European context are Lundval (2002) and Ivaldi and Verboven (2005).

7. A much more extensive survey is, for example, provided in Werden and Froeb (2005). See also Werden's introduction into game theory concepts in his chapter in this book.

8. The Cournot model can be analysed for any given number of firms in competition. Typically, it is laid out graphically for a duopoly. For the sake of the exposition below, we focus on a situation in which there initially are three firms in the market, so that we can illustrate the consequences of two of them merging. The exposition in the text is based on Martin (1994), Chapter 9.

9. When there are fixed costs, that is, to the point where each competitor makes zero economic profits – and equilibrium that establishes if entry and exist are free and costless.

10. Further influential papers on mergers in Cournot markets are Perry and Porter (1985), Davidson and Deneckere (1984), and Farrell and Shapiro (1990, 2001).

11. Later extensions include Kreps and Scheinkman (1983), and Davidson and Deneckere (1985).

12. See, for example, Hausman, Leonard and Zona (1994), Hausman and Leonard (1997), Werden and Froeb (1996) for an application to simulation models.

13. See Davidson and Deneckere (1985).

14. For an excellent survey on auction theory see Klemperer (2004). The backbone literature in auction models includes Vickrey (1961), Griesmer, Levitan and Shubik (1967), Ortega Reichert (1968) and Wilson (1969). More recent models were developed by Milgrom (1981), Riley (1989) and Maskin (1992). For an application to simulation models, see Froeb and Tschantz (2002).

15. It should be noted, however, that this logic is debatable, for the winning firm has, other things equal, no incentive to produce at higher costs than strictly necessary after winning the bid. X-inefficiency could nevertheless be substantiated by introducing a difference between firm objectives and manager objectives.

16. The recent literature on mergers in auction markets includes Brannman and Froeb (2000), and Dalkir, Logan and Masson (2000).

17. For an assessment of the implications of a consumer surplus standard versus a total welfare standard, see Neven and Röller (2005). The former standard is argued to be less prone to adverse lobby pressures in merger control.

18. A number of economics consulting firms, such as Charles River Associates, LECG, NERA and PriceWaterHouseCoopers have in-house developed merger simulation packages that are often quite advanced. Several of those are evaluated in Goppelsröder (2004).

19. For the EU decision, see Comp/M.3216-Oracle/Peoplesoft. For the US decision, see *United States of America v. Oracle Corporation*, No. C 04-0807 VRW. For an analysis of actual mergers in the airline industry using merger simulation techniques, see Peters (2003). See also Nevo (2000), in which simulation analyses are used to assess actual, as well as hypothetical mergers in the cereal

industry. For the use of simulation analysis during an actual investigation by an enforcement agency, even though it was not used in the decision, see Werden (2000).

20. Case 3386/Nuon-Reliant (2003). See also the contribution of Jan de Maa and Gijsbert Zwart, elsewhere in this book.
21. See Ivaldi and Verboven (2005), as well as Marc Ivaldi's contribution elsewhere in this book.
22. See Froeb and Tschantz (2002) for a survey. In the Oracle/Peoplesoft cases in the EU and the US, an auction model was used for simulation purposes.
23. See Fridolfsson and Stennek (2005).
24. Apart from the seminal papers already quoted above, sources for various dimensions in which models of strategic behaviour have been extended in economic theory are Tirole (1988), Martin (1994) and Motta (2004).
25. In 3386/Nuon/Reliant (2003), for example, the source code of the analysis carried out by an outside consultancy on behalf of the Netherlands Competition Authority was not disclosed, so that consultants working for the merging parties had to construct, on only loose instructions, their own replica of the original model. Apart from wasting resources, this did not facilitate the debate, to say the least.
26. See Baker (1999) for the use of econometric evidence and its acceptance in court.
27. A similar concern, including methods to remedy this effect by favouring simple econometric analyses over more complicated ones – even when the latter are objectively better – purely to avoid problems with insufficiently trained officials, is advocated in Bishop and Walker (2002). Although this is a sensible operational strategy in the field, it cannot be accepted as a long-term equilibrium. All parties have an obligation to mutual schooling to enhance future enforcement.
28. We are grateful to members of the Chief Economist Team of the European Commission for this suggestion. Obviously, the reliability of such submitted information remains an issue, see Lagerloef and Heidhues (2005).
29. Authorities opting for this possibility have typically set up and economics department with trained econometricians and economists. Examples are Denmark, Italy and Sweden. See also the contribution of Fabio Massimo Esposito, elsewhere in this book.
30. This approach is currently taken by the Italian Competition Authority, inside their economics department.
31. On the many insights obtained in this field, see Kehoe, Srinivasan and Whalley (2005).
32. This type of feedback learning has been taking place at the FTC, for instance – see Froeb, Hosken and Papalardo (2005). In Europe, and only very recently, the UK has started an *ex post* evaluation of several mergers that were cleared by the Competition Commission. In OFT, CC and DTI (2005), 2 of 10 investigated consummated mergers nevertheless turned out to have caused competition concerns, at least in the short-run.
33. See Werden (1996) and Froeb and Werden (1998), which lay out how CMCRs can be calculated on the basis of mark-ups and diversion ratios – which, in turn,

are based on own- and cross-price elasticities of demand – in, respectively, a Bertrand differentiated commodities, and a Cournot homogenous goods setting.

34. In some settings, the WFI may not be uniquely determined in that various combinations of CMCRs over the merger-implied commodities would regenerate the status quo. For example, the combination of large efficiency gains on one good and small ones on another may lead to the same outcome as the other way around. In such cases of multiple solutions, it seems natural to ask the merging firms to meet the lowest possible value of the WFI as a threshold (see text), since that would be a feasible cost savings – and it seems furthermore in line with the firm's objectives to materialize the largest possible post-merger cost savings.

35. Note that typically it will be part of the merged firm's post-merger strategy to discontinue or extend its product line. However, in establishing the WFI it is natural to assume that the range stays as it is, since the measure uses the *status quo* as its analytical base point. This is a further benefit of the measure.

36. Typically, log-linear and AIDS demand functions yield the highest changes in price and quantity, whereas linear demand functions come to more conservative predictions. See Crooke, Froeb, Tschantz and Werden (1999). Obviously, the WFI remains level-dependent of the class of underlying models.

37. In the case of DG Competition, of all Phase II investigations since the beginning of merger control enforcement in 1990, 26 mergers were cleared unconditionally (Art. 8(2)), 72 were cleared with conditions and obligations (Art. 8(3)), and only 19 were blocked (Art. 8(3)). (as on March 8, 2005) .

38. Obviously, we abstract here from the possibility that merger decisions are influenced politically, or otherwise efficiency unrelated. This may be a rather heroic assumption – if only because in the EU, market integration of Member States is an explicit objective of competition policy. The absence of a pattern in implied WFI values could, in fact, be a measure of non-economic arguments in merger control. Note in this context that Duso, Neven and Röller (2003) report indeed no significant political determinants.

39. The proposed application may require the determination of a second, upper-bound critical (delta) HHI value, such that a Phase II investigation is always entered when the merger surpasses this upper-bound threshold, irrespective of its WFI. The precise relationship between HHI and WFI, as well as the region(s) in which they discriminate under various conditions, is a topic of further research.

6. Merger Simulation Analysis: An Academic Perspective

Eric van Damme and Joris Pinkse[*]

Merger control is changing. In Europe, we have recently seen a change in the substantial test that is used to assess mergers. While the old test required the authorities to investigate whether a dominant position was created or strengthened as a result of the merger, the new test insists that it be investigated whether or not the merger would significantly impede effective competition. As has been widely discussed, this change brings European merger policy more in line with that in other jurisdictions such as the the US. The change in focus, from dominance to effective competition, roughly a shift in focus from Article 82 type tools to those used in the analysis of Article 81 cases, invites and enables the use of new techniques of economic analysis. At the same time, it raises old questions: what is competition and what do we mean by a significant impediment to effective competition? Is an impediment to competition equivalent to a reduction of total welfare or of consumer surplus? Or are these static notions from welfare economics too narrow and should we also consider dynamic aspects, i.e. treat competition as a process? Would a more dynamic approach do away with the possible divergence between competition and consumer welfare? These issues are discussed to some extent in the EU Guidelines on the assessment of horizontal mergers (European Commission, 2004), and also (at a more abstract level) by Boone (2004a), who argues that there is no obvious definition of 'competition' and that measuring the degree of competition is a nontrivial exercise.

Not only is the formal test for the assessment of the effects of mergers changing, the techniques for implementing it are changing, also. There is now more scope for the use of novel scientific methods. Merger control aims to prevent mergers that reduce consumer surplus by increasing the market power of firms. As economists are well aware, market share is a rather imperfect proxy for market power. Hence, methods that are based on market share criteria alone may induce both type I and type II errors, i.e. some anticompetitive mergers proceed and some non-problematic ones are disallowed. Targeting market power directly may be difficult and is moreover still circuitous. In a sense, the newer methods target the ultimate criterion, i.e. consumer surplus, directly: they investigate or estimate how consumer surplus changes as a result of a merger. The methods build on and integrate two branches of economics: game theory and econometrics. In this chapter, we discuss these two subdisciplines in the current context. In doing so, we explore the benefits and limitations of modern merger analysis, i.e. of merger simulation, from an academic perspective.

The first section deals with (game-)theoretical issues. We argue that a merger analyst must make several modelling choices, each with its own assumptions. Some assumptions are taken for granted in the (neo-classical) theoretical literature, others are implicitly made to maintain tractability in empirical work without full support from theory. We discuss the results of several experimental studies and some field studies which call the validity of several of these assumptions into question. However, since the subjects in such experiments are typically inexperienced students, not company executives, it is not clear what credible inferences can be made on the basis of such experiments (with respect to the plausibility of assumptions) when it comes to the analysis of actual mergers. See Götte and Schmutzler (2005) for an overview of experimental results related to mergers.

Section 2 explores the choices to be made in the empirical implementation. Typically, richer data sets yield results that are more precise, but that are also more expensive to obtain. We discuss the pros and cons of each choice, depending on the situation a merger analyst encounters. We argue that while calibration is cheap and can be done in a limited amount of time, it is less reliable than estimation and does not provide testability.

In the final section we conclude that the methods discussed in this book offer a potentially important improvement if valued against the benchmark of the "old-fashioned" market-share determined approach to merger analysis. We also warn against too mechanical a use of economic models.

1.   THEORY

What effect will a merger have on prices, quantities, consumer surplus and total welfare? A growing literature attempts to answer this question by means of model simulation. Such a simulation analysis requires three types of input: input relating to the demand side, to the supply side and to the mode of competition.

1.1 Pre-merger Data

In the first stage, the model is calibrated or estimated using pre-merger data. Usually, one begins by estimating a system of demand equations for all products under consideration. As the various chapters in this book testify, a great many possibilities exist. In section 2, several of these are discussed in some detail.

As a second important building block, the analyst assumes a form (mode) of competition between the firms. Frequently, the Bertrand model is used, as Bertrand (price) competition is often viewed as a good representation of the competitive situation. Alternatives abound: the Cournot (quantity setting) model may be used, or an auction model (and in that case there are several candidates to choose from), or one may use a supply function equilibrium model, in which bidders bid quantities depending on the price that will eventually result in the market. If one expects that the pre-merger situation is characterized by a certain degree of collusion already, one may start out with reaction function equilibria, or another type of equilibrium known from the "Folk Theorem", an important result in repeated game theory. Given the plethora of choices, it will be clear that knowledge about the industry is useful, indeed indispensable, to guide the proper choice.

The third relevant element of the pre-merger model relates to the supply side, that is, the (marginal) cost functions of the firms involved in the industry. Assuming profit maximization, one can frequently infer the marginal costs from the estimated elasticities and the form of competition. For example, in the case of monopoly we have

$$\frac{p-c}{p} = \frac{1}{\varepsilon} \tag{6.1}$$

where ε is the (absolute) price elasticity of demand, hence, if $\varepsilon = 2$ and $p = 10$ we must have that marginal cost is given by $c = 5$: we do not need to estimate marginal cost separately.

Note, however, that in order to infer marginal costs from prices, we had to use another assumption, i.e. profit maximization by firms. While this is a standard assumption to make in neo-classical economics, we know surprisingly little about actual price setting in real markets; see for example the large-scale ECB project on inflation persistence in the Euro area and in particular the background papers to the December 2004 conference.[1] Furthermore, we know (see e.g. Bartelsman and Doms 2000) that firms active in the same market can differ substantially in their productivity levels. Hence, competitive forces are apparently not always sufficient to guarantee that firms maximize profits. Related to this, the extensive discussions on corporate governance indicate that managers may well induce a firm to deviate from profit maximization. In short, the result that marginal costs can be inferred from other data relies on strong assumptions. It would therefore seem worthwhile to try to estimate marginal costs independently.

Thus, for each of the three types of data that are needed to conduct a merger simulation, there are a lot of choices to be made. One should hence be careful not to exaggerate the implications of one's analysis.

1.2 Equilibrium

In the best case, the constructed model will have a unique equilibrium, thus allowing an evaluation of the pre-merger situation in terms of total welfare or consumer surplus. One is not always so lucky. Repeated games and supply function models allow for multiple equilibria, in which case additional assumptions have to be made. (The chapter by Zwart and De Maa provides an example.) In the simulation of the Nuon–Reliant merger done by the NMa, the central prediction was based on the "median equilibrium", but this equilibrium concept is not solidly grounded in game theory. In fairness, game theory cannot currently provide an adequate answer to the authors' problem. In fact, while frequent references to selection criteria such as "risk dominance" and "Pareto dominance" occur in the (game theory) literature, one has to admit that, in general, the equilibrium selection problem is unsolved. Be that as it may, the selection of the "median equilibrium" is not based on any of the general selection criteria from game theory.

Let us assume that the mode of competition is Bertrand and that the equilibrium is unique. A merger brings different products under common ownership and it will in this case relax the competitive pressure on the merging firm, such that it typically will be able to increase prices. If *reaction functions* are upward sloping, as they typically are, other firms will respond by raising prices, also.[2] Consequently, all prices will increase and the consumers will be worse off, if there are no synergies.

1.3 Efficiencies

If the merger allows the merging firms to produce at (substantially) lower marginal cost, then, in the setting described above, the new firm may be a more aggressive competitor, and there can be downward pressure on prices instead. This shows that it is important to incorporate appropriate assumptions about the cost savings that are obtained as a result of the merger into the analysis. However, as the EU Guidelines on the assessment of horizontal mergers state: "cost savings are easily claimed but seldom demonstrated." The Guidelines insist that the efficiencies generated by the merger are likely to enhance pro-competitive behaviour that is ultimately to the benefit of consumers. Specifically, the efficiency gains have to benefit consumers, they should be merger-specific and they should be verifiable. These are formidable requirements.

The Guidelines further require (in paragraph 80) that marginal cost reductions are more important than reductions in fixed costs. This stance is justified in case the standard neo-classical assumption of profit maximization is appropriate but, as mentioned above, such an assumption is not necessarily accurate. Accordingly, it is possible that the pricing policy of the merging firms is such that fixed cost reductions can also result in lower prices. That this possibility should not be rejected out of hand is supported by the experiments conducted by Offerman and Potters (2000). The authors report on the results of Bertrand games in which players first have to pay to acquire the right to participate in the game. The payment to participate in a game is a sunk cost which, according to standard theory, implies that it should not influence the price that is charged.

Indeed, as Ricardo first argued, the market price determines the price one is willing to pay to enter the market, not the other way around. Offerman and Potters (2000), however, find that in their experimental markets it is in fact the other way around: if players have to pay more, they compete less fiercely and charge higher prices. Specifically, if the right to play is auctioned, then the higher the auction price, the higher the market price. More generally it might be true that higher fixed costs result in higher market prices, and consequently that a merger that reduces fixed costs also reduces prices.

Efficiency gains in the form of a reduction of marginal costs do not necessarily result in lower prices. This is the case if the cost savings are large enough and if the mode of competition remains Bertrand. But Boone (2004b) has argued that lower marginal costs do not necessarily lead to lower prices if the mode of competition changes. Consider, for example, the following setting in which there is inelastic demand $D(p) = 1$ if $p \leq 1$ and there are three firms with marginal costs $c_1 = 0$, $c_2 = 0.5$ and $c_3 = 0.7$. Boone argues that in this pre-merger situation, Bertrand competition is likely to result, and the market price will hence be $p = 0.5$. Now assume that firms 2 and 3 merge so as to produce a very efficient competitor of firm 1 with equal marginal costs $c_{23} = 0$. In the post-merger situation, competition is an unattractive outcome for the firms. Boone argues that the mode of competition will change to tacit collusion and that the market price will increase to $p = 1$. Consequently, consumer surplus is lower as a result of the merger. (Since we assumed demand to be inelastic, total welfare is unchanged.)

1.4   The Mode of Competition

The model of Boone (2004b) is a theoretical model. There is also some experimental evidence that shows that the mode of competition may change as a result of a merger. Huck et al. (2003) find that, in the experimental laboratory, a merger may have psychological effects. The authors consider a symmetric n-person Cournot quantity setting game that, in the pre-merger situation, is played for 25 rounds. Next, two of the players are randomly chosen and are forced to merge, without there being any cost reduction; after the merger an $(n-1)$-player Cournot game is again played for 25 periods. If the mode of competition would remain unchanged, the merger would be unprofitable, that is, the merging players would be worse off as a result of the merger. However, Huck et al. (2003) demonstrate that the actual result is different: the merged firm increases output and the other firms decrease output somewhat. There is a movement in the direction of the Stackelberg outcome, and the post-merger quantities are asymmetric even though the post-merger situation is a symmetric one. Huck et al. (2003) explain their results by referring to the fact the players adopt payoff aspiration levels during the first phase of the game and that they do not want to accept lower payoffs after the merger. If this effect indeed is present, and all players take it into account, then the outcome does indeed move into the direction as observed in the experiment. Of course, we do not know whether similar effects are at work in real world mergers, but they should not be excluded a priori.

1.5   Coordinated Effects

Competition authorities are well aware of the possibility that a merger may change the mode of competition: they typically worry not just about the unilateral effects of mergers, but also about so-called possible coordinated effects. In paragraph 39 of the Guidelines on the assessment of horizontal mergers in the EU, we read:

> In some markets, the structure may be such that firms would consider it possible, economically rational and hence preferable, to adopt on a sustainable basis a course of action on the market aimed at selling at increased prices. A merger in a concentrated market may significantly impede effective competition, through the creation, the strengthening of a collective dominant position, because it increases the likelihood that firms are able to coordinate their behavior in this way and raise prices, even without entering into an agreement or resorting to a concerted practice within the meaning of article 81 of the Treaty.

The next paragraphs of the Guidelines then discuss the forms that coordination may take and in what circumstances coordinated price increases or coordinated quantity reductions may become more likely. In this respect the document mentions four aspects in particular:

- the ease with which parties can arrive at a common perception of how coordination should work,
- the ease with which deviations from the "coordinated plan" can be detected,
- the availability of mechanisms to punish deviations from the plan, and
- the responses of outsiders, including the possibility of new entry into the market.

As the discussion in these Guidelines make clear, the conceptual framework underlying that discussion is the afore-mentioned Folk Theorem of repeated games, a theorem that states that under certain conditions any agreement that could rationally be reached by market parties can be obtained as a self-enforcing plan, i.e. as an equilibrium, of the repeated game. In this applied context, at least two remarks should be made in relation to this theorem. First, the assumptions underlying the theorem are quite strong and should not be forgotten, especially the informational assumption. The (standard) Folk Theorem assumes that, at each point in time, the history of the game is common knowledge: all players have the same information, all players know this, etcetera. In case players have private information, for example about their individual sales or about the (secret) price discounts they have given to their costumers, situations which are likely to occur in practice, this assumption does not hold, hence, the Folk Theorem result need not hold either; see for example Stigler (1964). Second, even if the assumptions are satisfied, the Folk Theorem is just a possibility result, coordination could be the outcome, but it does not necessarily arise. Standard game theory assumes that, if there are multiple equilibria, players will somehow succeed in coordinating on an equilibrium, but the theory is silent on how this will be achieved and which equilibrium will result.

In this respect, one should bear in mind that the Folk Theorem typically does not only allow for equilibria that are better than the equilibria of the one-shot game, but that it also allows for equilibria that are worse from the firms' point of view, i.e. ones that are better for consumers. In applied work, it is often assumed that the most profitable equilibrium is the one that is played. There is, however, little justification for that assumption in the formal game-theoretic literature. Experiments have shown, moreover, that in situations where the more attractive equilibria are also more risky, safer equilibria with lower payoffs can result; see van Huyck et al. (1990) and

Battalio et al. (2001). In short, in situations with multiple equilibria, the theory remains silent on why a specific equilibrium arises, or indeed why there should be an equilibrium at all. Experiments show that in such cases non-equilibria may indeed be the outcome and that if an equilibrium results it need not be the one with the highest payoff. In fact, it may be the one with the lowest payoff.

Sometimes, the caveats mentioned above seem to be insufficiently taken into account. For example, in Airtours/First Choice, the commission wrote:

> It is not a necessary condition of collective dominance for the oligopolists always to behave as if there were one or more explicit agreements (e.g. to fix prices or capacity, or share the market) between them. It is sufficient that the merger makes it rational for the oligopolists, in adopting themselves to market conditions, to act – individually – in ways which will substantially reduce competition between them. (paragraph 54)

The question is under what conditions it is rational for oligopolists to reduce competition between them. Is it sufficient if there is an equilibrium in which competition is reduced? The game-theoretic literature suggests "no", since in these cases the players will not necessarily succeed in reaching this equilibrium. The players may want to establish such a coordinated outcome, but the fact that coordination is a theoretical possibility does not imply that it will be practically feasible.

In short, the Folk Theorem shows that tacit collusion may be an outcome, but it does not state that such an outcome must necessarily result: there are a lot of practical barriers that stand in the way. Indeed, if there is one lesson coming out of the experimental economics literature on tacit collusion, it is that such tacit collusion is hard to obtain; see Haan et al. (2005). In particular, Dufwenberg and Gneezy (2000) and Huck et al. (2004) find that experimental markets are already competitive when the number of players exceeds two. This does not imply that tacit collusion, collective dominance and coordinated effects should not be aspects of concern; it just implies that such effects are not usually found in laboratory experiments, which should lead us to play down the value of these models for merger analysis.

2. DATA

2.1 Bias versus Variance

There are two factors determining the precision of the results of any empirical study: bias and variance. If there is a systematic tendency of a procedure to produce results which are off in one direction (upwards or downwards), then the procedure is biased. If empirical results are sensitive to changes in the data, then variance is a concern. Thus, high bias/low variance procedures produce results which systematically and substantially over- or under-state the "truth", whereas the results of low-bias/high-variance procedures are frequently off by large amounts in either direction. The ideal is hence a low-bias/low-variance procedure.

Model complexity plays a large role in the bias/variance tradeoff. Models which are too simple provide a poor description of competitive reality, thereby inducing bias. In models with more unknowns, on the other hand, the variance tends to be greater since more information has to be extracted from the same amount of data, causing more variability in one's results. Correspondingly, by increasing the amount of data the variance is reduced. Hence in larger data sets it is generally advisable to choose a somewhat larger model, such that both the bias and the variance are less than with a smaller data set.

The above generalities apply to all empirical scenarios when the objective is to obtain the most precise estimates/predictions. There are cases, however, in which it is preferable to accept more bias than is optimal in terms of estimation precision. Sometimes, the direction of bias is known or can be controlled. For instance, if an estimated price effect is known to be biased downward and its variance is small, then the exact price effect is immaterial if the price effect found using this procedure is large; it is already clear that the proposed merger is highly anti-competitive, the precise extent is irrelevant. If the price effect found is low, however, then a high-bias/low-variance procedure is inconclusive. So here a larger data set still produces better results than a smaller one since the bias is then less for the same amount of variance (or *vice versa*), thereby increasing the number of cases in which the proposed procedure provides a definite answer.

So richer data sets provide results which are more accurate and reliable, but which are also more costly to obtain. Below is a discussion of potential methods of merger analysis, starting with the least data-intensive.

2.2 A Pauper's Choice

If data are limited due to money and/or time constraints, the only option – absent reliable elasticity estimates in the literature – is a calibration analysis. Calibration entails the use of a minute amount of economic data to infer relevant quantities in a structured economic model. Calibration yields exact results if the model is a perfect description of reality and all relevant data correspond exactly to the variables in the model and are observed without error. If these assumptions are satisfied, then data requirements can be as little as a few aggregate price and (market) share numbers; see, for example,

Epstein and Rubinfeld (2004). More elaborate models can be calibrated with a few more data points: essentially one additional parameter per observation; Epstein and Rubinfeld's (2004) PCAIDS with nests model is an example.

Unfortunately, models are never exact and neither are data. Precision of the results of a calibration study is affected by the proximity of the model to the "truth", data quality, and model complexity. A simple model which is a good description of reality combined with reliable data yields the best results. For instance, a calibration study using a flat logit model may give reasonable results if it is known that market shares of any two products A and B change by the same percentage if any third product C were to be taken off the market.[3] The trouble with calibrating richer models is that there are unknown parameters whose values need to be inferred, thereby exacerbating the already serious variance problem resulting from the paucity of data. Consequently, a PCAIDS model with several nests is rarely advisable for a calibration study, and the same (to a lesser extent) applies to the nested logit model.[4] But a flat logit model may be a poor description of the market studied, and the tradeoff between generality of the model and the variance can be tricky.

Whether one calibrates or estimates, it is necessary to extrapolate one's results to the post-merger situation. Doing so relies on the validity of the elasticities obtained in the calibration (or estimation) exercise, on the assumption that only brand ownership changes post-merger, and on the assumption that the model is a good description of the market away from the current equilibrium, also. Any errors in the elasticities will be magnified in post-merger predictions. Errors in calibrated elasticities are generally greater than those in estimated elasticities.

Since with calibration there is no way to determine which model provides the best description of reality, or indeed which model is the optimal choice in the bias/variance tradeoff exercise, it is advisable to produce predictions using a variety of plausible model choices. Some models are known to consistently produce higher predicted price effects than others, e.g. flat logit versus linear, and it has been argued (for example Werden et al., 2004) that both numbers should be computed and the least favourable one selected as in Postema et al. (2004). Although this is good advice, there is no guarantee (or convincing argument to believe) that the true price effects will be inside the range so indicated.

The main problem with calibration is its implicit assumption that errors are absent from both the model and the data. This assumption is necessary since the presence of errors would invalidate the calibration procedure. Absent any errors there is no reason to evaluate the reliability of one's inferences. But even if one wanted to conduct some basic tests on the validity of either the model or inferences based thereon, the shortage of data would preclude one from doing so. In other words, there is no way to evaluate the validity of one's findings in any meaningful (formal) fashion.

Despite the limitations described above, a calibration study is valuable in a competition authority's decision as to which cases to pursue and is the method of choice if a more sophisticated/comprehensive analysis is not feasible.

2.3   A Yeoman's Choice

If the number of brands is large and/or product data are available for a number of different markets, one can estimate rather than calibrate elasticities. As with calibration, estimated elasticities depend on the model chosen and also on assumptions made about the relationship between errors (their existence is now allowed) and model variables. However, all such model assumptions are now testable. Moreover, the data can be used to determine formally which of several model specifications is the most appropriate. Finally, the precision of price effects imputed from an estimation-based study can itself be gauged and hence some upper and lower bounds on the likely price effects can be determined. The verification possibility is available with estimation due to the presence of more data points than are strictly necessary to estimate the coefficients in the model; with calibration the absence of such "slack" precludes testability.

As mentioned earlier, model choice should depend on the available data, with richer data sets leading to larger models. All models that are calibrated can, conditional on data availability, also be estimated. Some more complex models, such as the Berry–Levinsohn–Pakes (BLP, 1995) random coefficients model, require a considerable investment of time to estimate properly. The Pinkse–Slade (PS, 2004, see also Pinkse, Slade and Brett, 2002) nonparametric estimator, on the other hand, is straightforward to use, but requires the existence of a large number of brands; with a small number of brands and a large number of markets the PS model typically reduces to an equivalent simpler model.

All estimation procedures make assumptions about the relationships between various elasticities across brands and/or markets (e.g. cities or time periods), explicitly or implicitly. But again, all such assumptions are testable. The assumed structure of cross- and own-price elasticities is implicit in the structure of discrete choice models (such as logit and BLP), and explicit with AIDS (Deaton and Muellbauer, 1980) and PS. The need for such assumptions arises from the vast number of own- and cross-price elasticities: if there are g products in h markets then the number of elasticities is gh^2. Assuming that elasticities are the same in all markets reduces the number of elasticities to h^2, which is manageable without further restrictions when g is large relative to

h^2. Often, h^2 is still too large, and further assumptions are necessary to make the model estimable with the available data. With a logit model, for instance, the number of unknowns is further reduced from h^2 to 1, which is indicative of the restrictiveness of the assumptions made. At the other extreme, the PS methodology merely requires the number of unknowns to be small relative to the total number of observations, i.e. gh, a minimal condition for all unknowns to be estimable.

Model choice should also depend on the applicability of the underlying assumptions associated with each model. With the logit and random coefficient models, for instance, the model is structured in terms of individual consumers' purchase decisions of single products. Such models are most appropriate for the modelling of large ticket items, such as automobiles, but are less suitable for products which are purchased repeatedly in a small amount of time, in variable quantities, or in combination with similar products. Nevertheless, random coefficients models have been used to analyse competition in markets for such products as breakfast cereals (e.g. Nevo, 2000), which are bought on a regular basis, in variable quantities and at the same time as other breakfast cereals. The Hausman, Leonard and Zona (1994) procedure allows for variable quantities, but is in other dimensions more restrictive than is the random coefficients model.

A thorny issue is that of the potential "endogeneity" of covariates. There is often an implicit assumption in empirical work that prices and quantities depend on covariates, but not vice versa, but such exogeneity assumptions are questionable. Brand characteristics, for instance, are chosen to maximize future profits and the optimal choice of such characteristics will depend on other model variables, including (anticipated) prices and quantities. This problem can be finessed by the argument that brand characteristics are chosen long before the current pricing game and are expensive to change. Whatever the case might be, it is unquestionably true that in most instances a merger analyst will have bigger fish to fry, i.e. there are other problems which are likely to have a greater effect on her results.

The main limitations of estimation with market-level data, then, are the greater data requirements than those necessary for calibration, a greater investment of time, and the existence of a still better, albeit more expensive, alternative: estimation using consumer-level data.

2.4 A Prince's Choice

Models for market-level data are typically generated by aggregating a model for individual consumer choices across all individuals. Such aggregation can take various forms and is only valid if a number of (sometimes simplistic) assumptions are satisfied. For instance, in market-level random coefficient models consumer heterogeneity is represented by a random variable, which is integrated out over all coefficients. But even if aggregation assumptions are questionable, the implied market-level relationships can form a reasonable approximation to the actual ones, and the proximity of implied to actual is statistically verifiable.

It is nonetheless preferable to use consumer-level data (e.g. from supermarket scanners) if such data are available. Besides mitigation of aggregation problems, the sheer amount of micro-level data typically results in more accurate estimates despite the fact that consumer preferences are highly variable and scanner data only apply to a (potentially nonrepresentative) subset of consumers.

The main limitation of using consumer-level data is cost; such data when available from a commercial source are expensive and the time required for collection and analysis can be substantial. Indeed, the time requirements are likely to be prohibitive.

3.   CONCLUSIONS

None of the above is intended to discredit any other work in this book, or indeed to take away from the potential value of the "new tools" of merger analysis. Instead, we hope to have pointed out some of their limitations. Uncritical implementation of any methodology is foolhardy. Nevertheless, modern merger analysis methodology constitutes a useful addition to a merger analyst's arsenal. If "standard analysis" is limited to the mechanical computation of market shares and Herfindahl indices and the application of rigid rules (the merger is disallowed if the value of the index or the change thereof is sufficiently large), then the new methods are an indisputable improvement. They allow for a rational discussion of the issues that matter. If used appropriately, they provide credible information on the extent of the anticompetitive effects of a proposed merger, particularly if the analysis is based on a rich data set, if the results are verified using statistical procedures and/or the results are supported by more traditional methods.

NOTES

*   We thank Barry Ickes and Margaret Slade for their valuable suggestions.
1.   See http://www.ecb.int/events/conferences/html/inflationpersistence.en.html.
2.   A reaction function is a representation of one firm's response to another firm's pricing decisions.
3.   The independence of irrelevant alternatives assumption.
4.   The number of unknowns in a PCAIDS with nests model is generally greater than in a nested logit.

7.   Mergers and the New Guidelines: Lessons from Hachette–Editis

Marc Ivaldi

The motivation for this chapter is to be found in the new Guidelines on Merger control that stipulate the Significant Impediment of Effective Competition (SIEC, herein) as a new criterion.[1] The text of the guidelines is not really clear about what is actually meant by this test. As the text reads, and as is usual for merger inquiries, it calls for an investigation process, which involves the elaboration of hypothetical post-merger situation based on observed facts, data or documents, and compares it to the pre-merger situation or the post no-merger situation.

The new Guidelines provide some information on the ways and methods in which one should perform this counterfactual analysis. First, they strongly recommend measuring concentration level (using the Herfindahl–Hirschman Index) and change in the concentration level to screen merger cases. The text says that "Each of these HHI levels, in combination with the relevant deltas, may be used as an initial indicator of the absence of competition concerns. However, they do not give rise to a presumption of either the existence or the absence of such concern." Second, the Guidelines relate the SIEC test to a significant increase in market power and implicitly call for an evaluation of post-merger price increase ("non-coordinated effects"). The Guidelines do not prescribe specific tools to do these post-merger assessments.

Interestingly, the Hachette–Editis Case arrives at the watershed between the old and the new guidelines thus offering a unique chance to anticipate what the European Commission's future interpretation of significant impediment to competition may become. At least the method that has been deployed in this case offers an empirical way to assess the key parameters and to test a number of the crucial hypotheses that are often made explicitly or implicitly in the more sophisticated merger analyses. As a consequence the decision on Hachette–Editis is partly based on an explicit account of an econometric analysis of the unilateral effects of the proposed merger.

This chapter is structured as follows. First I will discuss the empirical and theoretical arguments for sophisticated empirical analysis. In the second section I will discuss the main features of the case and reflect on market structure and conduct. I will pay particular attention to data collection and related issues. The third section introduces and discusses the model and in section four the econometric results are presented assessing their relevancy for the case at hand. The final section draws some conclusions.

1. THE NEED FOR EMPIRICAL ANALYSIS

Clearly, the use of models in analysing the impact of the proposed mergers is in the start–up phase. The modelling industry has just entered the market. Although the learning curve is steep and the market potential definitely exists we have to acknowledge that this is not yet a mature industry. Methods have generally speaking not yet or insufficiently been tested by the courts.

The question is to evaluate whether these techniques can be helpful for the effectiveness of competition policy. The scope of this policy provides one important element to elaborate a reply to this question. This is why we look at the statistics on the merger policy, as illustrated by Table 7.1 that summarizes simple counts of notified mergers by the Commission. If one believes that only in second phase cases could sufficient time be available to do the more complex type of analysis, such sophisticated analyses could have been applied in 102 cases out of more than 2000 cases (i.e., 5 per cent). Actually, the numbers are even more sobering. Only 0.8 per cent of planned mergers out of more than 2000 notifications over the years 1990–2003 were prohibited or remedied by the Commission and of these only a very few arrived at the court.[2]

Table 7.1 also suggests that we cannot evaluate the type I error problem in merger control since the prohibition of actually procompetitive mergers occurs in less than 5 per cent of the notifications. Meanwhile type I errors receive considerable attention because of their political impact even although casual observation suggests that such cases have been extremely rare (less than 1 per cent).

What do the Numbers Suggest?

The numbers summarized in Table 7.1 suggest two plausible interferences that need further investigation. The first hypothesis is about the probability of error and the second hypothesis is about the question where simulation models such as the antitrust logit model developed by Werden and Froeb (1994) are most apt. The hypotheses are purely statistical and ignore the sources of error. Political economic considerations suggest that error may, for example, be influenced by the investigation capacity or by the institutional set up (such as the fact that investigation and sanction is performed by one and the same organization). First principles of Industrial Economics suggest that error will occur when the measure of dominance is given too much weight (a tropism refuted by economic theory) or alternatively if efficiency gains are not taken into account (note that measurement of such gains is remarkably absent in most cases). Of course these factors are relevant and need further investigation. However, from a purely statistical point of view the numbers in Table 7.1 may help to formulate hypotheses that are potentially relevant for competition policy makers.

Table 7.1 Notifications and decisions on mergers by the European Commission (September 1990–April 2003)

	Allowed	Remedy	Prohibited	Total
Phase 1	1879	98		1977
	83.4%	4.3%		87.7%
Phase 2	22	62	18	102
	1.0%	3.0%	0.8%	4.8%

Source: Data are drawn from the European Commission – DG competition website on mergers.

The second hypothesis is about the question of the most effective use of modelling tools and capabilities. More than three-quarters of the mergers that were notified in the period 1990–2003 were green light cases. It is well known that most of these cases have been accepted basically on *a priori* grounds. Although we can not conjecture from that figure either, it would seem reasonable to assume that the odds are against type II errors given the sheer number of accepted cases. It would thus seem reasonable to have very sophisticated models for cases where we want to eliminate type I errors and a relatively simple family of models for cases where type II errors may be relevant. Especially here calibrated models can add value as screening devices, essentially because calibrated models require less data and because they are relatively easy to use.

Important Theoretical Insights

So far I have advanced a number of mostly practical numerical arguments regarding the tools of proper economic analysis, but economic theory also offers relevant guidance for the issues that are at stake. Three contributions from theory are crucial for understanding the requirements of the proper economic analysis of dominance.

The first contribution is the seminal article by Williamson (1968). Williamson clarifies the need to consider the welfare trade-off of a merger. We need to weigh the increase in efficiency against the increase in market power. Importantly, already a small reduction in average costs could offset a large increase in prices. Taking Williamson's insights seriously requires an evaluation of both elasticities and marginal costs in order to arrive at a really meaningful measure of the effect of mergers.

The second contribution is Davidson and Deneckere (1985). They clarified that mergers will always have positive price effects in Bertrand models. Rising prices in the end reflect preferences and thus substitution elasticities are essential. The diversion ratio (that is the ratio of a product's own price elasticity to the cross price elasticity) thus becomes essential (the higher this ratio, the higher the price increase gets).

The third lesson from literature derives from Hausman et al. (1996) that showed that it is very difficult to apply the market test in practice if there are different types of consumers, so with heterogeneity of demand. Hausman clarifies that the profitability of a price increase is linked to the structure of the different customer segments. The results strongly depend on the ratio of inframarginal customers to intramarginal customers (i.e., of those that are sensitive to price changes and insensitive to price changes, respectively)

The Standard Approach Remains Important

Both from the practical side and the theoretical side there is a need to put numbers on competition policy issues, which means that we have to provide measures. This is the only way to evaluate the critical assumptions in the analysis. We need an empirical analysis

- to enlighten the critical assumptions and factors,
- to improve the accuracy of competition analysis and
- to provide a persuasive set of arguments by making them more concrete and better grounded on facts and theory.

Now, before proceeding with what we have done in the Hachette–Editis case, I would like to make clear that the increased use of sophisticated methods does not mean that I want to suggest that we can get rid of the standard analysis. We do not really care about the proper relevant market definition in an empirical approach since the model allows us to address this question of the size of the market. Indeed, in an empirical approach, we let the model decide which potential competing products are relevant and which are less relevant.[3] However, we can not proceed to the analysis when we do not understand the market and so careful case study remains the essential basis for the empirical analysis. We need the standard analysis to get a good feeling for the data and to estimate what is relevant. The information and data collected from business documents, interviews, marketing and economic studies and descriptive analysis of the market are key elements. This is true both for simulation models and for the econometric approach. For instance, when (as in the Hachette–Editis case) estimation requires the use of instrumental variables, understanding the industry is the key for picking the right instrument. Hence standard analysis is essential for a sound model-based empirical analysis.

2.　THE HACHETTE–EDITIS CASE

Hachette–Editis is one of the leading European mergers in 2003. This merger in the market for books written in the French language extends beyond the geographical boundaries of France. The geographical market is delineated by the assumption that a market only exists in the French speaking countries in Europe, which includes France, Luxemburg, the southern part of Belgium and the western part of Switzerland. The industry can be characterized as an oligopoly on which several groups of publishers operate. Each group is made up of a set of publishers of different sizes, acting on different market niches. For instance, Hachette and Editis are groups of different publishers that have their own clearly defined marketing strategies. Hachette comprises such publishers as Livre de Poche (the big brand for paperbacks that publishes the larger part of French literature), Grasset (a publisher of new novels in hardcover), and Stock, among many others. Likewise Editis comprises such famous publishers as Pocket, Laffont and Fleuve Noir.

In the analysis of this industry, horizontal and vertical issues are at stake. The vertical issues relate to the distribution channel that is characterized by the fact that all books are distributed via the so-called distribution platforms to the individual book stores. These platforms are to be seen as essential facilities and thus needed consideration in the actual merger case. Vertical issues are, however, beyond the scope of this chapter, so I will focus on the horizontal issues and more specifically how we used an econometric model in order to estimate the unilateral effects due to the merger in this industry. First, however, a closer look at the data is warranted as we are dealing with estimation rather than calibration.

Data Issues

One can argue against the use of econometric methods in merger cases because of the time-consuming and data-intensive nature of sophisticated empirical analysis.[4] How the case Hachette–Editis has been treated, however, appears to prove this wrong. We got involved in this case in March 2003. We had the data available by the end of May 2003. The first draft report was made available for the Commission by the middle of July 2003. So all in all probably four months were necessary to organize the data, to perform the analysis and then the reporting. Admittedly, this is a lot longer than the time span to do an informed simulation if the main parameters are available at the start of a merger case. Anyway here the analysis just took six weeks. My conclusion is that the econometric method is not too much more demanding and time consuming and should be considered where appropriate.

One particular problem that always emerges in discussion about the econometric method is the availability of data. In this case we used data that were provided by IPSOS and which can be described as the standard marketing data that one typically expects to be available in a case. Indeed in a great many markets (particularly for consumer goods) this type of data is available. Note that this data has been made available by the merging firms following discussions we have had with the parties on the appropriateness of the data. We decided that the IPSOS data set was sufficiently rich and reliable and so to say reflected best practice marketing data.

The data set provides a cross section related to 1500 hardcover titles and 5000 paperback titles sold in France in 2002 and covering roughly 50 and 85 per cent of the market, respectively. For each title we observe the sale volume and the price on the market (given the fixed book price regulation we know that this is the actual French transaction price). Clearly, this is a rich and highly disaggregated data set that allows for sophisticated analysis especially since we were able to add product characteristics, in particular the number of pages which is the main determinant of variable costs (in addition to the hardcover/paperback fixed effect). After correction for misclassifications we then have more than 3200 products. These products can be sold through three different distribution channels: supermarkets, large book stores (Virgin is an example) or the small and specialized book stores in the city centres. Since we are dealing with literature in general we would expect that the distribution channels matter with, for example, poetry or "difficult" novels selling in specialized bookstores, and bestsellers selling in railway shops and the like.

3.   THE MODEL

This market is studied with an approach where we have a nested logit model for the demand side and a supply side in which pricing is modelled as Bertrand competition between groups.

The Demand Side

As to the demand side, Figure 7.1 shows that the customer first decides on the type of book (science fiction, thriller, novel, humour, essay). Given the genre, he decides which title to buy.[5] Equation 7.1 is the demand equation corresponding to a nested logit model. The left-hand side is the logarithm of the quantity q of product j over the quantity of the outside good, defined as the total market N minus the inside goods, i.e. the French literature books.

Figure 7.1 The demand side

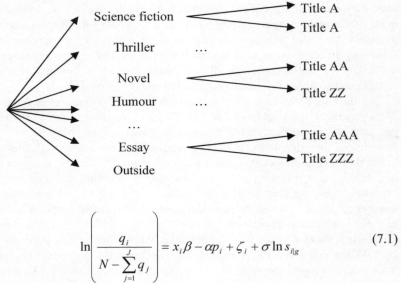

$$\ln\left(\frac{q_i}{N-\sum_{j=1}^{J}q_j}\right) = x_i\beta - \alpha p_i + \zeta_i + \sigma \ln s_{i|g} \tag{7.1}$$

Basically market share in this manner of demand system is explained by two components. The first component is the trade-off between price and quality, where quality is operationalized by a matrix x_j of dummies for distribution channel, author and publisher. It also includes a random term which accounts for unobservable quality. The second term relates to market differentiation, i.e. whether we are dealing with humour, a novel or an essay and so on. If the coefficient σ is significantly different from zero, we know that this manner of differentiation empirically matters.

Note that one parameter that is particular relevant in this equation is essentially unknown. N is not the turnover on books since we account in the analysis for the outside goods. This may be an alternative cultural good or a non-cultural good or one of those purely mathematic books that many of us love so much to write but which are obviously not in the data set. Such products should, however, be considered as being part of this particular relevant market in the sense that they potentially compete for the customer's money. The upshot is of course that an estimate from this model is very conservative for the merging firms thus providing a first safeguard against type I errors.

The Supply Side

$$\frac{p_j - c_j}{p_j} = \frac{1-\sigma}{\alpha\left[1 - \sigma s_{f|g} - (1-\sigma)s_f\right]p_j} \qquad (7.2)$$

The second equation is a pricing equation when one assumes Bertrand–Nash competition. The price-cost margin equals the inverse of the price elasticity. The willingness to pay depends on σ and α. Parameter α reflects the consumer's price sensitivity and parameter σ, as I explained earlier, indicates the impact and relevancy of product differentiation in the market. To fully specify the margin in equation (7.2), in addition to these two parameters, we only need the market share of the firm over the whole market and its market share in each specific node or genre. So thanks to the nested logit model, the number of parameters required to measure margins is small, which facilitates estimation and allows for a faster analysis. The price is a lack of flexibility. Note that marginal costs are assumed to be constant. In fact the methodology can accommodate different cost curvatures without too much difficulties.

Sensitivity Analysis and Simulation Options

Importantly, estimation of the model does not preclude that we can analyse different types of the model in the sense that we can allow for different types of equilibrium. If the merger control department, for example, has circumstantial evidence or simply wants to investigate the assumption that the market concerned is characterized by explicit or implicit collusion then you can derive a similar reduced form price equation for that case of collusion. The formula changes of course, but it can be done and in this example would reflect how prices at the margin are set due to the fact that collusion occurs. And the same could be done for Stackelberg price leadership if there is evidence for such a conduct and so on. So a valid research strategy would be to estimate the model under different assumptions to show the sensitivity or the robustness of the estimation results for different assumptions on market conduct behaviour. Then these equilibria have to be statistically compared in order to investigate which model performs best. Hence the approach allows both for simulation and in a sense detection.

4.   MAIN RESULTS

In discussing the main results I will not go into the econometric details but present the main conclusions that can be derived from this model. I see three important results that shed light on the merger case: the model's actual description of the market, the delineation of the market and the confidence interval for the unilateral price effects of the merger.

Description of the Industry

One particular strength of an econometric model compared to a calibrated model is that it allows one to actually identify some main features of the industry that can readily be checked in real life. You provide a good snapshot that the industry people and the judge will recognize. For example, in the demand side estimation we identify the effect of different writers among which are Agatha Christie, Arthur Conan Doyle and Barbara Cartland.[6] That is to say, we identify the most popular books on the French market. This offers a recognizable and convincing picture of the industry's main features.

Market Delineation

As to market delineation, the Commission argued on the basis of price distributions (Figure 7.2) that essentially two relevant markets should be discerned. Indeed we see two different frequency distributions for the prices of hardcovers and paperbacks respectively. Thus eye-o-metrics suggest separate markets for hardcovers and for paperbacks. This is, however, not self evident. For one thing, generally speaking the same book cannot be bought in paperback and hardcover at the same time. Publishers follow a strategy of intertemporal price discrimination, publishing the first edition as a hardcover in order to get the cream off the market and publishing later editions as paperbacks. But the customer can also make intertemporal decisions depending on relative prices, his time preference and income. The existence of these intertemporal substitution patterns suggests that markets may not be as separated as suggested by the price diagram. So the best way to deal with this issue is to follow the empirical method and let the data decide whether or not the two markets are sufficiently close.

The model could be used to run an equilibrium test (Table 7.2). The question is to evaluate the average price increase for all books in a monopoly and a duopoly. The equilibrium test is not an SSNIP test, but consists of running the model for a hypothetical monopoly model and for a hypothetical duopoly model where the set of hardcovers constitutes a first hypothetical firm and the set of paperbacks forms a second hypothetical firm. When you compare the two models you can observe that the price increases and the relative price changes under the two market structures have different outcomes (see Table 7.2). This could favour the Commission's decision to delineate two separate markets. For the econometrician the distinction does not seem relevant.

Figure 7.2 Partitioning of the market for literature by form and by price class (prices in euros)

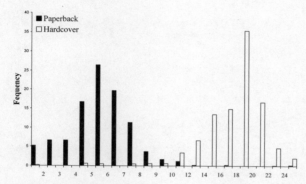

Table 7.2 Percentage price increase according to different assumptions on market delineation (equilibrium test)

	Duopoly	Monopoly
Paperback	13.6	26.5
Hardcover	1.4	8.2

Unilateral Effects

Consider Figure 7.3 that illustrates the unilateral effect of the merger. On the horizontal line we have market size (N), that is the turnover of the market. We estimated the effect of the merger for different market sizes including the outside good and find, for example, for 50 million units of books sold, that the average price increase (on the vertical axis) amounts to between 8 and 9 per cent. At a size of 100 million units of books sold the model predicts a 4.8 per cent price increase. And at a size of 360 million units of books sold the price increase is only equal to 3 per cent. In other terms, depending on the market size, the merger is or is not harmful for the consumer. Incidentally this question is a characteristic of all antitrust logit models and should always be addressed. At the end of the day we thus need an evaluation of N, that is the market size that includes the outside good. The problem is to find the "right" market size. We had several discussions with the parties to arrive at a good estimate. Finally we agreed on a 100 million market size and an average price increase of 4.8 per cent.[7]

Figure 7.3 distinguishes between the set of all books and the subset of paperbacks. The point to note is that the lines are close so that the conclusion is that the overall effect of hardcovers is empirically not very strong and that paperbacks are responsible for most of the average price increase.

Figure 7.3 Unilateral effects and market size

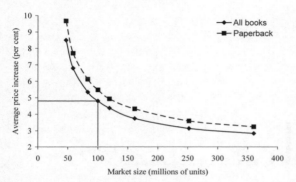

Next the model could be used to generate a frequency distribution for the predicted price increase using a bootstrap method running a good 1000 model simulations of the merger for a market size of 100 million units sold. The resulting price distribution (Figure 7.4) of course has an average of 4.8 per cent, but in addition gives us information on the 95 per cent confidence interval that runs from 4.0 to 5.4 per cent. This is of course one of the advantages of the econometric methods since you directly obtain the variance covariance matrix of the parameter that allows you to do these bootstrap estimations and to derive the confidence interval.

Figure 7.4 The bootstrap method

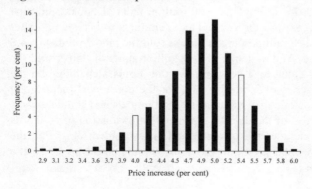

5.   CONCLUSIONS

The main lessons of the Hachette–Editis case for merger analysis are two-fold. First, empirical Industrial Organization has proven to be a powerful and complementary tool for the standard methods of analysis that are deployed by competition policy makers. Second we have seen that powerful and robust results can be achieved with econometric models that cannot be realized with calibrated models. Admittedly there is a clear price tag. Econometric methods are more demanding both in terms of time, data and effort. Especially the human factor provides a challenge for academic economists like myself. The new approach can only be viable if economic faculties succeed in providing sufficient well trained IO PhD's to the competition authorities. I am optimistic and expect that in a few years sufficient analysts will be on the market to ensure that sophisticated methods can be applied within the time span available in a merger case. Indeed this is the way forward to achieve that we can put numbers on the change in market that are fundamental in the assessment of what the new guidelines have labelled a significant impediment of effective competition.

NOTES

*   This chapter is based on joint work with Jérôme Foncel (University of Lille) and Valérie Rabassa (Chief Economist Team, DG Comp).
1.   See http://europa.eu.int/eur-lex/pri/en/oj/dat/2004/c_031/c_03120040205en00050018.pdf.
2.   Clearly, Table 7.1 sketches the Commission's perspective only. As Pieter Kalbfleisch argues in Chapter 3, we have more cases available if we look at the different jurisdictions in Europe and obviously much is to be learned from the different European experiences. However, the picture in terms of percentages does not change much by considering these cases.
3.   Werden makes the same point in Chapter 4
4.   See Göppelroder (2004) for an account of pros and cons.
5.   Different decision trees were tried during the estimation process adding the selling location or the difference between hard cover and paper back. We were unable to estimate these extended models. Of course this does not mean that it cannot be done. It only means that during the procedure and given the inherent deadlines the extended model could not be estimated, but this is something on which we plan to work further in the future
6.   Indeed (the translations of) English bestsellers are the top of the market of French literature.
7.   The model was also used to analyse efficiency gains and remedies, but the final decision of Hachette to sell a large part of Editis has nothing to do with the results of the model.

PART THREE

European Case Studies

8. Simulating Merger Price Effects Using PCAIDS with Nests: The Italian Aperitif Market

Fabio Massimo Esposito[*]

Merger analysis often has to deal with localized competition. When competition is localized, analysis based on market shares can easily be misleading: on the one hand, if markets are defined too broadly, then market shares alone cannot convey the increase in market power due to a concentration between owners of very close products; on the other hand, if markets are tailored around clusters of close products, the market shares may overstate market power.

Merger simulations with nests can help in dealing with localized competition, by grouping brands that appear closer to each other in nests and by modulating the substitutability between different nests so as to reflect the localized structure of competition.

The main problem with nests is to define appropriate "nest parameters" controlling for the substitutability between different nests. One possibility is to calibrate nests using brand margins (Epstein and Rubinfeld 2003, 2004). In this chapter, we apply this calibration method to a preliminary investigation[1] of a recent merger in the Italian aperitifs market.

The chapter is structured as follows. The first section briefly reviews the use of simulations at Autorità Garante della Concorrenza e del Mercato (AGCM). The second section illustrates the calibration of nest parameters using margin data, making several methodological considerations. The third section introduces the Italian aperitifs market and the merger the simulations were applied to. The fourth one deals with calibration of nest parameters. The fifth section discusses the merger simulations performed. The concluding remarks discuss some open problems and compare simulation results to the available information on actual market evolution. Actual data from a previous merger investigation used in the simulations are presented in the Appendix.

1. AGCM EXPERIENCE

AGCM learned for the first time of merger simulations at a workshop organized by the Swedish Competition Authority in Stockholm in May 2002, held by Greg Werden (US Department of Justice) and Luke Froeb (then at Vanderbilt University, now at the Federal Trade Commission). Later that year Roy Epstein provided AGCM with an Excel-based software running merger simulation based on Epstein and Rubinfeld's PCAIDS. The Excel interface – familiar to lawyers too – seemed useful to attract the interest of AGCM officers towards merger simulations and to promote a hands-on approach to such an important tool.

In autumn 2002, a difficult investigation of a merger between two insurance companies, SAI and Fondiaria, offered an opportunity to test the usefulness of merger simulations. The anticompetitive potential of the merger was thought to be high, as it would have put the first, third and fourth non-life insurance groups under the same control, but it was difficult to prove under a "dominant position" standard: structural indices were barely satisfied and additional indices of competitive advantage weakly supported the creation of significant competitive advantages for the new entity, who could actually rely only on the greatest network of exclusive agents in the industry.

AGCM, however, emphasized that a dominant position rests both on structural factors *and* on the ability of the firm to behave independently from competitors and customers. The ability of a firm to behave independently should reflect itself in its ability to raise the prices of the goods or services it sells. This argument opened the door to the use of merger simulations – which offered a method to "estimate" the likely increase in prices charged by the new group – under the "dominant position standard"[2] set out in the Italian Competition Act.[3] Merger simulations performed in the SAI–Fondiaria case indicated the potential for significant price increases for the new entity: PCAIDS predicted price increases above 10 per cent, while Logit predicted above 6 per cent by using the same assumptions and a price vector normalized to 1.

This result made people at AGCM aware of the potential of merger simulation. However, a hands-on attitude did not develop, and responsibility for conducting merger simulation eventually remained with the Market Analysis Office, a small economic unit that was established in March 2000. The Office engaged in a long-term project[4] directed to improve its ability to estimate demand elasticities to be used as inputs into simulations, using both the Almost Ideal Demand System (AIDS) and the Logit model.

In autumn 2003 the Office was involved in the formal investigation of a merger between the second (ETI, a state-owned enterprise) and the third (British American Tobacco) cigarette producers in the Italian market.

Simulations showing that unilateral effects would have been negligible were performed using data arising from a "natural experiment" (a Pall Mall price decrease induced a large increase in sales of the brand and attracted customers from Marlboro). The Office embarked on an unsuccessful[5] attempt to estimate the demand elasticities, in order to understand market segmentation and verify the "one relevant market for all cigarettes" hypothesis; after AGCM decided to investigate only the possible coordinate effects of the concentration (that is "joint dominance"), the efforts were directed to understand whether demand structure could have favoured tacit coordination between BAT–ETI and Marlboro, the market leader. That was the first time the Office engaged in this type of back-end work during a formal investigation.

During this investigation AGCM easily gathered data on cigarette brand margins to perform critical loss analysis; this prompted the Office to consider the use of margin data to calibrate merger simulations with nests, following Epstein and Rubinfeld's (2003) suggestion. This calibration method was at the heart of simulations performed in the preliminary investigation of aperitifs.

2.   CALIBRATING AND MARGIN DATA

Localized competition challenges traditional merger analysis based on market shares, that cannot adequately account for market power opportunities arising from the clustering of differentiated products around certain locations in the product space. It may seem natural to include several clusters into a relevant market, but in that case shares will understate the possible anticompetitive potential of the merger within clusters; on the other hand, defining clusters as a relevant market may overstate that potential (and may raise allegations of tailoring markets to make the merger look anticompetitive). Simulation with nests offers an attractive alternative to that analysis:

- it offers a natural framework to analyse localized competition;
- nest "distances" can account for substitution between product clusters (nests), thereby weighting and correcting market shares;
- the emphasis of the analysis shifts usefully from the definition of relevant market boundaries to the understanding of competitive relations among products, in order to construct nests and to determine nest distances plausible with available information on consumer tastes and firms' strategies;
- candidate relevant markets can be broadly defined; subsequent analysis of nest distances will tell whether some cluster is so weakly

substitutable with other nests as to be safely excluded from the relevant market;

The same definition of the relevant market becomes an outcome of the simulation process, through the determination of nest "distances".

The Method

Strict time requirements of merger investigations[6] require a method to simulate mergers with nests that can be implemented with minimal data in a short time but able to give parameter values reflecting closeness in competition. Models based on Bertrand competition and the Independence of Irrelevant Alternatives hypothesis (IIA) are very attractive in this respect. In the nested version of these models, "nest parameters" adjust odds ratios[7] to reflect the different substitutability between brands belonging to different nests. This enables a relatively parsimonious parameterisation to be kept: there are only two elasticity parameters and a reasonable number of nest parameters to calibrate, instead of a whole elasticity matrix to estimate.

PCAIDS, in particular, has a nest parameter for every pair of nests, as every parameter modifies the way sales are diverted from a brand in one nest to a brand in another nest; this allows a nest to be close to some other nests and farther away from others. While this may be problematic when there are many nests – a case where Logit, who has only one parameter per nest, is preferable – it allows a greater diversification of cross elasticities among products put in different nests.

PCAIDS assumes a symmetric nest parameters matrix in order to preserve the symmetry of the parameter matrix of the underlying AIDS system. This is a natural assumption when the parameters are interpreted as distances, even if it can appear somewhat restrictive when one thinks in terms of the switching behaviour of consumers: substitution often is not symmetric.

Epstein and Rubinfeld (2003) suggested using margin data to calibrate nest parameters, although in a later paper (Epstein and Rubinfeld 2004), however, they outlined a complete procedure for calibration. In the meantime, AGCM's economic consultant[8] developed the same ideas and wrote a *Matlab* code allowing the calibration of one brand elasticity and the nest parameters using available brand margins.[9] Both of them calibrated nest parameters as the parameters that minimized the sum of squared differences between actual margins and margins simulated by PCAIDS.

The basic idea behind the *Matlab* code was, however, a little bit more general: discussions of merger simulations overlook that in many instances (and very often with non-nested models) more brand margins than the number of parameters to be calibrated will be available. Given that it would not be informationally efficient to (arbitrarily) discard part of the evidence, a method is needed to use all available evidence to calibrate the parameters needed. Choosing parameter values that minimize some loss measure – for example a quadratic loss function – is therefore a general approach to use all available evidence.

In particular, calibrating parameter values as the values that minimize the sum of squared differences between actual margins and simulated margins is a method that can be applied both to nested and flat simulation models like PCAIDS and Logit.[10]

More formally, PCAIDS pre-merger first-order conditions imply that the following relation holds between actual brand margins (m^*) and nest parameters (w) (Epstein and Rubinfeld 2004):

$$m^* = - S^{-1} [B(w, e, e_{11}) S^{-1} - I]^{-1} s \qquad (2.1)$$

where B is the AIDS coefficient matrix – whose elements depend on nest parameters w, market elasticity e and one brand elasticity e_{11} –, s is the pre-merger shares vector and S is a diagonal matrix with shares on the diagonal. Provided that a number of actual brand margins at least equal to the number of parameters to be calibrated is available, nest parameters and brand elasticity will be chosen[11] as the values that minimize the sum of squared differences between actual margins (m) and margins implied by first order conditions, under the constraints that $m^*_i \in (0, 1) \ \forall i$ (implying that marginal costs are positive) and $w_k \in [0, 1] \ \forall \ k$:

$$w = \text{argmin} \ [\Sigma_i \ (m_i - m^*_i)^2] \qquad (2.2)$$

The closer the nest parameter is calibrated to zero, the farther are the nests and the more likely that the candidate relevant market has been defined too broadly. On the contrary, for a calibrated nest parameter close to 1 the corresponding nests can be taken to belong to a larger nest including both of them.

The minimized sum of squared deviation is the calibration loss. This loss provides a useful guide to find the best vector of parameter nests for given nests and varying values of actual margins, market elasticities etc.[12] "Best" here means that it minimizes the deviations between calibrated and actual margins – that is, simulated margins fit with actual margins. These deviations are important because small deviations imply that the model is better able to replicate pre-merger market conditions and therefore it is an acceptable, albeit simplified, representation of the market under study.

A useful measure of fit based on the calibration loss is a familiar R^2 type of measure, defined as one minus the ratio of the minimized loss to the sum of squared deviations of actual brand margins from their average; this measure can be computed also by weighting deviations with actual brand shares, in order to give a greater weight to large deviations on more important brands; this "pseudo-R^2" varies between 0 and 1, although satisfaction of constraints may prevent perfect fit.

Methodological Remarks

Four final methodological remarks are in order with respect to the present method.

First, a good fit is good for calibration, as it implies that the model replicates pre-merger market conditions, but does not say anything about the precision of the nest parameters values, when they are thought of as "estimates" of true parameters. While it is true that calibration is not estimation, it would be desirable to know how much confidence can be put on those values. Bootstrapping procedures might be the appropriate techniques to answer this problem, but it is unlikely that they could be applied when there was no econometric estimation behind the simulation model,[13] unless there are many margins and very few calibrated parameters. In most cases, information about the confidence that can be put into nest parameters and, more importantly, on the robustness of simulation results based on them, would be gained only through some sort of sensitivity analysis.

Second, margin data currently appear to be the more readily available data source to calibrate brand elasticities and nest parameters; thanks to standard accounting software (SAP, Oracle and their small competitors) it should be easy even for medium-sized firms to provide required margin data, detailing items that were subtracted from prices to get those data. Therefore, the data needed should be available by the first two weeks of a formal merger investigation.

Third, calibrating nest parameters to margins implies that nest distances will reflect the way firms think about competition when setting prices, advertising and promotions; this is in general desirable as this is the distance structure that will determine the competitive effects of the merger; it is even more important when there is a completely autonomous distribution sector between firms and distributors which will filter the merger to consumers, so that it is important to focus the analysis at the producer/distributor level. Moreover, calibration to margins makes nest parameters consistent with the underlying cost conditions, which determines the scope of firms' positioning choices.

Fourth, the nest parameters' calibration results depend on fundamental model assumptions (Bertrand competition, simplified AIDS demand, IIA etc.) and on margin accuracy. Modelling hypotheses can prevent satisfactory fit, and the whole procedure can produce surprising results. Therefore, it is crucial to compare calibrated nest parameters and the implied distances between nests with independent relevant evidence, in order to understand whether results are reasonable and consistent with market evidence. Since nest parameters should reflect the way firms think of competition, a useful piece of information can be gathered by asking each firm to rank, in order of importance, competing brands for every controlled brand. Evidence on consumer tastes – which has to be consistent, but not coincident, with that gathered from firms – can also be useful.

3.   THE CAMPARI/BARBERO MERGER

The calibration method outlined above was applied to a preliminary investigation of a merger in the Italian aperitifs market, involving Davide Campari Milano SpA (Campari), the owner of the sixth group in the worldwide spirits industry and producer of the internationally renowned *Campari* bitter, and Barbero 1891 SpA (Barbero), whose well-known *Aperol* and *Aperol soda* brands were among the main alternatives to Campari in Italy. I will first briefly describe the Italian aperitifs market and then the merger.

The Italian Aperitifs Market: Production, Consumption and Distribution

Aperitifs are the kinds of drinks consumed before a meal. There are three main types of aperitif: (i) alcohol-free, non-fruit carbonated bitters (AFCB), sold both in single-serve 10cl glass bottles (mainly branded aperitifs) and 1.5 plastic bottles (only unbranded aperitifs); (ii) spirits, divided into bitters (AB), sold in 0.75- or 1-litre bottles, often served mixed with other beverages or water, and carbonated aperitifs (ACA) – mainly based on bitters,[14] sold in single-serve 10cl glass bottles; and (iii) vermouths (V) (white or red sweet wines flavoured with herbs, consumed mainly as aperitifs). Fruit and tomato juices, tonic water and sparkling wines are also consumed occasionally as aperitifs. AFCB, AB and ACA are produced from infusions of herbs, root and fruits, giving the aperitif its distinctive, often bitter, taste.

In 2001 the launch of Bacardi–Martini's *Bacardi Breezer*, a ready-to-drink mix of fruit juices and rum, started the development of a new segment, including "ready-to-drink" mixes of fruit juices and spirits (bitters or rum) sold in 33cl beer-like bottles, to be consumed before or after meals in every "get together" situation. While this kind of drink was not unknown in Italy

(Barbero launched *Corky's* mix in 1995), it met success only after Bacardi–Martini's move. In 2002 Campari successfully launched its own *Mixx* brand (a mix of *Campari* and fruit juices), and other firms have jumped into this promising segment. Campari claimed that ready-to-drink mixes are a type of aperitif, as they are consumed during "*happy hours*" before dinner, and that therefore the relevant market included at least traditional aperitifs *and* RTDs.

According to an independent research by Euromonitor, on the contrary, *Bacardi Breezer*, the RTD segment leader, "is a product which competes directly with cocktails, beer and wine, and is targeted especially at young people, particularly women, attending night bars and clubs … Carbonated aperitifs are not in competition with alcopops [Euromonitor's name for the products like Bacardi Breezer], which are consumed in the evening, while carbonated aperitifs are mostly consumed before dinner." Inclusion of these flavoured alcoholic beverages into the aperitif market was therefore dubious.

Table 8.1 shows the volume of sales for traditional aperitifs and for ready-to-drink mixes, both in litres and in servings.[15]

Table 8.1 Volume of sales of aperitifs

	millions of litres			millions of servings		
	1993	2001	2003	1993	2001	2003
Traditional aperitifs	111	79	77	1496	996	1036
Alcohol-free carbonated bitters	47%	52%	51%	35%	41%	40%
Alcoholic carbonated aperitifs	18%	23%	23%	13%	19%	18%
Alcoholic bitters	14%	9%	10%	21%	15%	16%
Vermouths	21%	16%	16%	31%	25%	26%
Ready-to-drink mixes	0	1	19	0	3	58

Source: AGCM estimates based on firms' data

The market for traditional aperitifs has clearly shrunk since 1993, but it has now stabilized (in terms of servings). A general trend away from alcohol consumption has penalized in particular the segments high in alcohol, alcoholic bitters and vermouths. The rise of ready-to-drink mixes, whose alcohol content is similar to beer, draws on this trend too.

According to data gathered by AGCM in 1994 – apparently not contradicted by recent independent studies of this sector –, aperitif consumers are very brand-loyal; demand elasticity both at the brand and at the segment level was low (see Appendix).

The most important distribution channel is bars, followed by supermarkets. Branded aperitifs in single-serve bottles are mainly sold to bars, but the supermarket share is growing, also because bar owners sometimes find it more convenient to buy from large supermarkets than directly from producers. Unbranded alcohol-free carbonated aperitifs sold in supermarkets in 1.5lt plastic bottles account for more than one-third of the total volume of sales in that segment.

Technology is not a barrier to entry. Branded products are sustained by heavy advertising expenditures, directed to create and maintain a strong brand image capturing the minds of consumers. Promotional expenditures are often high, to sustain trade relationships.

Firms and Market Shares

The main players in the aperitif market are just four firms, accounting for 80 per cent of total volume sales: Campari, San Pellegrino (controlled by Nestlé), Martini&Rossi (part of the Bacardi–Martini group) and Barbero. Table 8.2 shows the volume of shares and main brands for these firms in 2003.

Table 8.2 Volume of shares and main brands of major producers, 2003

	(1) AFCB[a]	(2) ACA[b]	(3) AB[c]	(4) V[d]	(5) (1)–(4)	(6) RTD[e]	Total
	Crodino	*Campari soda*	*Campari, Campari Biancosarti, Cynar*	*Cinzano*		*Mixx*	
Campari	41.0	82.9	46.1	2.6	44.7	15.8	38.9
		Aperol soda	*Aperol*			*Corky's*	
Barbero	–	14.3	35.7	–	6.8	1.1	5.6
San Pellegrino	*Sanbittèr, Gingerino* 40.5	–	–	–	20.7	–	16.5
		Baby Martini		*Martini*		*Bacardi Breezer*	
Martini& Rossi	–	2.7	–	62.7	10.9	74.9	23.6
Others	18.4	0.1	18.20	34.7	16.9	8.2	15.2

Notes:
a. AFCB: alcohol-free carbonated bitters
b. ACA: alcoholic carbonated aperitifs
c. AB: alcoholic bitters
d. V: vermouths
e. RTD: ready-to-drink

Source: AGCM estimates based on information provided by merging companies

The positioning of firms is very different. Campari is the overall market leader and the only firm with well-known brands in all segments. The other main players have a stronghold in one or two segments, and almost nothing elsewhere. This structure is partly due to the successful acquisitions made by Campari in 1994 (the acquisition of the Italian branch of the Dutch group Koninklijke Bolswessanen Nv – the "Campari/Bols merger", see Appendix –, which allowed Campari to consolidate its position in the AB segment (*Cynar* and *Biancosarti*) and to expand into the AFCB (*Crodino*)) and 1999 (Cinzano).

The Merger

On December 1st, 2003, Campari notified the AGCM of the acquisition of Barbero 1891 SpA ("Barbero"), whose well-known *Aperol* and *Aperol soda* brands were among the main alternatives to Campari's aperitifs in Italy. Merging companies submitted that, in their opinion, the acquisition was below the notification thresholds and therefore it was not subject to the application of Italian competition law. AGCM questioned some of companies' calculations and requested additional information.

The concentration strengthened Campari's leading position in the Italian market for aperitifs, virtually eliminating competition from two of the segments the aperitifs market is traditionally divided into, carbonated alcoholic aperitifs and alcoholic bitters (see Table 8.2 above). Table 8.3 reports the merger's structural indices. The concentration had a significant impact on the market for all aperitifs, increasing Campari's quota from 39 per cent to 44.6 per cent, almost twice that of the nearest competitor. Considering only traditional aperitifs, Campari's quota would have reached 51.5 per cent. Under the dominant position standard, structural indices for dominant position creation were clearly satisfied when only traditional segments were included, but the case was less clearcut with RTD included. Under the revised Merger Regulation and the new Merger Guidelines, there was a clear potential for significant unilateral effects under both market definitions.

Table 8.3 Structural indexes for the Campari/Barbero concentration

	Relevant market	
	only traditional	traditional segments + RTD
Pre-merger HHI	2606	2393
HHI change	606	439
Cumulated share	51.48	44.56
Ratio to first competitor	2.49	1.88

Therefore, during the three months of the informal investigation, AGCM's Market Analysis Office produced a preliminary assessment of the competitive effects of the concentration, using a PCAIDS simulation model *with nests* calibrated on margin data.

Given the preliminary stage of the investigation and the doubts on the necessity to submit the operation to an antitrust scrutiny, the Office could not ask for new information and data and it therefore had to rely on evidence on consumer behaviour and extensive margin data collected in 1994 during the Campari/Bols formal investigation and on publicly available information.

Preliminary assessment suggested that the merger could have a significant impact on prices, and therefore a formal investigation was needed to gather updated information and carefully assess the competitive effects of the merger. However, after carefully reviewing the merging companies' financial and accounting data, AGCM acknowledged, on March 11th, 2004, that the operation was below the thresholds and therefore it could not open a merger investigation.

4.   CALIBRATION OF NEST PARAMETERS

The natural starting point for merger simulation in the Campari/Barbero case was the relevant product market defined by AGCM when it passed the Campari/Bols merger in 1994. Drawing on the results of a survey of aperitif consumers, evidence of substitution across segments and answers to questionnaires sent to firms, AGCM used a chain-of-substitutes argument to establish that the relevant market included all traditional aperitifs.[16]

It was not clear, however, whether the chain-of-substitutes could be extended to also include the RTD segment. More importantly, firms' positioning, differences among the characteristics of aperitifs, strong consumer preferences for brands belonging to a given segment and substitution not proportional to market shares clearly indicated that competition in this market is localized. Chain-of-substitution arguments, while not necessarily at odds with localized competition, may lead to correctly broaden the market, but then a method is needed to represent the competitive relations implied by the chain-of-substitutes (market shares are not appropriate to it).

In addition, critical elasticity and critical loss-relevant market tests performed on 1994 data hinted that relevant markets could be smaller than the market for all aperitifs: competition emerged which was so localized that in the chain of substitution there appeared breaks that the former investigation did not recognize and that required a different configuration of the relevant market. Therefore, the chain-of-substitutes argument may have been pushed too far, overlooking the gaps created by the strong local character of competition.

The availability of margin data collected during the 1994 Campari/Bols investigation provided the opportunity to re-evaluate the relevant market for aperitifs, testing the just developed calibration method based on margins.

Our strategy was therefore the following: (i) use the 1994 brand margin to obtain sensible estimates of nest parameters for a market including all four traditional aperitif segments; (ii) simulate the price effects of Campari/Barbero mergers using those nest parameters and available 2003 data; (iii) test how these effects would change if the RTD segment was included, using different sets of nest parameters.

Brand Margin Data

During the Campari/Bols investigation the main firms operating in the industry were asked to provide details on production costs of each brand. Specifically, firms had to indicate, for each aperitif brand produced, the share of mill average price represented by each of the following cost items: raw materials, energy, labour (not including administration and other staff), promotions and agency commissions, transportation costs, advertising, administration, depreciation, other costs.

These data were used to construct four different margin measures, both net and gross of excise duties:

- *Gross margin*: mill price net of excise duties and discounts – raw material, energy and labour costs
- *Margin net of variable sales costs*: gross margin – promotions and commissions – transportation cost
- *Margin net of all sales costs*: margin net of variable sale costs – other sale costs
- *Trading profit*: margin net of all sales costs – advertising expenses.

The accounting margin closest to the economic notion of "margin over variable costs" is the "contribution margin" (measuring the proportion the revenues from a given product contribute to cover fixed costs). Our best approximation to this margin was the margin net of variable sales costs, as: (i) Gross margin is gross of variable sales costs, (ii) the nature of "other sale costs" was too uncertain, (iii) trading profit is net of advertising expenses, which are actually a fixed cost as they do not change with sales. However, it was decided to experiment also with the *gross margin*, as this is a readily available measure in every firm. Table 8.4 reports for each aperitif brand the ranges (for confidentiality reasons) within which net margins fell, along with the owner, the segment they were commonly thought to belong to and the value share.

Market Elasticity

To implement our method a sensible estimate of market elasticity is needed. During the Campari/Bols investigation, Campari commissioned Nielsen to carry out an econometric study of the demand for aperitifs. Nielsen estimated very low own demand elasticities for the traditional aperitif segments, seemingly consistent with behaviour emerging from AGCM own consumer survey (see Appendix).

From these elasticities it was possible to obtain a market demand elasticity below 0.5. Therefore, we decided to perform simulations using the following grid of values: [0.3, 0.5, 0.7, −1].[17]

Table 8.4 Margins (net of taxes) and segment of aperitif brands

Owner	Brand	Value share (%)	Gross margin	Margin net	Trading Profit
	Crodino (AFCB)	19.23	[71–80]	[61–70]	[51–60]
Bols	Cynar (AB)	1.69	[61–70]	[41–50]	[11–20]
	Biancosarti (AB)	1.52	[61–70]	[41–50]	[21–30]
	Riccadonna (V)	0.80	[41–50]	[21–30]	[11–20]
San Pellegrino	Sanbitter (AFCB)	12.79	[71–80]	[51–60]	[41–50]
	Gingerino (AFCB)	3.53	[61–70]	[51–60]	[51–60]
Zucca	Rabarbaro Zucca (AB)	0.47	[51–60]	[21–30]	[1–10]
Martini	Martini (V)	17.00	[61–70]	[41–50]	[11–20]
	Martini Bitter (AB)	n.a. (< 1)	[41–50]	[21–30]	[1–10]
Campari	Bitter Campari (AB)	7.02	[81–90]	[71–80]	[51–60]
	Campari Soda (ACA)	20.61	[71–80]	[61–70]	[41–50]
Aperol	Aperol (AB)	4.52	[81–90]	[61–70]	[41–50]
	Aperol Soda (ACA)**	0.04	[71–80]	[41–50]	Negative
Coca-Cola	Beverly (AFCB)	n.a. (< 4)	[41–50]	[11–20]	[11–20]
Average			65.2	47.6	
Standard deviation			12.2	18.4	

Notes:
* net of variable sale costs
** 1995 budget figures

Calibration of Nest Parameters

Nests were exogeneously specified. We considered several alternatives, ranging from simple two-nest structures (alcohol free *vs.* alcoholic aperitifs; aperitifs mainly sold in single-serving bottles (AFCB, ACA) *vs.* other aperitifs) to five-nest structures (separating *Cynar* only, or it and *Rabarbaro Zucca* from the AB segment because of their more bitter taste – akin to digestive bitters – and of the fact they were consumed both before and *after* the meals). With only two nests, simulated margins fitted actual margins very badly, implying that this structure was too simplified to reproduce acceptably the actual market structure. A three-nest structure (lumping together ACA and AB segments) performed better, but the best results were obtained with four or five nests. Five-nest structures produced, however, nest parameter matrices implying competitive relationships that were not consistent with available data.[18] Analysis therefore focused on the four-nest structure corresponding to traditional segments; the assignment of brands to segments/nests was that reported in Table 8.4. Further interesting specifications could not be tried due to the lack of margin data. In particular, it would have been interesting to enlarge our candidate market to include at least wines or, better, wines, tomato and fruit juices and tonic water.

Some of the brands for which the margins were available were very small. This was a potential problem: by excluding them, we would have foregone the potential advantages of overfitting, while inclusion could have introduced an additional source of instability of nest parameter values. We identified a base case including only the seven biggest margins – just as many margins as the number of parameters in the four-nests case. The margins of minor brands were progressively added to the base case, and several different combinations of margins were tried. Results can be summarized as follows:

- Gross margins (GM) were fitted better than margins net of variable sale costs (MNVSC); this was due to the smaller variability of GM;
- margins, in particular MNVSC, were better fitted using low values of market elasticity (e.g. -0.5);
- calibration in the base case gave a very good fit of actual margins, but some of the implied competitive relations were inconsistent with data;
- the inclusion of *Beverly* margin (assigned to "other AFCB") and of the *Riccadonna* margin affected nest parameters significantly, allowing values more consistent with the available evidence; this was obtained at the price of a loss of fit, more significant for MNVSC;

- calibrated nest parameters implied a substantial independence of the AFCB segment from all other segments and a stronger substitutability between the ACA and V segments than ACA and AB; the AB segment also displayed a substantial independence from other segments, except vermouths; this was true for calibration based on both MNVSC and GM;
- once the *Beverly* margin was assigned to "other AFCB", substitutability relationships implied by nest parameter values remained very stable; values calibrated on GM changed only little as different combinations of margins were added to the *base + Beverly* one; nest parameter values calibrated on MNVSC changed more, but never enough to support different substitution relationships.

Table 8.5 reports the percentage of deviations of simulated margins from actual margins, "pseudo R^2" for the base case and the most convincing calibrations based on MNVSC, while Table 8.6 reports the corresponding nest parameter values. Using GM, we obtained very similar nest parameter values with smaller deviations; brand 1 elasticity, corresponding to *Crodino*, was approximately equal to −1.4 in all specifications.

Deviations are of a tolerable magnitude for important brands, while large for smaller brands. However, inclusion of smaller brands was necessary to get nest parameter values reasonably consistent with the available evidence.

Table 8.5 Calibration of nest parameters
(Margin net of variable sale costs, computed on revenues net of excise duties)

	Base case	Case 1[a]	Case 2[b]	Case 3[c]
Crodino	0.0484	0.1313	0.1439	0.0773
Vermouth Riccadonna	−	−	−0.4827	−0.5764
Sanbitter	0.0002	0.0975	0.1140	0.0388
Gingerino	−0.0268	0.0732	0.0901	0.0128
Martini Vermouth	−0.0328	−0.0843	−0.0742	−0.0461
Bitter Campari	0.0044	0.0122	0.0289	0.0294
Campari Soda	−0.0103	0.0336	0.1069	0.0831
Aperol	0.0022	0.0052	0.0232	0.0115
othersAFCB (*Beverly*)	−	−0.9906	−0.9241	−
e11 (*Crodino*)	1.66	1.82	1.84	1.71
Industry elasticity	0.50	0.50	0.50	0.50
Pseudo-R^2	0.9760	0.7492	0.7546	0.8275

Notes: a. base case + Beverly assigned to "othersAFCB" b. case 1 + Riccadonna
c. base case + Riccadonna

Table 8.6 Nest parameter values

Base	AFCB	ACA	AB	V	Case 1	AFCB	ACA	AB	V
AFCB	1				AFCB	1			
ACA	0	1			ACA	0	1		
AB	0	0.065	1		AB	0	0	1	
V	0.32	1	0.21	1	V	0.12	0.79	0.027	1

Case 2	AFCB	ACA	AB	V	Case 3	AFCB	ACA	AB	V
AFCB	1				AFCB	1			
ACA	0	1			ACA	0	1		
AB	0	0	1		AB	0	0	1	
V	0.05	0.85	0	1	V	0.11	1	0.11	1

Nest Parameter Values Reflect Firms' Perception of Competition

Alcohol-free carbonated bitters are depicted as very far from other aperitifs. This distance seems consistent with at-home consumer behaviour (only one-third of consumers shifted to another aperitif in the event their preferred choice was not available, and most stayed within the category when the category price was increased), less with away-from-home behaviour. It is strongly consistent, however, with firms' perception of competition; when asked about the competitors of their brands, firms answered as follows for AFCB brands:

AFCB brand	Competing brands (listed in decreasing order of importance)
Crodino	Sanbitter (AFCB), Gingerino (AFCB), Private Label (AFCB)
Sanbitter	Crodino (AFCB), Beverly (AFCB), Campari (AB), Aperol (AB)
Gingerino	Crodino (AFCB), Beverly (AFCB), Campari (AB), Aperol (AB)
Beverly	Crodino (AFCB), Campari (AB), Sanbitter (AFCB)

Crodino, leader of the segment, listed only other AFCBs as competitors; the two followers listed Campari only as third.

Vermouths emerged as much closer to carbonated alcoholic aperitifs than to alcoholic bitters, something that does seem inconsistent with consumer choices. Again, this is strongly consistent with firms' perception of competition; actually, when asked to list their brands' competitors, they answered as follows:

Vermouths	Competing brands (listed in decreasing order of importance)
Campari Soda (ACA)	*Martini (V), Bitter Campari (AB), Cinzano (ACA)*
Martini (V)	*Campari Soda (ACA), Aperol (AB), Cinzano (V)*

Campari soda and *Martini* perceive themselves as each other's most important competitor. At that time, the ACA segment was almost monopolized by *Campari soda*, while the vermouth segment was dominated by *Martini*. *Campari soda* was therefore priced not in competition with other brands in the same segment, but against competitors from other segments. To Campari, Martini&Rossi was the closest competitor and a *Martini* with soda water could have been the best alternative to *Campari soda* for people not too fond of *Campari*'s taste.

Finally, the relative independence of the Alcoholic Bitters segment was consistent with firms' perceptions (*Cynar*, *Zucca* and *Aperol* listed as competitors other ABs; Campari listed as competitors of its *Bitter* its own *Campari soda* and *Martini* first, and then *Aperol*, another AB).

The four-nest parameter structure had the very appealing feature that it showed nest relations *as firms perceived them*. Therefore, it was not arbitrary but represented very well the competitive relations in the industry, as they emerged from positioning strategies incorporated into margins.

Nest parameter matrices for the four-nest structure implied therefore a very fragmented market for aperitifs. In particular, it appeared that the AFCB segment was *not* in the relevant market and that the AB segment enjoyed a relative independence from the remaining two segments, alcoholic carbonated aperitifs and vermouths.

5.   SIMULATING PRICE EFFECTS[19]

Armed with nest parameters, we turned to the Campari/Barbero merger. Given the preliminary stage of investigation, our aim was to give AGCM's commissioners advice on whether or not to open a formal investigation.

Under the "dominant position standard", simulated price effects can be taken as a manifestation of the degree of independency of the new firm formed by the merging companies (the "newco") from the remaining competitors. A greater weight may be given to the price increases predicted for the "newco" than to market price increases, since what is analysed is the potential for *individual* independent behaviour. Provided that PCAIDS has a tendency to overestimate price effects, we decided to use the following rule of thumb: a formal investigation should be opened if the model simulates a price increase of at least 5 per cent at the market level and of at least 10 per cent for the "newco" formed by the merging firms.

Merger Simulations Without Nests

First, a merger simulation without nests was run. For industry elasticity we used the previous grid again. For brand elasticity, we found useful data in Campari's *Half-yearly Shareholders Report at June 30, 2003*, which reports gross margins and trading profits for three product categories: spirits (AB, ACA, RTD), wines and soft drinks (there was no way to recover contribution margin estimates). Among them, the most homogeneous is the spirits category, where *Campari soda* accounts for 68 per cent of volume sales in Italy. The gross margin for spirits was therefore taken as an approximation of the *Campari soda* gross margin. Its value, corrected for fixed production expenses estimated from the balance sheet, was equal to 73.4 per cent, close to the 1994 gross margin. It implied a brand elasticity of -1.36. Merger simulation without nests including only traditional segments gave an average price increase for the new merged entity Campari+Barbero of 15.3 per cent and a price increase of 8.8 per cent at the market level. When RTD were also included, simulated price increases reduced to 11.1 per cent and 5.6 per cent respectively, still greater than our rule-of-thumb thresholds.

Merger Simulations with Nests without RTDs

We then turned to simulation with nests. Under the hypothesis the relevant market does not include ready-to-drink mixes, the merger would have certainly deserved close scrutiny if the alcoholic bitters segment were significantly independent of the others, as suggested by the calibration of nest parameters. Actually, in this case the merger would have created a quasi-monopoly in the segment.

In the four-nest case (AFCB, ACA, AB, V), the calibration of nest parameters strongly suggested that AFCB was not in the relevant market. However, one nice aspect of merger simulation with nests is that it can handle, through nest parameters, also apparently weak substitutes, without worrying about relevant market definition. Simulations were therefore run including AFCB, and using several vectors of nest parameters – some of them with zeros for AFCB.[20] AFCB inclusion also allowed us to check how substitutable it should be to affect merger simulation results significantly.

When the AFCB segment was included, price effects were above 9 per cent at industry level and above 15 per cent for the newco, even for nest parameter values like those of the base case, favourable to the merging companies. Price effects stayed above 5 per cent at the market level and above 10 per cent at the merging firms level even if nest parameters for AFCB were increased up to 0.5, keeping the others constant.

Merger simulation signalled high potential unilateral effects and a large potential for independent behaviour for the new firm.[21] Therefore, a formal investigation to ascertain the possible creation of a dominant position able to restrict competition would have been necessary.

Merger Effects when RTDs are Taken into Account

Finally, we studied what happens when new possible types of aperitifs, namely ready-to-drink mixes, are included in the candidate relevant market.

Given that we had no margins to calibrate nest parameters with RTD, we constructed the nest parameters matrix by augmenting the nest parameter matrices which emerged from the previous analysis for the three-nest (ACA, AB, V) case with a row representing nest parameters for the RTD segment. We used the same brand elasticity and market elasticity employed for the simulations without RTD.

The purpose of the simulations performed was to ascertain how substitutable RTD had to be with the other segments in order to make it unlikely for the merger to restrict competition appreciably.

Assuming for simplicity that RTDs were equidistant from other segments, simulations showed that in order to have price effects below the thresholds given by our rule of thumb, RTDs have to be close enough to other segments – that is, nest parameters have to be above 0.4. However, if RTDs were closer to some segment bur farther from others, the picture changed significantly. For example, if RTDs were very far from alcoholic carbonated aperitifs (i.e. nest parameter value for the pair (RTD, ACA) below 0.25), even if the other segments were relatively close to other segments (i.e. with nest parameter values above 0.4 but below 0.75) PCAIDS would have simulated price increases above the thresholds.

Our results suggested that the inclusion of RTDs in the relevant market could have made a difference, but only to the extent that subsequent analysis would have shown a sufficiently high substitutability between RTDs and other segments – in particular alcoholic carbonated aperitifs. Only in that case would the RTDs have been able to sufficiently constrain the exploitation by Campari of market power resulting from virtual elimination of competition in the ACA and AB segments. Available evidence, however, emphasized a limited substitutability between RTDs and traditional aperitifs – the RTD segment is increasing more because it identified a niche which was poorly exploited previously, than because of reducing sales of traditional aperitifs.

Nests indicated the importance of the degree of substitutability between RTDs and traditional segments in the evaluation of the merger. A formal investigation was therefore called for a deeper understanding of current market conditions.

6.   CONCLUDING REMARKS

Merger simulation is a very useful tool for analysing merger effects. The use of nests in simulations seems, however, to be necessary to handle markets with well-defined segments or hazy boundaries.

Building on a suggestion by Epstein and Rubinfeld, AGCM developed a method to calibrate nest parameters through margins. Although developed in connection with PCAIDS, the method is general and can be easily applied to nested logit too.[22]

The method was tested on a merger between the two leading producers of aperitifs in Italy, using old margin data, yielding sensible and robust results; calibrated nest parameters fitted well with firms' perception of competition between brands. Nest parameters were then used to simulate merger price effects through PCAIDS; simulated price effects were large enough to suggest that a formal investigation should have been opened, but emphasized that the true issue was nest distances.

We dealt with the choice of the appropriate nest structure by using a measure of fit and evidence on brand competition as perceived by firms. Although we focused on an estimation of the brand contribution margin, we found that the best fit was obtained when the gross margin (mill price net of excise duties and discounts – raw material, energy and labour costs (excluding administrative personnel costs)) was used. This was likely due to a lower variability of gross margins, that allowed our model, based on the IIA hypothesis relaxed through nests, to perform better. Future research on calibration through margin data will have to understand which is the best price with respect to which the margin has to be computed. Our results hint that the use of margins computed on mill prices, that is net of distributors' policies, will likely reflect the way producers think of competition, and that this perception may be somewhat different from that held by consumers, who face retailers' prices. As long as a merger between producers is dealt with, analysis should focus first on the effects at the production level, so it is the producers' perception that mostly matters.

However, in case large potential anticompetitive effects emerged at this level, then the analysis should focus on whether distributors' and retailers' behaviour – including buyer power – can actually weaken anticompetitive effects at the consumer level; at this level, possible differences between firms' perception of competition and actual substitution by consumers will have to be taken into account.

Eventually, the best test of merger simulation models is their ability to predict the size of the competitive effects of mergers. In the case of aperitifs, available evidence on post-merger market evolution points to very low price effects, a result which is at odds with those obtained in the simulations. So large a difference cannot be explained only by government invitations to branded goods' producers to refrain from increasing prices. The key point is that our simulations did not take into account the downward trend of demand for traditional aperitifs, that would obviously discourage firms from increasing prices. Is there any simple way to deal with this problem in the context of our simulations? To the extent that the downward trend can be assimilated to an increase in market demand elasticity, the answer is yes.[23]

Simulating the merger assuming very high (given our estimate of brand elasticity) market elasticities (e.g. 1.2, 1.25) actually decreased a lot of simulated price effects, bringing them significantly below our thresholds;[24] therefore, according to our rule of thumb, a formal investigation should not have been opened, as the merger was not likely to have significant competitive effects.

So revised, merger simulation results do seem consistent with actual market evolution. This make us confident about the usefulness of simulations in preliminary merger analysis. There is still some work to do, however, to get precise the estimates of the merger price effects.

APPENDIX: THE CAMPARI/BOLS MERGER

In 1994 Campari bought the Italian branch of the Dutch group Koninklijke Bolswessanen Nv (Bols), owning some of the best-selling brands at that time: *Crodino*, *Biancosarti* and *Cynar*. This merger allowed Campari to become the market leader, ahead of the Bacardi–Martini group.

The operation was notified to AGCM, who conducted a 45-day formal investigation on concentration competitive effects. During this investigation, AGCM collected extensive data on the aperitif market, through (i) questionnaires sent to firms, asking about sales, competitors and costs, and (ii) a consumer survey administered through Nielsen.

The consumer survey revealed very brand-loyal consumers, with a very low demand elasticity. When asked what they would do in the event of a 10 per cent increase in the price of their preferred brand for at-home consumption,[25] only 17 per cent of consumers who replied said they would switch to another brand, while another 8 per cent would cease to consume aperitifs altogether. Thirty-five per cent of all respondents (about 47 per cent of those that would not switch brand) would not diminish consumption in that event.

Looking at the switchers, 56 per cent of consumers whose first choice was
an alcohol-free carbonated bitter would switch to another brand in the same
segment if the price of their preferred brands were to increase by 10 per cent;
the others would distribute evenly among the available alternatives. Fifty-two
per cent of vermouth consumers would switch to another vermouth, while
another 21 per cent would switch to an alcoholic bitter. On the other hand,
only 15 per cent of alcoholic bitters' consumers would switch to another
alcoholic bitter, the main alternative being an alcohol-free carbonate bitter.
Very few carbonated alcoholic aperitif consumers would stay within the
category (at that time, monopolized by *Campari soda*), the main alternative
being an alcohol-free carbonated aperitif (about 50 per cent of switchers).

Consumer behaviour in the event of a 10 per cent increase in the price of
all brands belonging to the segment of their preferred aperitif showed a very
similar pattern. Demand elasticity at the segment level was therefore low.

Respondents were also asked to indicate their second-choice brand or
aperitif type for home consumption. About one-third of consumers of
alcohol-free carbonated bitters stayed within the segment, while another third
chose a drink different from those usually or occasionally consumed as
aperitif. Half of the remaining third chose alcoholic bitters and only a very
few chose a carbonated aperitif. Carbonated aperitif consumers (at that time,
the segment was monopolized by *Campari soda*) mainly chose alcoholic
bitters. Twenty per cent of consumers of alcoholic bitters indicated as their
second choice another alcoholic bitter. Most of the others chose a vermouth
or an alcohol-free bitter. Vermouth consumers (at that time, *Martini*
dominated the segment) almost always switched segment, choosing mainly a
drink different from those usually or occasionally consumed as an aperitif or
an alcoholic bitter.

As to away-from-home consumption, consumers were asked to name the
aperitif they would have asked for if their preferred choice were not
available. Behaviour was not very different from that in at-home
consumption. People preferring alcoholic bitters seem to stay within that
category more at bars than at home, while those preferring alcohol-free
aperitifs switch to alcoholic bitters far more often at bars than at home.

In addition, Campari commissioned Nielsen to produce a study of demand
for aperitifs. Nielsen estimated a set of log–log demand equations, which
produced the following estimated elasticity matrix:

	AFCB	ACA	AB	V
AFCB	−0.147	0.212	0.189	
ACA	0.506	−1.256	0.734	
AB	0.488	0.507	−1.954	0.609
V			0.518	−1.063

AGCM established that the relevant market included all drinks produced to be used mainly or exclusively as an aperitif, that is non-fruit carbonated alcohol-free bitters, carbonated alcoholic aperitifs, alcoholic bitters and vermouths. Fruit drinks and sparkling wines were excluded as they were used only occasionally as aperitifs. The four types of aperitif were put in the same market on the basis of a chain-of-substitutes argument, drawing on the results of a survey of aperitif consumers, evidence of substitution across segments and answers to questionnaires sent to firms: at one extreme there were alcohol-free bitters and at the other end the vermouths; in between, alcoholic aperitifs with carbonated alcoholic aperitifs closer to carbonated alcohol-free bitters thanks to gas and their low alcohol content.

In particular, AGCM emphasized the following elements:

- changes in relative prices of aperitifs moved consumption from one segment to another;
- consumers' second choice brands do not necessarily belong to the same segment, and often they do not;
- high correlations between prices;
- producers indicated among their brands competitors' aperitifs belonging also to other segments;
- the pattern of cross-elasticities estimated by Nielsen.

Value market shares are reported in Table 8.A.1.

Table 8.A.1 Value of market shares, 1993

	Overall	Non-fruit alcohol-free carbonated bitters	Carbonated alcoholic aperitifs	Alcoholic bitters	Vermouths
Bacardi-Martini	17.0	–	–	n.d. *(Bitter)*	17.0 *(Martini)*
Bols	23.24	19.23 *(Crodino)*	–	1.69 *(Cynar)* 1.52 *(Biancosarti)*	0.8 *(Riccadonna)*
Campari	27.63	–	20.61 *(Campari)*	7.02 *(Bitter)*	–
San Pellegrino	16.32	12.79 *(SanBittèr)* 3.53 *(Gingerino)*	–	–	–

Barbero (Allied Domecq)	4.56	–	0.04 *(Aperol soda)*	4.52 *(Aperol)*	–
Cinzano (IDV Grand Met)	0.76	–	0.23 *(Cinzano)*	–	0.53 *(Cinzano)*
Zucca	0.47			0.47 *(Rabarbaro Zucca)*	
Others	10.02	4.28	0.1	1.75	3.89
Share	100%	40%	21%	17%	22%

Note: Reported values are somewhat different from those in the cited decision as allowance has been made for the fact that, according to producers, only ¼ of Cynar and Zucca volumes were consumed as aperitifs (the remaining being consumed as "amaro", after the meal)
Source: estimates based on average mill price and volumes in litres by brand as reported in answers to questionnaires sent to firms

Campari and Bols were clearly complementary: the merger would have significantly reduced competition to *Bitter Campari* and allowed Campari to extend in the vermouth and, above all, in the alcohol-free segment, strengthening its competitive and bargaining position.

The merger had its major effects in the alcoholic bitters segment, where it left only one well-established competitor, *Aperol*, with a 26.6 per cent share against Campari's 60.3 per cent share.

In the relevant market established by AGCM, the merger raised HHI by at least 700 points, creating a firm with a 50.9 per cent share in value and 37.3 per cent in servings. In value terms, the measure probably best suited for differentiated products, the new entity share would have been almost three times that of the closer competitor. From a purely structural point of view, the concentration would have created a dominant firm.

AGCM decided to pass the concentration, however, because it did not think that the dominant position would have eliminated or restricted competition appreciably and on a lasting basis, because of the following considerations:

- presence of competitors with well-known brands, included in the assortment of any point of sale;
- different segment trends, reflecting taste evolution opening opportunities for product and marketing innovations;
- potential competition from drinks which are currently consumed only occasionally as an aperitif, to which consumers could switch in the event of a significant increase in prices;

- very low technological barriers to entry.

NOTES

*   Ideas expressed in this chapter do not purport to represent either the opinions of members of Autorità Garante della Concorrenza e del Mercato or the expected course of merger investigations conducted by Autorità's staff. I am indebted for useful comments to Mario Forni, Pierluigi Sabbatini and Joris Pinkse. The usual disclaimer applies, of course.

1. We refer to "preliminary investigation" to indicate the "Phase I" investigation aimed to decide whether or not to open a formal investigation on a notified merger.

2. The "creation of a dominant position" requires that a change in the mode of competition is brought about by the merger. Standard merger simulations based on the Bertrand model with differentiated products, which assume no change in competition mode, can therefore be seen as a sort of baseline case: if a switch to a less competitive interaction model occurred, then the likely increase in prices could not be lower.

3. The Italian Competition Act is still not aligned to the new EU Merger Regulation.

4. As part of this project, both Ariel Pakes and Marc Ivaldi held seminars on empirical methods in antitrust analysis.

5. There was not enough price variability in the data, so both AIDS and Logit estimates were very unreliable.

6. AGCM has 30 days to decide whether to open a formal investigation after a complete notification has been received; a formal investigation lasts 45 days.

7. Assume there are three brands, with shares 30 per cent, 40 per cent, 30 per cent. Under IIA, If brand 1 price increases, $(40)/(100-30) = 57.1$ per cent of lost share will go to brand 2 and $30/(100-30)= 42.9$ per cent will go to brand 3. The ratio 57.1/42.9 is called *odds ratio*. By modifying it, it is possible to represent the fact that, for example, brand 1 is actually closer to brand 3.

8. Mario Forni, Professor of Economics at University of Modena and Reggio Emilia (Italy) and CEPR fellow.

9. Inputs to the program are market shares, market elasticity, brand allocations to nests and at least as many brand margins as the number of nest parameters plus one.

10. Given that with four or more nests the nested logit model requires less nest parameters than PCAIDS, with a given number of actual margins the nested logit actually allows exploration of finer nest structures.

11. If exactly as many margins as the number of parameters to be calibrated are available, then the method actually amounts to solving a system on n equations in n unknown under the specified constraints.

12. Calibration loss may also be used to determine the best allocation of brands to a given number of nests. Currently a *Matlab* code to endogeneously allocate brands to nests is under study. The current version allows only two or three nests.

13. For an application of bootstrapping in the context of merger simulation, see Capps, Church and Love 2001.

14. Popular carbonated alcoholic aperitifs are just an alcoholic bitter with soda added and some minor adjustment in the recipe: *Campari soda* is based on *Campari*, *Aperol soda* is based on *Aperol*, and so on. There are also carbonated alcoholic aperitifs based on vermouths, like *Martini baby* and *Cinzano soda*.

15. Servings may provide a better comparison, as several aperitifs are also used as mixers and the alcoholic aperitifs servings are usually smaller.

16. Evidence of substitution and of direct competition among brands suggested that alcohol-free bitters were closer to carbonated aperitifs than to vermouth and non-carbonated bitters; that vermouths were closer to non-carbonated bitters; that carbonated aperitifs were close to bitters (sharing the basic composition). Therefore, the four segments could be put ideally on a line, at one extreme of which there were alcohol-free bitters and at the other end the

vermouths; in between, alcoholic aperitifs with carbonated alcoholic aperitifs, the latter closer to alcohol-free aperitifs.

17. Data collected from Istat (the Italian Central Office of Official Statistics) did not reach the level of industry detail needed to perform an independent estimation of industry demand.

18 Nest parameters implied the same relationships described in the main text among AFCB, ACA, AB (without *Cynar* and *Zucca*) and V, but a very strong substitutability/competition between AFCB and the Cynar–Zucca nest, which was supported neither by the AGCM consumer survey nor by brand competitors lists provided by firms.

18. For purposes of comparison, an attempt to simulate the merger through a flat logit model was made. It was, however, unsuccessful: with the same hypothesis on elasticities and using Campari's and Barbero's actual prices and realistic estimates of other companies' prices, we got negative marginal costs. Inserting on the contrary a vector of equal prices normalized to 1 gave very low price increases.

19. Performing the simulation including the AFCB segment with nest parameters set very close to zero or without it makes some difference, as shares change. In cases like ours, where the excluded segment was not interested by the merger and included a strong competitor, simulation results are more favourable to merging companies when the segments with zero nest parameters are included.

20. Of course, simulated price increases must not be taken at face value. High numerical values, such as those here, should be taken as an indication of large expected increases at the actual price level, where an actual 10 per cent increase may be already considered "very large".

21. We do not think there is any *a priori* reason to prefer Logit or PCAIDS merger simulations. In the flat case they have exactly the same elasticity matrix as a starting point, and their different predictions depend on the fact that PCAIDS does not impose IIA on post-merger elasticities. In the nested case, however, nest parameter structures do differ between them, so future research should focus on understanding the differences in the performances of the two models due to different nest parameterization.

22. A decreasing demand trend can be thought of as a series of downward parallel shifts of the demand curve. In the case of linear demand curves, this implies that, for a given price, demand elasticity increases.

23. For example, without RTDs – the worst case for merging companies – simulated price increase for the newco was only 6.4 per cent, while at the market level it was 3.5 per cent.

24. As all aperitifs are priced the same in bars where away-from-home consumption mainly occurs, it did not make sense to ask this question for this type of consumption.

9.   Simulating the Effect of Oracle's Takeover of PeopleSoft

Claes Bengtsson[1]

The hostile takeover of PeopleSoft by Oracle was not an everyday business transaction. The assessment of the transaction by the European Commission was also a process that was special for a number of reasons. It was an unusually long procedure where the clock was stopped twice.[2] It was also one of the last transactions to be assessed under the old merger regulation.[3] Furthermore, in parallel with the assessment by the Commission, the US Department of Justice asked the District Court for the Northern District of California in San Francisco to prohibit the transaction and lost.[4] This chapter deals with none of these particularities. Instead it describes the choice of merger simulation model that was developed by DG Competition in the course of the assessment and how it influenced the thinking about the transaction.

The model presented below indicated that the transaction potentially could lead to significant harm to customers, yet the Commission ultimately decided to clear it. This should not be seen as a general hostility towards merger simulation models, rather it was due to the particular circumstances in this case. The simulation model relied on a narrow definition of the relevant market, whereby the merger could reasonably be described as a strict reduction from three to two players. Relatively late in the procedure, the Commission concluded that it was inappropriate to exclude other players from the relevant market. Since the narrow market definition was perhaps the most fundamental assumption in the model, it could no longer be relied on to predict the effect of the merger. Though the model ultimately had little relevance for the final outcome, it may serve as an illustration of a case where actual modelling potentially can be both possible and useful.

There are many different ways in which the effect of a merger can be modelled. The choices made should to the greatest possible extent reflect the particular characteristics of the market in question without compromising the mathematical tractability of the exercise. In this particular case a number of observations regarding the market were informing the choice of model. These characteristics are described in Section 1. Section 2 outlines the structure of the model and its basic mechanics. In Section 3 some results from the simulation of the merger are shown.

1.   MARKET CHARACTERISTICS

Oracle and PeopleSoft are two of many companies active in the part of the software industry that is called Enterprise Application Software (EAS) which provides software that facilitate all the different aspects of corporate activities. One can broadly distinguish between different pillars of software, depending on whether it aims at managing customers (Customer Relationship Management, CRM); staff (Human Resource, HR); transactions (Financial Management Systems, FMS) or input and production (Supply Chain Management, SCM). While some firms provide point-solutions to particular tasks within the firm, both Oracle and PeopleSoft are among the companies providing integrated suites that deliver broad packages of solutions to most or all of the firms needs within a pillar as well as across pillars.

The difficulties in defining the relevant market in this case related inter alia, to the fact that customers varied greatly in terms of the kind of software they could use, which in turn depended on a number of factors including their size, their industry, their internal organization, their global presence etc. At the point in time where the model was developed the Commission worked under the assumption that for large enterprises with complex needs only Oracle, PeopleSoft and SAP were competing for FMS and HR. Yet, for a number of reasons that are mentioned in its final Decision,[5] the Commission ultimately decided that this hypothesis could not be upheld and that the market also contained other firms.

A number of characteristics of the market are outlined below which guided the decision on how to model competition in the market. To illustrate different points, references are sometimes made to witness statements from the trial in the District Court in San Francisco. This is done out of convenience since, contrary to many other types of evidence, the testimonies are in the public domain.

Individual Bidding Process

The procurement process by which large enterprises select their EAS provider takes place in a way that can appropriately be understood as a bidding contest. The customer decides how to structure the process based on individual preferences and other constraints. In many instances it may acquire expert assistance from an independent advisor.[6] The procurement process usually contains a number of stages including the definition of the scope of the tender and a number of selection criteria as well as negotiation and selection rounds. There does not appear to be a general market-wide practice as to how the process should be designed, rather the process chosen in a given situation appears to be specific to the particular tender and the particular circumstances. In order to take this diversity into account, it is not appropriate to make very detailed assumptions about how the procurement process takes place. It appears more robust to choose a model that is sufficiently generic to take all the variations into account.

Competitors are Known

From internal documents it appeared that in many instances each bidder becomes aware of the identity of its competitors in a particular bidding contest before they decide on their final offer. Discount approval forms from Oracle very often contained references to the identities of other bidders in the contest. Similarly, PeopleSoft had submitted bidding data to the Commission indicating the identity of their competitors in given bidding situations.

Most Cost are Sunk Before the Bidding Contest

The main cost components of an EAS supplier are the development of the software and sales and marketing activities. Apart from the sales commission, these types of cost are all incurred by the EAS supplier prior to the entering into a contract. This is confirmed for instance by the testimony of Ms Catz (one of the two presidents at Oracle) before the District Court in San Francisco. When asked about Oracle's gross margin, she replied:

> ...on a million-dollar deal for example, regardless of what the software is, I might have to send a CD pack or a few CDs to the customer. That would cost maybe $30. Many of our customers don't ask for a CD pack because they download the software from our web sites or they already have it in-house. In addition, I have to pay commissions to my salesmen. And depending on which product line, the commissions for – including the salesmen and the sales manager and all the way up would be anywhere from six percent to maximum nine or ten percent. So, from a million dollars, from a million-dollar deal, $900,000 or so drops to the bottom line, maybe more.[7]

This is different from many other industries where most of the costs of delivering the services are incurred only by the winner and only after the bidding contest. As an example, in procurement contracts for cleaning services the main part of the costs of delivering the services are not known when the bidding contest takes place. This is an important distinction since in most existing models of procurement bidding markets the uncertainty about future costs forms a very central component of the competitive process.[8]

Sales commission is a marginal cost but since it is incurred as a fixed proportion of the final sales price, it does not affect bidding behaviour in the model and can therefore be ignored.

In addition to the licence fee that is paid up front, the customer can also purchase subsequent maintenance of the software, including updates and patches that repair bugs when identified. The price for the maintenance is usually decided as a fixed annual fee calculated as an agreed percentage of the licence fee. The costs related to deliver these services are unknown at the point of bidding (as is the exact content of the service), but since they are generic updates, it appears reasonable to assume that the costs of providing them will be incurred regardless of whether a particular bid for a particular customer is won or not. This means that these costs, though uncertain at the point of the procurement, should not be considered as marginal costs and are therefore not important for the model.

It therefore appears to be a reasonable starting point to understand a particular bidding contest as one involving zero marginal cost. It should be noted that this assumption is not an exact replication of the facts in that it ignores some adaptations of the software to the particular needs of the customer. Most of the costs related to those kinds of services are offered either by the consulting arm of the suppliers or by third parties awarded via separate contracts, often on a per hour basis.[9] Winning a software contract may thus have an additional impact on the consultation arm of the firm, which is not taken into account.

Each Contest is Unique; Relative Fit of Each Alternative is Uncertain

The requirements of each customer are highly dependent on the particular way the company is organized. This makes the identification of the best technical solution for the customer a complex process in which the software providers invest significant resources. While the bidder appears in most cases to have reliable knowledge about the identity of the competitors in the market, each bidder has less reliable information about how much better (or worse) its proposed solution fits the needs of the customer compared to the competitor's offer. During the tender process the supplier will get a certain feel for the needs of the customer, and perhaps some ideas about what competitors are offering. But throughout the process the customer will have an incentive to put pressure on each competitor by "exaggerating" the quality of the available alternatives. Such pressure, if successful, will lead to either lower prices or a higher quality offer from the bidder. When submitting the "final bid" the supplier does not know for sure exactly what reduction is necessary to win the deal. This uncertainty stems both from the lack of knowledge of the prices from other bidders but also from the lack of knowledge about how much the bidder is willing to pay extra for a better fit. Ms Catz's testimony illustrates this, when during cross examination she discusses what is known to Oracle and what is not:

> ... I think we would love to know how our customers value our product versus our competitors' products, we would love to know that, but we could not possibly know that, because they're not going to tell us. So we're going to look, you know – we're going to try to do our best to learn as much as we possibly can, and if they share with you, they'll share with us something, but they're negotiating with us. So they're not that motivated to tell us everything, and to tell us everything exactly right.[10]

2. THE MODEL

Based on the above observations the Commission designed a model to best capture the potential effect on prices of the proposed merger. A model must necessarily be based on a certain number of simplifications and assumptions. It will not be able to exactly predict the effect in any particular bidding process, but to the extent that it captures the essential characteristics of the market, it can be seen as a good approximation of the average effect of the proposed merger.

The model chosen was a sealed bid auction model with a relatively simple information structure. It has one stage in which the customer receives a sealed bid from each of the three potential suppliers. The customer then compares the three prices with the value (or quality) he attaches to each of the three products. Exactly what quality he attaches to each of the three offers is individual to that particular customer and is unknown to the bidders. Though the bidders do not know exactly what the quality of each of the bids will be, they have an idea of the ranges. Formally, it is assumed that the actual quality of each bidder's offer is private information to the customer, but is drawn from a normal distribution with a commonly known mean and standard deviation. Quality in this context should be understood very broadly to also include the customer's expectations about how the supplier will behave in the future (in terms of providing maintenance, new relevant innovations etc.).

Based on these expectations about the quality of each of the three products the bidders have to decide on what price to ask for his product. It is assumed that this price is selected in order to maximize the expected profit for the bidder. The simulation model illustrates the fundamental trade-off that a vendor is facing when deciding what price to offer to the customer in a situation of imperfect information. A high price increases the risk that the vendor will not be chosen by the customer but at the same time will result in a big profit if he is, while a low price will increase the probability of being selected but result in a lower profit.

The importance of trying to find out about the preferences of the customer in order to optimize the bidding strategy is illustrated inter alia, by the testimony of on customer, Mr Wolfe, the CIO of the state of North Dakota. He testified about the behaviour of Oracle and PeopleSoft when they were left as the two final bidders in a competition:

> ...they both did what they could to determine where the evaluation process was and how they were ranking. Oracle in particular were very aggressive about trying to find out how the evaluation was going, how they stood, and what their ranking was and what the comparisons were with PeopleSoft.[11]

The same point was also dealt with by Ms Catz, when explaining what information the sales representatives extract during the sales process:

> Well, what they learn often is what the customer tells them about what modules and functionality and features they're looking at. What the customers don't tell them, though, is how they value the different differences between our different products and the features, and in fact, as you know, I have been here, and I've noticed that none of the customers wanted to actually share their actual TCO[12] and internal valuation numbers because they actually said they didn't want the vendors to find out.[13]

The model has an implicit assumption that neither of the bidders have any private information about the relative performance of their software compared to that of the competitors.[14] This assumption greatly simplifies the tractability of the model.

Sealed Bid Versus an Open English Auction

The main model choice was to use a sealed bid auction model.[15] Though the entire procurement process may involve a number of selection and negotiation stages, one should not immediately draw the conclusion that a sequential English auction model is the most appropriate way of capturing the competitive process.

The key in this context is rather whether bidders can always expect to be given the chance to respond with an improved offer if they are on the verge of being eliminated from the contest, or whether they risk being eliminated even before they have reached their pain threshold in terms of how low they would go on prices. In an English auction a bidder stays in the race until the price offered by a competitor is so low that he becomes impossible to beat without losing money. In a sealed bid auction, each bidder may actually regret that he did not give a lower bid after the contest is over.[16]

Since marginal costs were negligible, the English auction model would predict that losers would bid all the way down to a price close to zero, and this rarely appeared to be the case. Rather what appeared to be occurring was that bidders were sometimes eliminated because their bids were too high, which would be consistent with a sealed bid model.

The sealed bid model should not be seen as an attempt to mimic the final round of a long procurement procedure only, but rather as a simplified approximation of the entire bidding process. This is important because it would be inappropriate to ignore the part of the competitive process that takes place prior to the final round. Customers also extract benefits from the competition among bidders earlier in the process, where bidders risk being eliminated if the quality of their offer or the (preliminary) price they ask is not satisfactory. The fact that the competitive pressure does affect the price that a customer can obtain even when it does not result in a direct bidding contest was provided by Mr Wesson, the CIO from the largest owner and operator of apartment buildings in the US, AIMCO. He explained in the US Court proceedings how AIMCO had obtained a very substantial discount from PeopleSoft (70 per cent) in return for closing the deal very fast.[17] Such a deal would appear to suggest the presence of only one competitor in the final round, but it is unlikely that AIMCO could have obtained a similar discount absent significant competitive pressure on PeopleSoft as represented in a model including bids from all market participants.

Furthermore, the elimination of one bidder before the final round cannot always be considered a final decision. So bidders in the final round may be more compelled to offer an attractive price if they perceive a risk that too high a bid may lead the customer to reconsider previously eliminated options. In the US trial Mr Cichanowicz, Vice President of Business Systems Integration for Nextel testified that they had not invited SAP into the final round but stipulated:

> We felt, though, that the fact that there were three viable alternatives out there still gave us an opportunity to look at SAP, if, in fact, negotiations would fall apart with PeopleSoft or Oracle.[18]

It would not be possible to account explicitly for all these different types of procedural details in the model. In general, what appeared to be the case was that the buyer could or would not commit to a fixed selling procedure and could not credibly commit to transfer information to the bidders. In such a context a sealed bid model seems to be an attractive way to capture the general uncertainty that bidders are facing.

Customer Surplus or Quality Adjusted Prices?

In many cases the effect of a merger is described by the effect on prices, possibly adjusted for changes in quality. In the context of this particular model, it is possible to calculate directly the effect on costumer surplus.[19] This is because the model includes specific assumptions about the quality of the product and thus captures the actual value of a transaction for the customer. The distinction between these two measures became particularly important because the merger would lead to the elimination of the PeopleSoft product from the market.[20] The loss of variety would thus not show up in a quality adjusted price measure, but only when measuring customer surplus.

The Commission formed the view that it would be incomplete to restrict attention only to the effect on prices. The risk of restricting attention only to prices can be illustrated by an example. Imagine a market with only three restaurants where two are very close substitutes (say McDonalds and Burger King) and the third is distinct from the other two (say a Chinese restaurant). One would expect the two burger restaurants to compete aggressively and have very low prices compared to the Chinese restaurant. If Burger King bought the Chinese restaurant and closed it down, this would likely lead to no (or very little) effect on prices and probably even a reduction in the average price paid for a meal, but at the same time to significant harm to those customers who prior to the transaction preferred the Chinese alternative.

The fact that Oracle stops developing a new PeopleSoft product of course leads to fixed cost savings that would have to be included in a total surplus assessment. The fact that efficiencies are only taken into account if they are passed on to customers illustrates that this is an area where the customer welfare standard bites.

Efficiencies

The predicted prices in the model will depend on what is assumed initially about the average quality (monetary value to the customer) of the software solutions of Oracle, SAP and PeopleSoft as well as the uncertainty about these respective values for bidders prior to issuance of the final bid. To predict the effect of the merger, it is also necessary to make assumptions as to what will happen to the average quality of Oracle's software once it has acquired PeopleSoft.

The acquisition of PeopleSoft's know-how and source code may allow Oracle to enhance its own product. Oracle argued that it would be able to combine the complementary strengths of the two product offerings after the merger to put an even better product on the market. Though this process requires a complete rewrite of the source code, it may be easier for Oracle to do it with PeopleSoft staff than from scratch. It is difficult to assess whether this effect will be of any significance, in particular in light of the countervailing integration costs that must also be incurred in order to be able to offer a new product that is compatible with the previous products of both PeopleSoft and Oracle. The simulations below offer both scenarios in which: (i) the only effect of the transaction is that PeopleSoft's product disappears; and (ii) the acquisition of PeopleSoft will allow Oracle to improve its quality.

The model does not address in an integrated way, how the merger may affect the incentives to innovate in the industry. Such an analysis would likely show that the increased market share of both Oracle and SAP would lead to improved incentives to offer add-on innovations to its existing customer base, but decreased incentives to provide fundamental innovations intended to win over new clients, because they would also cannibalize existing contracts.

3.   RESULTS

Based on assumptions about the parameters in the model – the average quality and uncertainty about the actual quality for each of the three suppliers – it is possible to predict how each bidder will bid in a particular context as well as the probability that the customer will pick each of the three. The bidding prices, the average payment by the customer and the expected utility derived from the transaction can then be calculated.

For a given level of uncertainty the quality parameters can be adjusted to produce market shares that correspond to the observed situation prior to the merger. Once the calibration is done, the model can then predict how the disappearance of PeopleSoft will affect the bidding behaviour of Oracle and SAP as well as estimating the impact on average prices and costumer surplus.

The results presented below are split into three cases. In the first, it is assumed that the qualities of the three products prior to the merger are identical. This serves as a baseline. In the next case it is assumed that the products of SAP and PeopleSoft are of a higher quality than Oracle's. This is done to reflect the conditions in a bidding contest for a HR solution, where SAP and PeopleSoft appear to have a higher market share than Oracle. In the third case it is assumed that SAP has a product that is of higher quality than Oracle and PeopleSoft. This is intended to reflect the conditions in bidding contests for FMS suites, where SAP appears to have a stronger market position than the two others. Throughout it is assumed that the uncertainty is symmetric for the three products.

A Symmetric Case (Baseline)

A reasonable starting point would be to analyse the case where all three products are of equal average value and the inherent uncertainty is the same for all products. The predicted effect of the merger will depend on how much uncertainty is related to the actual value of the three offers. Table 9.1 below illustrates the results of a base scenario under different degrees of uncertainty.

Table 9.1 Effect of merger baseline (symmetric case; quality = 1)

Uncertainty (st.dev)	0.1	0.2	0.3	0.4	0.5	0.6	0.8	1
Prices								
-post-merger	0.18	0.35	0.52	0.64	0.72	0.79	0.93	1.06
-pre-merger	0.12	0.24	0.35	0.47	0.58	0.67	0.84	0.99
Effect (%)	50.0	50.0	48.0	35.5	23.8	16.8	10.3	7.6
Probability of sale (%)								
-post-merger	100	100	99.68	96.63	91.80	86.89	78.58	72.38
-pre-merger	100	100	100	99.92	99.19	97.46	92.59	87.83
Effect (%)	0.0	0.0	−0.3	−3.3	−7.5	−10.8	−15.1	−17.6
Customer surplus								
-post-merger	0.88	0.76	0.64	0.59	0.58	0.58	0.60	0.63
-pre-merger	0.97	0.93	0.90	0.87	0.84	0.84	0.86	0.90
Effect (%)	−9.0	−18.7	−28.3	−31.9	−31.5	−30.6	−29.7	−29.4

The table shows that a reduction in the number of players may have a very substantial effect on both prices and customer surplus. Each column shows the result of the simulations under one set of assumptions regarding the average uncertainty. All prices in the table are expressed with reference to the average quality.[21] In the first column the uncertainty (measured as the standard deviation of the quality) is set to be 0.1 or equal to 10 per cent of the average value. In this case the bidders would all ask 12 per cent of the average value prior to the merger but 18 per cent after the merger. This would correspond to an increase in the price of 50 per cent.[22]

Since the customer in both cases will derive the lion's share of the benefits from the transaction, the effect on customer surplus is more modest (9 per cent). It should be noted that the customer surplus not only measures the loss due to higher prices, but also captures the loss due to reduced choice. In those instances where PeopleSoft's solution would have been the preferred solution by the customer, there would be a loss, even if the second-best solution had been available at the same price.

The effect on prices (measured relatively) is most substantial when there is little uncertainty, but as uncertainty increases (towards the right in the table) the loss in customer surplus becomes more and more important, rising to around 30 per cent. When uncertainty increases the suppliers will have an incentive to increase their prices, which leads to a decrease in the probability of a sale actually occurring. This would be the case if all three bids turned out to be less valuable to the customer than the prices submitted.

The probability of a sale actually occurring will decrease after the merger due to a combination of two effects. First, the prices asked by each bidder will be higher after the merger. This increases the probability that none of the offers will bring a positive net benefit to the customer. But even if prices remained unchanged after the merger, the probability of sale would decrease due to the second effect, which stems from the fact that the probability of sales occurring is based on the joint probability that at least one of the bids will provide positive net benefits. The probability that at least one solution out of three will be satisfactory exceeds the probability that at least one of two will be so.

Calibration

A situation in the model where no sale occurs would in the real world correspond to the situation where the bidder, based on the submitted offers, decides either to postpone the acquisition or find a solution outside the relevant market. From the Commission's market investigation it was established that this sometimes happens in actual bidding contests. This makes it possible to calibrate the level of uncertainty in the model so as to correspond to a realistic frequency of sales not taking place.

The Commission had no quantitative evidence available regarding how often customers actually decide not to buy. But it appeared reasonable to assume that such an event is rare, though not extremely rare (i.e., it occurs with a frequency of between 0.01 per cent and 10 per cent of tenders). The level of uncertainty in the model could thus be bounded to an interval that produces probabilities of sales corresponding to this range. In the case of symmetric bidders the appropriate interval for the standard deviation can be delineated from 0.2 to 0.8. Below this interval an actual sale happens virtually always, whereas above this interval the probability of a sale drops well below 90 per cent.[23]

Based on the above, it is fair to conclude that a merger from three to two in a symmetric market with three equally strong suppliers is likely to lead to significant price increases as well as substantial loss in customer welfare absent substantial efficiencies.

First Asymmetric Case (Resembles HR)

The effect of the merger will to a certain extent depend on the relative strength of the product that is taken off the market and the products that remain. Historically PeopleSoft has enjoyed a relatively strong position within HR compared to the other pillars. Below is analysed whether the conclusion from the symmetric case also holds for an asymmetric case designed broadly to capture the market conditions with regards to tenders for HR suites.

Each column in table 9.2 represents a simulation in which the quality of SAP and PeopleSoft has been normalized to one while Oracle's quality has been adjusted in order to arrive at a distribution of market shares where Oracle holds 12 per cent of the sales prior to the merger. For instance in the simulation where uncertainty is captured by a standard deviation of 0.5, Oracle's average quality must be 0.45 to generate a market share of 12 per cent. This should not be understood as assuming that Oracle's product only has 45 per cent of the features that SAP and PeopleSoft have, but rather that the relative differences are so important that on average customers true willingness to pay for Oracle's product is 45 per cent of that of SAP and PeopleSoft. Since customers themselves depend on doing at least as well as their competitors, they may be willing to pay a lot not to have systems that are even marginally inferior to those of their competitors.

Table 9.2 Effect of merger in HR (quality of SAP and PS=1)

Uncertainty (st.dev.)	0.1	0.2	0.3	0.4	0.5	0.6	1
Quality of Oracle	0.886	0.772	0.658	0.5475	0.4500	0.3635	0.050
Market Share Oracle (%)	12.0	12.0	12.0	12.0	12.0	12.0	12.1
Effects on price (%)							
Pessimistic	48.6	48.5	39.4	21.1	11.3	6.8	1.5
Optimistic	37.5	37.5	35.7	25.5	17.9	14.1	9.0
Probability of sale (%)							
Pre-merger	100	100	100	99.5	97.2	93.7	80.5
Effect on customer surplus (%)							
Pessimistic	-12.1	-26.2	-37.8	-39.0	-38.2	-37.8	-38.1
Optimistic	-5.5	-12.0	-18.6	-19.2	-17.0	-15.5	-13.5

As in the case above, it is assumed that Oracle after the merger will stop actively selling PeopleSoft's product but instead sell one Oracle-based product. The effect of the merger depends on what is assumed about the quality of the new Oracle-based product. Two scenarios are considered: one in which Oracle's product in the future will be unaffected by the merger (pessimistic scenario) and one in which Oracle will be able to recode the Oracle HR suite so it reaches the same level of quality as PeopleSoft's product (optimistic scenario). In principle the optimistic scenario would require the Commission to find that Oracle's claimed efficiencies were substantiated to the requisite standard.[24]

If the probability of sale pre-merger is used as indicator for the range of the most likely level of uncertainty, a range from 0.3 to 0.6 appears to be reasonable. Throughout the realistic range of uncertainties, the loss in customer welfare will be significant even in the most optimistic scenario. When the uncertainty is at the high end of this interval, the price increase will be 6.8 per cent in the pessimistic scenario and 14.1 per cent in the optimistic scenario.[25] Due to the reduction in choice, the customer welfare will be reduced by 15.5 per cent even in the optimistic scenario, whereas the loss will be 37.8 per cent in the pessimistic scenario. At the other end of the range, when uncertainty is low (st.dev.=0.3) the increase in prices will be 35.7 per cent in the optimistic scenario and 39.4 per cent in the pessimistic scenario. Though the percentage increase in prices is higher for low uncertainty, it is against a background of relatively low price levels. The negative effect on customer surplus of 18.6 (37.8) per cent in the optimistic (pessimistic) case are thus comparable to those found under a high uncertainty scenario.

Second Asymmetric Case (Resembles FMS)

While the situation in the market for HR solutions appeared to have two competitors of roughly equal strength and one relatively weaker offer, the FMS market appears to be characterized by one particularly strong supplier (SAP) and two less strong suppliers (Oracle and PeopleSoft). Table 9.3 shows the effect on customers in such a market situation when the two less strong competitors merge.

Each column contains a simulation for a particular standard deviation in which the quality has been adjusted to allow the market share of Oracle and PeopleSoft pre-merger to be around 15 per cent. The probability of sale in the pre-merger scenario appears to be in the realistic range if the standard deviation is kept between 0.3 and 0.5.

The effect on price and customer surplus in each column has been considered under two possible scenarios: one in which the merger does not create any synergies and one in which the merger would allow Oracle to improve the quality of the product by 10 per cent.

Table 9.3 Effect of merger in FMS (quality of SAP=1)

Uncertainty (st.dev.)	0.1	0.2	0.3	0.4	0.5	0.6	1
Quality of Oracle and PS	0.842	0.685	0.528	0.405	0.308	0.217	n.a.[26]
Market Share of Oracle and PS (%)	15.0	15.1	15.0	15.0	15.0	15.0	
Effect on price (%)							
No efficiencies	41.9	41.9	29.9	18.5	14.3	12.1	
10 % efficiencies	27.3	34.8	28.0	17.8	13.9	11.9	
Probability of sale (%)							
Pre-merger	100	100	99.72	95.88	89.64	83.51	
Effect on customer surplus (%)							
No efficiencies		−8.1	−19.3	−25.2	−21.4	−19.2	−18.1
10 % efficiencies		−2.5	−13.8	−21.8	−19.3	−17.9	−17.3

The table shows that in the relevant range the merger is likely to increase prices significantly (14.3–29.9 per cent without efficiencies and 13.9–28.0 per cent with efficiencies). Similarly the merger would significantly reduce customer surplus (19.2–25.2 per cent without efficiencies and 17.9–21.8 per cent with efficiencies). Based on this it is fair to conclude that in the market for FMS the merger will significantly harm customers, even with substantial efficiencies.

Model Fit

Compared to other models this one did not rely on a large number of quantitative data. That could be perceived as a weakness by some. Since the cost side of the model is irrelevant, the most obvious absence of data is on the demand side.

But the lack of extensive data requirements does not necessarily prove that the model does not adequately take the characteristics of the market into account. On the contrary, the model was tailor-made to take account of a number of particular qualitative characteristics of the particular market in question.

In addition, the model does capture a number of existing patterns observed in the market. SAP is widely perceived to have the highest prices. The model predicts that the bidder with the highest market share (SAP) is also the bidder that on average submits the highest price. Though prices in this market are inherently difficult to compare, some of the estimates that were mentioned in expert reports appeared to be fairly in line with what the simulation model predicted.[27]

Furthermore, as already mentioned, the model predicts that some customers decide not to buy from any of the suppliers. Other models based on other sets of assumptions would not produce the same results and would therefore be less suitable for predicting the effect of the transaction in this particular case.

Finally, the model predicts that customers who generally attach a high value to the software[28] will pay a higher price than customers who generally attach low value to it. This corresponds to the observed fact that the pricing structures chosen by each of the suppliers appear to be designed primarily to reflect the utility of the product to the customer. Pricing is mainly linked to proxies for the value of the software to the customer such as the number of users or the intensity of the usage of the application.

4.   CONCLUSION

A number of circumstances particular to the software industry made it possible to simulate the effects of the merger in a model that was both tractable and a reasonable approximation of how competition works. The fact that marginal costs can be ignored and that what constrains bidders is essentially uncertainty about customers' relative valuations, minimizes the need for data both on the supply and demand side.

In the guidelines for horizontal mergers, the Commission put quite some emphasis on the need to establish closeness of substitution in mergers with differentiated goods. The model illustrated that when a product is likely to disappear after the merger, the role of closeness of substitution takes on a different role.[29] If the merger is between close substitutes[30] the effect on price may be high, but the loss of choice from removing one of them will be low. If, on the other hand, they are distant substitutes then the effect of removing one of them depends on whether the remaining competitor's product is close to the product that stays in the market or the one that disappears. In the first case,[31] customers will be harmed mainly due to the loss of choice, while in the latter[32] the harm will mainly be due to higher prices.

Had the Commission found that the relevant market only contained Oracle, SAP and PeopleSoft, it would be fair to say that the model for realistic calibrations would have predicted a significant decrease in customer welfare. In all instances where there are no efficiencies due to the merger, the loss would likely exceed 18 per cent. Even if the merger would lead to moderate efficiencies for the new combined product, the merger would still lead to a loss in customer welfare in excess of 10 per cent.

NOTES

1.   The views expressed in this article are personal and do not necessarily reflect those of the Chief Economist, DG Competition, the Competition Commissioner or the Commission.
2.   The transaction was notified on 14/10/2003 and a clearance decision with no commitments issued on 26/10/2004.
3.   Council Regulation (EEC) No 4064/89 of 21 December 1989 on the control of concentrations between undertakings.
4.   US District Court for the Northern District of California. United States et al. versus Oracle Corp. Opinion handed down by Judge Walker on 09/09/2004.
5.   See M.3216 – ORACLE / PEOPLESOFT art. 8(2) Decision of 26.10.2004 Section IV.A.3.
6.   Such as for instance Accenture, Cap Gemini, Ernst & Young, Deloitte, IBM Global Services or Bearing Point etc.
7.   3460:24-3461:10 of the transcript of the US court trial.
8.   See for instance Dalkir, Logan and Masson (2000) and Waehrer and Perry (2003).
9.   One exception is where the development of a particular solution to an identified need has strategic value for the supplier. This would be the case where the supplier believes that the particular solution could subsequently be sold as a core solution to future customers. In such contexts the suppliers may enter into a joint development project in which they share the cost and risks of developing the solution in return for subsequent ownership rights.
10. 3517:25-3118:9 of the transcript of the US court trial.
11. 1560:8-15 of the transcript of the US court trial.
12. TCO means Total Cost of Ownership.
13. 3518:23-25 of the transcript of the US court trial.
14. Technically, the assumptions are: no private information and common priors about the relative performance of the three offers.
15. How the assumption of whether bidding takes place via sealed bids or in an oral auction matters, is analysed in Tschantz, Crooke and Froeb (2000).
16. Generally, open auctions are believed to have superior efficiency properties, because they always allocate the contract to the best supplier.
17. PeopleSoft wanted to close the deal fast in order to be able to include the deal in the sales for that particular quarter.
18. 1068:13-17 of the transcript of the US court trial.
19. Customer surplus is a better term in this context than consumer surplus. Since the software purchase is essentially a fixed cost, the effect on customers in the antitrust market in question is unlikely to be passed on in a straightforward way to the final consumers. The customer surplus measure applied in this case comprises the monetary gain that the customers extract from the trade in the antitrust market in question.
20. Oracle had publicly announced it would continue to support PeopleSoft customers, but cease to sell the product actively. See for instance the Oracle Press release from June 20 2003 "Oracle Makes Public Commitment to PeopleSoft Customers". In this context it should be noted that what is important for the modelling is not whether Oracle in future bidding rounds will offer a solution under the name Oracle or PeopleSoft or whether it will consist of a source code from one or the other of the existing products. For the purpose of simulating the effect of the merger the central assumption is that in the future, Oracle will provide one and not two alternative solutions..
21. In asymmetric simulations, the average quality of SAP is normalized to 1.
22. Table 9.1 shows that generally low levels of uncertainty result in low levels of prices. When the standard deviation is 1, the prices are close to 1, whereas when the standard deviation is 0.1 the prices are less than 0.1. This illustrates that the intensity of competition is dependent on certainty. If there were no uncertainty in the model (standard deviation goes to 0) and no asymmetry between the bidders (as in this example), then prices would be 0 even with only two bidders as is the case in traditional Bertrand competition.
23. The pre-merger probability is the relevant one for comparing with the observation that historically it has sometimes happened that a sale does not occur.

24. See Section VII of the "Guidelines on the assessment of horizontal mergers under the Council Regulation on the control of concentrations between undertakings" *Official Journal* C 31, 05.02.2004, pages 5–18. It should be noted that the Guidelines in principle only apply for the new merger regulation, which had not yet entered into force at the time of notification.

25. For large values of the standard deviation, the average price will be higher in the optimistic scenario than in the pessimistic scenario. The opposite is the case for low values of the standard deviation. In the optimistic scenario the higher average quality of Oracle will have two effects: it will put pressure on SAP to lower its price and it will also lead Oracle to charge higher prices. The higher the uncertainty, the stronger is the latter effect. It should be noted that the prices are not quality adjusted. Since the higher prices by Oracle correspond to a higher quality, customers will prefer the optimistic scenario regardless of the level of uncertainty (cf. the effect on customer surplus).

26. This simulation has not been performed because it would require the assumption of negative quality on average. Such assumptions did not appear realistic.

27. Had reliable price information been available, the calibration could have been further refined by attaching a different uncertainty to each product. That would allow the model to replicate both observed market shares and prices.

28. In terms of having high average valuations of the software packages.

29. In many instances the potential reduction in choice may not be a source of concern, because one can reasonably rely on firms to provide the range of products that customers want.

30. This would correspond to Burger King and McDonalds merging.

31. This would correspond to a Burger King buying the Chinese restaurant and closing it.

32. This would correspond to the Chinese restaurant buying Burger King and closing it.

10. Modelling the Electricity Market: Nuon–Reliant

Jan de Maa and Gijsbert Zwart

The merger case between Nuon and Reliant involves the take-over of the power stations in the Netherlands owned by US power company Reliant by one of the Netherlands' largest integrated power utilities. The buying company, Nuon, is active in all segments of the Dutch electricity market, ranging from the upstream business of power generation, through power trading and retailing for end consumers, to regulated activities in the management of the electricity grid. The take-over target was mainly active in the power generation business, having bought a large portfolio of plants from public owners after the deregulation of the power generation sector in the late 1990s (see e.g. ECN 1999).

The Dutch competition authority NMa assessed the take-over. Part of the assessment was carried out by using simulation models to evaluate the competitive effects of the operation. NMa decided to make use of the models of external consultants Energy Study Centre ECN and Frontier Economics. Both models had already been developed and had been tested and used for other studies. The ECN model contains specific data and knowledge about the Dutch electricity sector. The model developed by Frontier Economics has previously been used in several other merger control cases. Given the expertise of both organizations and the relative short time frame for merger control, NMa made use of both these models instead of developing a sector-specific model itself. Both studies were done in co-operation with and under the supervision of NMa. NMa determined the scope of the studies, made sure that the relevant data were used and discussed the assumptions of the models. In consultation with both ECN and Frontier Economics the results of the studies were interpreted. After consultation it was decided which types of sensitivity analysis were necessary.

To monitor these types of studies a very close co-operation and a good understanding of both the industry and the modelling itself is necessary. For this reason the merger control department of NMa made use of internal expertise from the Dutch energy regulator (DTe).

After these investigations, the take-over was approved subject to Nuon making some of its generation capacity available to its competitors (NMa 2003).

Our aim here is to discuss the relevance of simulation modelling for mergers in the electricity industry, and to give a description of the models used in this case. In our discussion on the use of models in the analysis of this merger we focus on the horizontal effects of the merger in the wholesale market for electricity. In section 1 we will argue that simulation modelling adds value to the analysis of competitive effects of mergers in the electricity sector. Traditional structural measures fail to capture some of the particularities of this industry. A useful perspective on models of electricity markets is that they provide yet another structural measure of market power, similar to the often-used HHI or market share indices. The difference is that the measure in this case is tailor-made to the specific characteristics of the market, and is constructed so as to make optimal use of the detailed data that are available. In section 2 we discuss two types of models that are common in the analysis of wholesale electricity markets, the Cournot model and the supply function model. Finally, in section 3 we explain how these models were implemented in this case and what the results were.

1. ELECTRICITY MARKETS AND MARKET POWER

Market power in the electricity market reflects the physical and economic characteristics of electricity. Electricity can not (easily) be stored, so that demand and supply balance continuously. Failure, in real time, to balance the supply of electricity into the electricity grid with off-take by consumers from the grid can cause extremely costly electric system collapse. The demand for electricity, moreover, fluctuates (to a large extent predictably) over a wide range during the day and year (see Figure 10.1 for a typical weekday demand pattern). Typically, demand is low during nights, and high in the day time, and in the Netherlands electricity consumption in winter is significantly higher than in the summer, mainly due to extra use for lighting.[1] Due to the balancing requirement, supply is equally variable, which leads to large price variations over the day.[2]

Figure 10.1 Typical daily electricity demand pattern in the Netherlands (third Wednesday in April 2003)

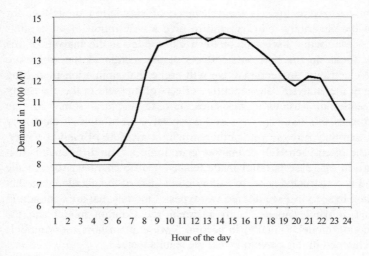

Hour of the day

Source: Data provided by UCTE

In the short term, demand is quite inelastic to prices. Small consumers do not observe the real time price of electricity, but only face average (annual) prices. They therefore lack the information to respond to short-term price fluctuations. Some large firms are metered continuously and do observe real time prices. However, the marginal value of electricity consumption for their production processes is typically many times (i.e. one or two orders of magnitude) higher than generic prices of electricity (Deloitte 2004). Only under extreme price spikes do they have an incentive to respond by reducing consumption.

Focusing next on the supply side of the market, the generation system is composed from units of various types, ranging from relatively inflexible but low marginal cost coal plants, running continuously in both low and high demand hours, to high marginal cost flexible gas-fired plants only serving the day-time peaks in demand. The larger production companies each have a portfolio of plants of different types. As demand for electricity increases during the day, the units of higher marginal costs are started up. The marginal costs of production are therefore an increasing function of supply to the market.

In liberalized power markets such as the Dutch market, contracts for supply of electricity are typically traded on a multitude of market places (see also NMa (2003) for an overview). A large part of end users' (or retail supply companies') demand for electricity is satisfied by longer term contracts for electricity. These contracts, often traded in the OTC (over-the-counter) market, are for delivery of electricity for example in the next month, quarter or year, mostly standardized to provide a constant supply of electricity in all hours (base load contracts) or in all day-time hours on working days (peak load contracts), against a fixed price. Trade is not only between suppliers and consumers, but also and increasingly between traders arbitraging, and speculating in, the various markets. Trade is driven by suppliers and demanders of contracts quoting their bid/ask prices and volumes, either through voice trading or through electronic bulletin boards run by intermediaries.

At the day-ahead stage, most consumers would have purchased a large part of their electricity needs for the following day. In order to match more closely their expected consumption patterns during that day, electricity contracts for individual hours are traded on the Dutch power exchange, the APX. Also traders arbitraging the price differences between the Netherlands and (electrically) connected countries, Belgium and Germany, take part in this exchange. On the APX, for each hour participants enter their supply or demand curves, after which the market operator clears the market at a uniform price per hour by intersecting the aggregated curves. The format of trade here is thus that of an explicit (double) auction with bids consisting of price quantity pairs.

On the hour of delivery itself, when demand is virtually inelastic, the independent electricity system operator (TenneT, in the Netherlands) runs a balancing market, where it makes sure that total production and consumption are in balance at all times. Producers offer supply curves for marginal increases or decreases of production, which the system operator uses to correct imbalances arising through unforeseen changes in consumption and production. This again is an auction, single-sided this time, where producers bid supply curves.

Clearly these markets are interrelated. Producers, consumers and traders can freely choose on which market to buy or sell their electricity. Expected prices on the various markets should therefore not diverge to a large extent.

Trade between countries occurs over transmission lines owned by the transmission system operators in the various regions. Due to the physical characteristics of these lines, transport of electricity is subject to strict constraints of capacity.[3] We see, therefore, that capacity limits play an important role in the economics of electricity: due to the technical requirement of balancing at each moment, the lack of demand elasticity and the small substitutability of electricity consumption over time (no storage), at every instance production plus net imports should match demand. These two sources of electricity, on the other hand, have relatively low marginal costs

up to a strict technical capacity limit. Also on a longer time scale, these
capacity limits are unlikely to be easily slackened, as investment in both
generation and transmission capacity is capital-intensive, and associated with
lead times of several years.[4]

These peculiarities of the market give rise to some difficulty in
establishing relations between market concentration and market power:
players having only relatively minor market shares may occasionally possess
strong market power. When the gap (reserve margin) between demand and
available capacity decreases, many suppliers may individually exert
significant influence on prices offering their marginal capacity only at high
prices. The fact that in such periods small changes in the reserve margin can
lead to large effects on price is evidenced by the various price spikes that
have been observed on power exchanges across the world, and may lead to
incentives to artificially create market tightness by keeping plant offline.
Indeed, in investigations into the use of market power in the power markets
of England and Wales (Patrick and Wolak 2001) and California (e.g. Joskow
and Kahn 2002), evidence was brought forward that power producers
withheld generation capacity to influence prices. Finally, the existence of
capacity constraints on cross-border power transmission lines leads to a
situation where relevant geographic markets may be dynamic. At moments
when import is not congested the market is physically and economically
different from times when the import constraints are binding or almost
binding. Effectively, in the absence of congestion, the market is open to a
larger number of competitors than in periods of congestion. Market power
will therefore vary over different time periods.

1a   Structural Measures of Market Power

These features of the wholesale market make it difficult to take a
conventional approach to analysing market power. Indices on market share,
specifically the Herfindahl–Hirschman index (HHI, calculated as the sum of
the squares of each player's market share), traditionally have a prominent
place in merger analysis. To account for the differences in competitive
landscape during different periods of the day and year, and different degrees
of congestion, concentration indices should be differentiated according to
time of day. One then potentially would have to determine what the
consequence should be of HHI being low most of the time, but high during a
limited number of (super)peak hours during the year.

Other quantitative structural indicators may be of some aid as well. Given
the good predictions that can be made of total electricity demand, and the
available data on production and import capacities, alternative structural
measures that are more sensitive to the importance of capacity constraints can

be computed as well. One may consider in particular indices measuring what percentage of the time any supplier or group of suppliers is essential to serving system load (i.e. total load exceeds the cumulative capacity of all competitors). In the light of the low elasticity of demand, during such periods the players who are essential for serving total load may have considerable market power.

In the judgement on the Nuon–Reliant case, NMa (2003), both market share indices and a measure involving the capacity constraints were analysed. The latter, the "time not fragmented index" (TNFI), measures in what percentage of time, which share of capacity possessed by the three largest players is essential for meeting demand, given the total (predicted) demand and total capacity available to competitors (and imports). The results of that computation can be compared before and after the merger, see Figure 10.2. One observes, for example, that before the merger (the lower curve), in the 15 per cent highest demand hours of the year (the horizontal axis), at least 40 per cent (vertical axis) of the capacity of the largest three producers is required to run. This is assuming that all other producers (and imports) are supplying at full capacity, and, hence, will not be able to increase production further. After the merger, the same situation occurs for a much larger percentage of time, approximately 30 per cent. Comparing other demand levels as well, one observes that as a result of the concentration, this share approximately doubles for the highest load hours.

Figure 10.2 The necessity of top three players, pre- and post-merger (calculations based on data by ECN)

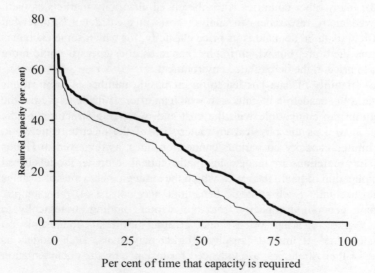

Per cent of time that capacity is required

On the basis of the qualitative analysis of the merger and these structural measures, it was concluded by the competition authority that the transaction was unlikely to be allowed without further measures to decrease potential market power. However, in order to get a deeper insight in the nature and extent of market power increases, the analysis was extended by using a modelling approach to the measurement of market power.

1b Strategic Models

In assessing the impact of mergers on market power one would preferably estimate the effect on prices of such concentrations directly. In most markets the information required to more directly estimate price cost indices, such as detailed cost data, are not easily available. One therefore has to rely on coarser structural indicators such as the ones described above.

In the electricity production sector, however, most data necessary to explicitly model oligopolistic price equilibria are available. This opens the way for direct estimation of mark-ups instead of having to rely solely on structural indices. In the electricity sector, production capacities are well defined and to a large extent publicly available.[5] Especially for those companies that previously were part of the SEP, the co-ordinating body for electricity production prior to liberalization, good estimates of data necessary to estimate short run marginal costs for each production unit are available. These are primarily data concerning the efficiency levels of generation units, as well as start-up costs. Furthermore, total demand on the grid can be measured to great accuracy. This situation of data accessibility, which is typical for many other countries with liberalized electricity markets as well, has allowed many researchers to analyse costs in great detail.[6] Somewhat more difficult data on demand is its price elasticity, for which some estimates exist in the literature, but which might change as consumers become more sensitive to price in the deregulated environment.

This availability of data has led to an increasing number of publications appearing in the academic literature, in which an effort is made to predict the price equilibrium compatible with the cost and ownership structures of the industry, as well as the physical characteristics of the electricity network, such as limited capacity on various connection lines, as reviewed in Hobbs (2001). The predictions are made using mathematical computer models based on the application of game theory, in which the strategic behaviour of firms is taken into account.[7] Such strategic behaviour may consist of, for example, withholding generation capacity from the market, bidding strategically to increase market clearing prices, and creating artificial congestion on transmission lines of limited capacity. Market players use such models as guidance for their strategies, as evidenced for instance by the documentation on gaming in the California market released in the Enron investigation in the United States (CAISO 2002). Some of these models have been used for assessment of the effects of restructuring in various liberalized markets.[8]

The ability to directly model prices allows one to tackle some of the difficulties specific to electricity mentioned above. First, it is straightforward to include the constraint that at any moment total load should equal total generation, given the capacities of individual generation units. Transmission constraints between regions can be naturally incorporated in computer models. In particular, strategic price models do not rely on definitions on geographic markets that may be too limited: as wide a geographic market as possible may be taken into account in the model, together with an explicit representation of available transmission capacity and its allocation, and competitive structure in the cross-border markets. The solution of the model will under the various conditions of congestion represent the various degrees of competition from generators located behind transmission links that are sometimes constrained. As to the distinction between product markets associated with different load levels (e.g. base load markets, peak markets), models typically will have as an output a collection of prices for each modelled load level. In this way one may more directly estimate price effects at various times of the day, and identify what time spans constitute the relevant differentiated product markets.

In a Cournot model approach adopted for the description of the California market (Borenstein and Bushnell 1999), the authors compute equilibrium prices for different levels of demand. They then compare these prices with HHI calculated from market share at these demand periods for the modelled firms. One result is that price–cost margins may increase quite suddenly and dramatically as demand increases, and the second that the HHI do not correlate with these price fluctuations. In the particular configuration modelled (including specific assumptions on demand elasticity) the authors observe Lerner indices increasing to about 100 per cent. HHI at the same time remains in a range of 1000 to 1200.[9]

2. MODELS OF MARKET POWER IN THE ELECTRICITY MARKET

2a The Cournot Model

The two most common models of strategic behaviour are those of Bertrand and Cournot competition (see Goppelsröder and Schinkel, chapter 5 in this volume). In the former, players simultaneously post prices at which they are willing to sell their products. In the Cournot model, conversely, players deliver chosen quantities to the market, and receive for their products the price that is required to balance total demand and aggregated supply. In both cases, the game-theoretic (Nash) equilibrium is the combination of strategies (prices respectively quantities for each player) such that, given all opponents' strategies, each player's strategy maximizes its individual profit.

The use of Bertrand models is unsuitable for electricity market modelling. The fact that in pure Bertrand models, players commit to deliver any desired quantity at the posted price, does not go together well with the presence of increasing marginal costs of production and capacity constraints. The latter may be incorporated in the model to obtain a so-called Bertrand–Edgeworth game, but this leads under some assumptions to outcomes similar to a Cournot game (Kreps and Scheinkman 1983). The use of Cournot models in electricity modelling is much more common. Cournot models with capacity constraints are more tractable. The very existence of capacity constraints (which put limits on quantities to be offered to the market) is sometimes quoted as a motivation for describing the market by competition in quantities. Furthermore, in analyses of the exercise of market power in electricity markets in the UK and California, the withholding of available generation capacity has been identified as an important method of driving up prices. Finally, Cournot models can be argued to provide an upper bound on the results of supply function models, as will be discussed below. In addition the computability of Cournot models, their ability to take into account precise cost and capacity characteristics of real plants and transmission lines, and to simulate markets with potentially thousands of different plants, has made them a useful tool for investigating the effects of market power.[10]

The Cournot model represents a game between producers who each strive to maximize their individual profits. The choice variable they have is, in each period, the amount of electricity they want to put onto the market. The producers choose these volumes simultaneously, after which the market clearing price is determined (including the, perhaps small, reaction of demand). A Nash equilibrium of this game is a set of quantities – one for each producer – such that, given the quantities produced by its competitors, each player maximizes its own profits.

If we denote the quantities by q_i, the market price clearing the market by $P(\Sigma \ q_j)$, and each player's variable costs of producing q_i by $c_i(q_i)$, we can formulate each player's optimization problem as

$$\max \ [q_i \ P(\ \Sigma \ q_j\ ) - c_i(q_i)] \text{ with respect to } q_i, \qquad (10.1)$$

subject to a set of constraints, such as the requirement that the produced quantity cannot exceed available production capacity. In solving this maximization problem, each player would compute the first order (Kuhn–

Tucker) conditions and those of its competitors. The joint solution to the resulting equations form the Nash equilibrium of the game.

In simple situations, the solution to the Cournot game is that price mark-ups are given by the HHI divided by the demand elasticity, and it would seem that there would be no need for simulation. The reason for carrying out the explicit computation in this case is that the relevant HHI is highly variable and cannot be computed without simulation. First, the equilibrium market shares that go into the HHI are variable, and cannot be obtained without carrying out the computation for each demand level. Second, whenever a capacity constraint (of production or transmission capacity) is binding, a producer cannot respond to higher prices by raising production and this capacity effectively "drops out" of the HHI, invalidating the simple result, and giving an "adjusted HHI" corresponding to a much more concentrated market (as explained e.g. in OECD 2003).

In applications of this model, one would therefore need the number of players, their installed production capacities and cost structures, and information on market demand. In practice, often only the larger firms are modelled as "strategic": for small firms, the equilibrium behaviour predicted by the model does not differ much between their behaving strategically (i.e. anticipating that their production decision will affect the market price), and acting as price takers. Simplifying the game by treating them as price takers then makes no essential difference to the model results. The question which players are to be modelled as strategic is an empirical modelling question (does one get significantly different results for the two different assumptions) and is independent of any assumptions one might have about the real attitude of firms.

In electricity market models, typically equations are added describing the characteristics of the electricity grids (and the physical laws governing electricity flow), as well as the activities of traders in the system, that buy electricity in one region and sell it in another (see Hobbs (2001) for an overview). In this way also the interactions between countries (imports and exports) are taken into account.

2b The Supply Function Model

A second approach to modelling market power in electricity markets is that of supply function equilibrium. In this approach one more closely follows the actual structure of part of the electricity market (the spot and balancing markets), in that producers' strategies are allowed to be supply curves. A supply curve or function is a set of bids of price–quantity pairs, allowing producers to indicate that, the higher the price a buyer is willing to pay, the larger the amount of electricity the producer will commit to sell at that price.

Supply function equilibria were explored by Klemperer and Meyer (1989) in a model of demand uncertainty. The concept was later applied to the English spot market by Green and Newbery (1992), and subsequently has received more attention in the electricity market literature (e.g. Bunn and Day 2001; Baldick and Hogan 2002; Rudkevich 1999). The set of available strategies to producers in this game form is much larger than in the standard Bertrand and Cournot games. Whereas in those traditional games, a strategy is one number (a price or quantity), so the strategy space is one dimensional, in the supply function context producers choose from a strategy space that is a set of functions, which is infinitely dimensional. In general the supply function model is therefore more difficult to solve (both analytically and numerically) and therefore more approximations and assumptions are generally necessary.

In the supply function model, producers again strive to maximize their individual profits. The difference is that each producer's choice consists of a function $q_i(p)$. Since their marginal production costs are increasing with volume, producers would like to differentiate the amounts of electricity they want to offer: a producer will only want to generate electricity using his cheap coal-fired plants if prices are low (and hence will not offer more than the capacity of these plants), while at higher prices he would wish to increase production using higher marginal cost gas-fired plants.

The aggregate of all producers' supply functions forms the market supply function. In the supply function model this curve is intersected with the downward sloping demand curve (which may be almost vertical in the electricity market). This again results in a market price. The process is quite like the procedure followed on the real electricity spot market APX, described above.

In determining the Nash equilibrium of this game, one again optimizes all players' profits, given their opponent's supply functions $q_j(p)$:

$$\max \{q_i(p) P[\Sigma q_j(p)] - c_i[q_i(p)]\} \text{ with respect to } q_i(p). \qquad (10.2)$$

Constraints on the optimization are again that a player's offered quantity can never exceed his capacity. In addition, the functions $q_i(p)$ are required to be upward sloping.

The difference with the Cournot model is that the profit function depends not on a set of quantities, but on a set of functions. The joint solution of the first order conditions for each producer again provides the Nash equilibrium: the situation where each producer could not improve on his profit by changing its own supply function, given the supply functions of its competitors.

The mathematical structure of this optimization is much more complex than in the Cournot case. It can be shown that a solution to the first order conditions must satisfy a set of differential equations, relating the slope of the aggregated supply curve of a player's competitors to the supply of the player itself:

$$\frac{\partial\left(\sum q_{i\neq j}\right)}{\partial p} = \frac{q_i(p)}{p - c_i'[q_i(p)]} + D'(p) \qquad (10.3)$$

where $D(p)$ is the demand curve, the inverse of $P(\Sigma\ q_i)$ used above.

The properties of this equilibrium equation have been studied in Klemperer and Meyer (1989). It turns out that a whole family of solutions to the problem exists, as depicted in Figure 10.3. Here each curve represents a possible equilibrium supply function for a player, giving, for each price p (vertical axis) the corresponding quantity q (horizontal axis). One observes that part of the equilibrium supply curves are convex, curving up until vertical at some quantity, whereas the other half of solutions is concave, becoming horizontal at some point, and curving down afterwards. Steep supply curves indicate that a relatively large price increase only triggers a modest increase of quantity offered to the market. Where the curves turn vertical, behaviour is therefore similar to Cournot behaviour, where quantities are fixed and independent of price. On the other hand, horizontal parts of the supply curve are reminiscent of the Bertrand model, where a price increase above the offer price calls forth a supply sufficient for the whole market. Indeed, the straight bold lines connecting the vertical, respectively horizontal parts of the curves correspond to the price quantity pairs that would result from pure Cournot and perfectly competitive behaviour.

All curved supply functions either bend downward (competitive curves) or backwards towards the p-axis (Cournot curves). Realistic supply curves however should be increasing functions, as one would expect producers to offer more products at a higher price.[11] This means that only the supply curve "in the middle", separating the region of upward and downward sloping curves, is a solution for all demand levels. However, given that expected demand is bounded at some finite level, also curves that remain increasing up to the maximum demand are regular equilibria.

The resulting multitude of Nash equilibria is of course unattractive. The supply function model does not give rise to a unique prediction about actual behaviour, but leaves one with the problem which of the many equilibria the players will choose. One result is that equilibrium prices will lie between the upper straight line in the figure, where supply curves turn vertical, and the lower one where they are horizontal. As pointed out, these lines coincide with the Cournot price (upper line) and the competitive price (lower line) at each quantity. One may therefore interpret the Cournot results as an upper bound to the supply function model. Studies on the likelihood of the various equilibria suggest that in dynamic games one may expect cycling of equilibria around the "centre" equilibrium.[12]

Figure 10.3 Examples of equilibrium supply functions in a simple model

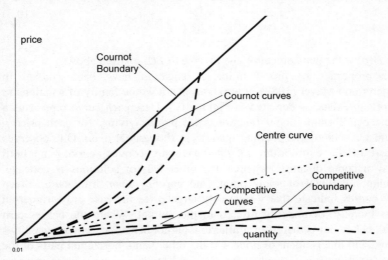

Applying the supply function framework in realistic cases one encounters more difficulties than in the Cournot approach. Incorporating capacity limits in the model makes the exact solution to the maximization problem intractable, and one is forced to impose additional assumptions in order to obtain numerical solutions. The additional complexities involving treatment of multiple regions connected by transport lines of limited capacity are even harder to model. For situations focusing on effects in one region only (such as the merger case at hand), the cross-border interactions can be simplified to be incorporated in the model. Applications of supply function models to real electricity markets are found in models of various organizations, such as the MARS model of Danish transmission system operator Eltra (used in the Commission's analysis of the Sydkraft/Graninge merger case, EC (2003)), and models by various consultants, such as Kema and Frontier Economics.

3. USE OF MODELS IN THE NUON–RELIANT CASE

In the Nuon–Reliant case it was decided to use both a Cournot model and a supply function model, since both have their drawbacks and advantages. Furthermore, robustness of modelling results could in this way also be tested against the choice of model: one would expect robust conclusions to be shared by both models. Here we will describe the outlines of both models employed in the investigation.

3a The ECN Model Competes (Cournot)

The Dutch energy study centre ECN developed a Cournot model for the Northwestern European electricity market. In the model, electricity generators in the Netherlands, Belgium, Germany and France are represented, including their capacity limits (at the individual plant level), as well as the main electricity transmission lines connecting these countries. Electricity transports are required to satisfy the physical flow equations, and are constrained by the maximum allowed flow levels on the various transmission lines. The scarce transmission capacity in the model is rationed by an auction by the transmission coordinator: generators or traders desiring to transport electricity from one country to the other will pay this system operator if the demand for transmission services exceeds supply.

The model is solved by computing the first order conditions for all agents (generators, traders and transmission operators). Here one explicitly takes into account the capacity constraints on players' generation plants and transmission lines. As explained, in this way one captures the varying levels of competition for varying levels of demand. For the larger generators in each country, the Cournot assumption is made with respect to the price of electricity: they anticipate that as they change output, they will affect electricity price. The smaller generators, as well as the transmission companies and traders, are treated as price taking in the model.

The equilibrium is computed for various levels of demand, each resulting in a set of prices and production and transport levels. In this way one accounts for the various levels of competition at different demand levels, as producers' and transmission capacity constraints become binding.

Outcomes of the model computations are sensitive to the assumed reaction of demand to higher prices, or the level of demand elasticity. For realistic levels of short-term demand elasticity (very small), the outcomes of the Cournot model tend to be relatively high compared to realistically observed prices. This is often attributed to the fact that generators are not quite following Cournot rules, but do assume that in equilibrium a deviation from their equilibrium strategy will not only trigger a response from demand (which they took into account in determining their optimal strategy), but will also lead their competitors to slightly adjust their bids. Such behaviour could in principle be modelled by incorporating a conjectural variations term in the first order conditions for the producers (see e.g. Day, Hobbs and Pang 2002, and note 10) and also in the supply function model, all equilibria below the maximum one exhibit some supply reaction from other producers. Other reasons for Cournot prices exceeding observed prices might be longer term considerations (e.g. fear of excessive entry), or fear of regulatory intervention at too high prices.

A practical approach to this overestimation is to calibrate the model using the demand elasticity in the Cournot model as a parameter, as explained e.g. in Stoft (2002).[13] In line with this reasoning, the elasticity parameter in the ECN model was chosen at 0.2, reproducing approximately the prices available in the market. After that a scenario was run in which the ownership relations were changed to reflect the effect of the merger. This led to a prediction for price effects of the merger.

The results of the model exercise in this case are presented in Table 10.1. Modelled prices before and after the take-over are displayed, differentiated by periods. Each period consists of a set of hours during the day in various seasons. One observes from the table that the forecast of price effects of the merger differ per period, and are highest in peak hours.

Table 10.1 Forecasted price increases

	Price before takeover (Eur/Mwh)	Price after takeover (Eur/Mwh)	Price increase (%)
Winter			
Super peak	62.5	65.4	4.7
Peak	59.8	64.5	7.9
Shoulder	43.6	46.4	6.6
Base	40.0	42.2	5.5
Shoulder season			
Superpeak	59.4	61.9	4.3
Peak	47.4	50.4	6.3
Shoulder	42.5	44.9	5.7
Base	39.1	41.1	5.2
Summer			
Superpeak	49.8	52.9	6.2
Seak	49.1	52.2	6.3
Shoulder	42.7	45.1	5.6
Base	42.5	43.9	3.4
Average	44.9	47.5	5.9

3b   The Model of Frontier Economics (Supply Functions)

The other model used in the case was a model by consultant Frontier Economics, which is based on a game in supply functions between the producers. In this case the model is restricted to the Dutch generation park, while interactions with neighbouring countries are represented by "power plants on the border": imports are assumed to arise whenever the Dutch price exceeds a certain level, with the existing capacity of the import lines as a maximum.

The Dutch system is again modelled in terms of individual power plants, each with a known marginal cost, aggregated into portfolios per producer. Competition now takes place by producers offering supply functions to the market (a curve of price quantity pairs), with market price (at a given demand level) constructed by intersecting the sum of all supply curves with demand. Different supply curves may be offered for each hour of the day (i.e. each expected demand level). Producers now optimize their supply curve bids by finding a situation where they all simultaneously maximize their profits, a Nash equilibrium. To keep the model computable, the possible supply curves are restricted to correspond to the marginal cost curves of the producers, multiplied by a constant mark-up factor chosen from some finite set. In this way, the lowest offer for a producer would be to offer his plants at marginal costs, while higher offers correspond to a mark-up factor times these costs. This effectively converts the infinite supply function game into a finite game.

Figure 10.4 Diagrammatic analysis of Nash equilibrium strategies in a hypothetical supply function game

Strategies player 2

	1* marginal costs	2* marginal costs	3* marginal costs	4* marginal costs
1* marginal costs	(1,1)	(3,2)*	(2,1)	(2,0)
2* marginal costs	(2,3)*	(2,2)	(3.1)	(3,0)
3* marginal costs	(1,2)	(1,3)	(3,3)*	(2,2)
4* marginal costs	(0,2)	(0,3)	(2,2)	(1,1)

Strategies player 1

The Nash equilibrium at a demand level is then computed by calculating, for each combination of mark-up factors for all producers, the profits for each producer. A combination where all producers cannot improve on their profit by unilaterally changing their mark-up factor is a Nash equilibrium. A hypothetical example is given in the diagram of Figure 10.4. Profits for two firms are displayed as a function of their mark-ups on marginal costs. The boxes marked with an asterisk are Nash equilibria: neither firm can obtain higher profits by unilaterally changing its strategy. Notice that multiple Nash equilibria can coexist.

The computation is repeated at each possible demand level, which results in a set of equilibrium prices. An example is given in Figure 10.5, for both the pre-merger and post-merger cases. On the horizontal axis total electricity demand is plotted, which ranges between 6000 MW at night to 17000 MW in winter peak hours. For each level of demand the sets of bid strategies are computed that constitute Nash equilibria. The dots in the graph represent the resulting prices at each of these equilibria. Not surprisingly, there may exist multiple Nash equilibria at a given demand level.

Interpretation of the model is more difficult than in the case of the Cournot model. One perspective on the effect of the merger on the resulting equilibria can be obtained by looking at the cluster of equilibrium price points in the graphs before and after the merger (Figure 10.5). One observes that the range of equilibria can be qualitatively divided in three regions: for low demand levels, prices are close to marginal costs (also depicted in the figure). At two consecutive demand levels ("steps") one sees first a shift towards a region with modest mark-ups on costs, followed by a region where rather extreme price equilibria occur. Such steps occur both in the scenarios before and after the merger. The location of the steps, however, shifts to the left, so that equilibria with higher price occur earlier (and hence more often). In the results for winter seasons, graphed in the figures, one sees that the pre-merger analysis predicts the extreme price equilibria whenever demand rises above some 15300 MW, while the possibilities of such high-priced equilibria after the merger already exist as demand exceeds 14200 MW.[14]

The second approach is investigating shifts in the distribution of prices and in the average prices over the year. One now has to make a choice from the multiple available equilibria. In principle the occurrence of any equilibrium at a given demand level will be governed by a probability distribution. As discussed above, the question of equilibrium selection is still unresolved, though some evidence points into the direction that actual equilibria may cycle over time. We focused on maximum, minimum and median price levels to obtain insight into the possible range of prices.

These maximum, minimum and median prices at various demand levels were converted into price duration curves, as in Figure 10.6. In such duration curves, prices for each hour of the year (given observed demand) are plotted, ordered from high to low. In the investigation, attention focused on the median price equilibria. This was mainly motivated by the fact that the median price distribution was fairly close to the actually observed price distribution on the APX (although the APX exhibits some higher peaks than the model).[15]

Figure 10.5 Plot of equilibrium prices for each demand level, pre-merger (upper panel) and post-merger (lower panel)

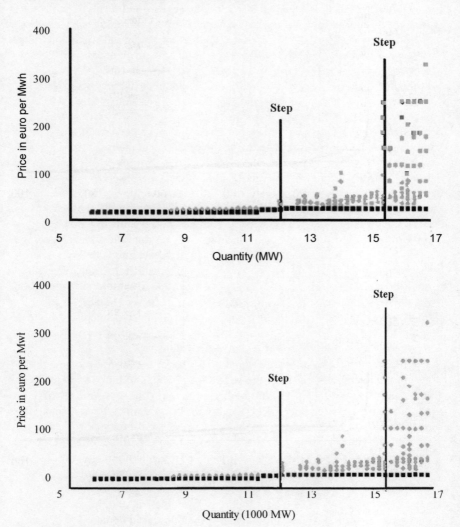

Source: Frontier Economics 2003, Figures 7 and 8

Figure 10.6 Price duration curves for minimum, median and maximum equilibria, compared to observed APX prices. Scenario 1 (upper panel) and 2 (lower panel)

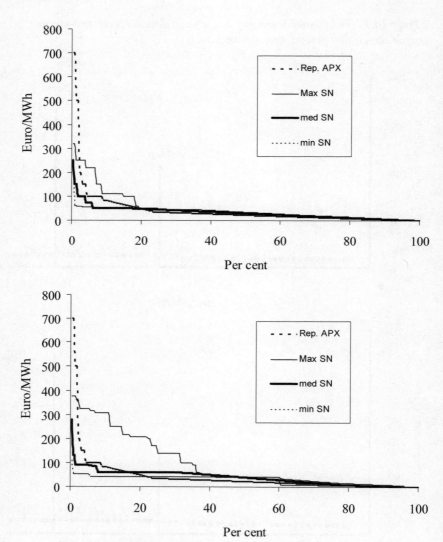

Source: Frontier Economics 2003, Figures 5 and 6

Price increases at the median level as a consequence of the merger were 13 per cent, averaged over all hours of the year. Focusing only on the lower bound on prices resulted in hardly any price increase, while the upper potential for exercise of market power was significantly higher.

To test the robustness of the results, various sensitivities were analysed. In particular the price effects were somewhat reduced if allowance was made for the existence of some realistic price responsiveness of industrial demand. These would be expected to decrease consumption when electricity prices exceed the value of electricity in their production process, typically starting at prices of several hundreds of euros per MWh. In this case price effects on average were closer to the results obtained by the Cournot model.

4. CONCLUDING REMARKS

In the Competition Authority's decision, the model results were interpreted as giving further evidence that the concentration would likely lead to a strengthening of the dominant position in the Dutch power generation market. This remained the case under various alternative assumptions (sensitivities) that were studied. An area where furthermore the use of the modelling technique offered more help was in assessing the effectiveness of the various remedies that were proposed by the parties to obtain permission for the transaction. Due to the detailed quantitative character of the modelling tool, a more insightful assessment of the (dis)advantages of various forms of remedy can be made than with the more traditional techniques.

The concentration was ultimately approved at the end of 2003, subject to the auctioning of part of the resulting company's access to generation capacity. While preparing this auction, Nuon chose to sell part of its contracted capacity to a competitor, and the requirement on further auctioning was first reduced, and finally removed (NMa 2005). The District Court of Rotterdam annulled the decision of NMa after Nuon lodged an appeal against the decision. It stated that the simulation models do not give an indication of a dominant position and that the possibility of a price rise does not justify the conclusion that a dominant position will be created or strengthened. NMa lodged an appeal against the Court's decision.

NOTES

1. Electricity consumption is rising in summer due to the increasing use of air conditioning equipment.

2. Hourly price patterns can be observed at the website of spot market operator APX, www.apx.nl.
3. In the Netherlands, transmission operator Tennet publishes the hourly available capacities on its website, www.tennet.nl.
4. As an example, in early 2004 an initiative was presented by producer Delta to build a new gas fired power plant, Delta (2004). It is expected to come on line only in 2007. Power company Electrabel, when discussing investment in new coal-fired plant, mentions investment paths including licensing procedures of six years (Electrabel 2004). A transmission line providing import capacity from Norway, currently being constructed by system operator TenneT, is expected to come online in 2008 (TenneT 2004).
5. TenneT reports on its website capacities of all production units above a certain capacity.
6. See for instance the study by Wolfram (1999) on price–cost mark-ups in the English electricity spot market. The general data availability can for a large part be explained by the fact that generation equipment is fairly standard across the world, and hence many consultancy firms possess detailed cost information on types of generation plants.
7. Evidently the task of constructing a model to capture the characteristics and interrelations of all real market places with their different rules is a formidable one. The approach commonly used in the extensive literature on gaming in electricity markets is to represent this complex real market in a reduced form where all interactions take place in a single market place, with a simplified set of rules, based on the more traditional paradigms of the game theory literature.
8. For example, Borenstein and Bushnell (1999) concluded that given the pre-restructuring industry structure in California, there would be potential for significant market power in some hours. Similarly, Bergman and Andersson (1995) found that the Swedish electricity market would be vulnerable to market power after deregulation.
9. Similar results, using a different mathematical model, are presented in Williams and Rosen (1999), who model both the New England and the Missouri/Kansas Region. Using a supply curve equilibrium model, this study analyses the effect of potential mergers in these markets in terms of both the change in price–cost margin, and in HHI. Little relation between the two is found, with HHI measures typically underestimating the effect on prices.
10. A generalization of Cournot models is that of conjectural variations. In the Cournot model, players choose quantities, and an equilibrium is a combination of strategies (quantities) such that no player would deviate from its chosen quantity, under the assumption that competitors will keep their quantities fixed. In the conjectural variations setting, players assume that competitors will react to a change in their strategy choice: if they reduce their quantity, competitors will respond to some extent by increasing their quantities to fill up the supply gap. A "competitiveness" parameter is included describing the measure of reaction. In the Cournot case, this parameter is zero, so that a reduction in volume by one player is not compensated by an increase of competitors' supplies. At the other extreme, one describes a perfectly competitive situation where one player's reduction will be completely substituted by competitors' supplies, and all players can be viewed as price takers, offering capacity at marginal costs.

    Strictly speaking the conjectural variations model is not a Nash game. It might, however, be considered to represent a reduced form of a repeated game, as explained by Cabral (1995). The model shares the good computability of the Cournot game, but for typical parameters produces lower prices than pure Cournot competition. The choice of "competitiveness" parameter is arbitrary, and might be tuned to reproduce observed prices and quantities. A drawback of the model, however, is that it fails to fully capture the importance of the capacity constraints. At all times players assume their competitors will make up for decreases in production, whereas precisely when capacity constraints are binding this assumption is violated. In practice it would therefore seem more natural to vary the response parameter for different situations. The Cournot assumption might be too strict in low demand hours (when capacity bounds are not reached), and a greater competitive reaction might be called for. On the other hand it may be more realistic in high demand situations. These issues seem to be more adequately captured by modelling market power in electricity markets in the supply function equilibrium framework. This introduces a quantity reaction into the behaviour of players, as in the conjectural variations framework, but with a variation parameter varying in a consistent fashion as a function of total production.

11. Technically, the downward sloping curves do not satisfy the second-order conditions (i.e. locally they give profit minima, instead of maxima) invalidating them as Nash equilibria.

12. Various studies have attempted to shed more light on the issue of equilibrium selection in the supply function model. As noted already by Klemperer and Meyer, if one allows for large demand uncertainty all supply curves other than the centre curve separating both regions become invalid, as they fail to be monotonically increasing. Demand uncertainty therefore helps to focus available supply functions around this special curve. More recent studies have tried to explain equilibrium choice as a result of "learning". In reality the game is repeated numerous times, each hour on each day. One may expect market participants to guide their choice of strategy, at least partially, by observed behaviour in the past, i.e. to learn from past behaviour. In models describing this learning process, strategies are adapted, after each model period, towards the best response to the previously observed aggregated supply curve of one's competitors. A numerical simulation study by Day and Bunn (2001) involving a particular kind of learning reveals a convergence towards the highest, Cournot equilibria. Similar studies by Larson and Salant (2003) and Bower and Bunn (1999) suggest that in reality, cycling behaviour, with both higher and lower equilibria occurring, takes place. This is consistent with theoretical work by Baldick and Hogan (2004) which indicates that no equilibrium is stable in the sense that small deviations from a chosen equilibrium lead to reactions that are even further from this equilibrium. Current work on the issue of equilibrium selection seems not quite conclusive.

13. The idea is, that while it is hard to predict absolute levels of prices using the model, what one is usually interested in is the relative effect on prices of some change (a merger in this case). As Stoft (2002) argues, although it may be hard to determine the effect of deviations from Cournot equilibrium from first principles, it seems not unreasonable to argue that this effect might be constant under changes in market structure. This suggests calibrating the model by adjusting the elasticity parameter so as to reproduce roughly the ex ante observed level of prices, and using this value to predict the change in prices as a consequence of the merger.

14. These demand levels above which high price equilibria become sustainable occur in roughly 15 per cent of time in a typical year for the pre-merger case, while post-merger these equilibria are accessibly in roughly 30 per cent of all hours of the year.

15. A further reason for not relying on average levels is to avoid the results being too sensitive to outliers.

11. Modelling Danish Mergers: Approach and Case Studies

Carsten Smidt

Merger simulation models are frequently applied in evaluating the effect of mergers. So far the modelling has concentrated on simulating horizontal mergers but the simulation models can also be helpful in SSNIP tests, vertical mergers, the assessment of horizontal agreements and cartels. The conspicuous output of a typical merger simulation is estimates on how the merger will effect prices. However the knowledge of the market which is generated during the process of modelling the market is just as important.

Models from the industrial organization literature can be very helpful to illustrate competition matters on a market. Of course you have to be very careful when you try to fit the actual market into a standardized economic theory. However the process of modelling a market compels the case handler to consider the most important conditions for competition on the market. The process of modelling the market can solely contribute to a better understanding of the functioning of the competition on the market.

When modelling a market the first considerations concern the choice of a competition model. The question is which model (Cournot, Bertrand, Supply Function Equilibrium and Conjectural Variation etc.) will mirror the actual market?

When a suitable competition model is found, many considerations need to be made on the explicit design of the model – including the explicit form and parameters of demand functions and marginal costs, the level of the price elasticity and cross-price elasticities, prices, market shares etc. All these considerations can be troublesome but necessary for having a suitable model of the market.

The Danish Competition Authority plans to continuously improve its knowledge in developing and applying merger simulation models, since the application of merger simulation models for the assessment of a merger can be very helpful. However the result of the merger simulation is no more than an indication of the likely merger effect.

On the one hand one should be prudent when applying merger simulation models. On the other hand one should not be blind to applying market simulation models within other fields of the competition area. A brief comment on this can be found in section 3.

During the last decade tools have been developed to analyse competition cases and a prevalent understanding has grown of the use of industrial organization models – particular in merger cases. Merger simulation models have for more than a decade been used by the Department of Justice in US merger cases. However a lot of other countries have within the last few years begun to apply merger simulation models.

Merger regulation was introduced into Danish competition law on 1 October 2000. The Danish merger regulation applies when a merger has no Community dimensions but the combined turnover in Denmark of the merging firms exceeds 0.5 billion euros (3.8 billion DKK) and at least two of the parties have a yearly turnover in Denmark above 40 million euros (300 million DDK).

In line with the EC Merger Regulation[1] a Substantial Lessening of Competition test was introduced in the Danish merger regulation on 1 February 2005.

The Danish Competition Authority has applied merger simulation models since early 2001. In the following section we present the merger simulations in Danish mergers. In section three we focus on merger simulation in a resent merger (Elsam/NESA) on the power market. In the last section we present some alternative ideas on the application of simulation models.

1.   MERGER SIMULATION IN DANISH MERGERS

In 1999 the Danish Competition Authority formed a separate economic unit, whose function among other things would be to assist in economic analyses in larger cases. Merger control has been in effect in Denmark since October 2000. In many merger cases economic analysis has been warranted, so since 2001 the group has focused considerable effort on merger analysis.

Economic Analysis and Merger Simulation Models

The decision on whether (and under what conditions) to approve a merger rests on a number of different analyses. Among others, these include analyses of legal conditions, market conditions, participants, and analyses of the probable effects of the merger.

Analysing the effect of a merger often calls for the use of economic analysis. In many of the larger cases, the Danish Competition Authority has specified a merger simulation model, which has contributed to analysing the effect of the merger. Merger simulation models do not stand alone in assessing the effects of the merger. They are used as an integrated part of the assessment – and the decision typically rests on a number of other analyses as well.

With the increasing experience with the practical use of merger simulation models, the Danish competition Authority has applied such models to a growing number of cases. Since 2001 the authority has used merger simulation models in five cases, see Table 11.1. This is almost half of the number of cases in which approval of the merger has been made contingent on remedies.

Table 11.1 Merger simulation models used in specific cases

Merger	Strategic parameter	Model
Carlsberg/Coca Cola bottling activities (2001)	Beverage prices	Bertrand
Danish Crown/Steff-Houlberg (2002)	Prices on fresh pork	Bertrand
DLG/KFK (2002)	Quantities of feeding stuff for pigs, cattle's and poultry	Cournot
Nykredit/Totalkredit (2003)	Prices on mortgage loans	Bertrand
Elsam/NESA (2004)	Supply curve of power on spot market	Supply Function

The authority has evaluated the effect of the merger in each of the five cases listed in Table 11.1 using a tailor-made market simulation model. The choice of the different economic models used (Bertrand, Cournot or SFE) was based on an evaluation of the market characteristics of the particular case.

Based on input of market data the models generate an output, which in each case has been used to evaluate changes in market shares and prices. The models require inputs such as product prices, market shares, marginal costs and the price elasticity. In the Elsam NESA case data were also required on production capacities and capacities on the cables connecting the different markets.

The data are mainly collected from the parties involved in the merger. But information from sector studies, sector organizations and statistical institutions is also used. Danish courts have not assessed the authority's use of economic evidence, simply because no parties have yet appealed against a merger decision.

The Reliability of Merger Simulation Models

It is important to understand the limitations of a merger simulation model. The output of a model does not yield a certain and precise prediction of the effects of a merger. First, the quality of the output will be no better than the quality of the inputs – so a model can yield reliable outputs only where reliable inputs can be ascertained. Second, a model is based on a number of simplifying assumptions, which restrict the reliability of the output. A model may fail to consider certain effects altogether. Or it may be unable to reliably estimate other effects, such as for example the more dynamic effects of a merger.

For these reasons, the authority considers the output of a merger simulation model only as an indication of the likely effects of the merger. Merger simulation analysis is complemented with other forms of analyses, as well as common sense, to ensure a reliable prediction.

The Process of Specifying a Merger Simulation Model

Applying merger simulation models require a solid understanding of the functioning of the market in question as well as a quantitative description thereof. The combination of the two leads to valuable information on the market and may fine tune the understanding of the functioning of the market.

A number of considerations and decisions need to be made when specifying a model of a market. Among these are the functional form and the explicit level of the parameters in the demand and marginal cost curves.

Another important issue is how to determine cross price elasticities. Explicit decisions on these matters, and especially consideration of the uncertainty of the model inputs, provide detailed knowledge about the functioning of the market.

Predicting the Effects of Remedies by Use of Merger Simulation Models

The Danish Competition Authority has also used merger simulation models to predict the probable effects of imposing remedies on the merging parties. The effect of an imposed remedy may be predicted by deriving the probable outcome of a merger both with and without the remedy in place. Again, the reliability of such predicted effects is uncertain and subject to the limitations of the model.

In order to evaluate the reliability of such predictions, the Danish Competition Authority has initiated a study of the *ex post* effects of imposed remedies. The study may be applied to evaluate the reliability of predictions by comparing the actual (*ex post*) effects of remedies with the predicted (*ex ante*) effects derived from merger simulation models. This comparison may improve the authority's ability to build models that yield reliable predictions, e.g. by including effects that were not previously taken into account.

The study considers all remedies applied in Danish mergers since merger control was introduced in October 2000. The findings were published in the authority's 2004 publication on competition issues. This shows that it may yet be too soon to study the effects of imposed remedies – in many cases the remedies have not yet taken effect, while other cases do not yet yield reliable data.

2.   THE ELSAM–NESA MERGER

In March 2004 the Danish Competition Authority (DCA) approved a merger between Denmark's two largest electricity companies – Elsam and NESA.[2]

After an investigation the merger was approved, conditional upon a package of remedies that was negotiated with the parties. The DCA found the remedies sufficient to neutralize the anti-competitive effects of the merger.[3]

The Firms and the Merger

At first glance the two merging firms Elsam and NESA are different in several ways. Their activities are located in distinct and non-overlapping areas of Denmark. Elsam's activities are located in Jutland and Funen (West Denmark). In contrast, NESA is located in Zealand (East Denmark).

Elsam's main activities are also different from NESA's main activities. Elsam primarily produces and trades electricity in the wholesale market in West Denmark. NESA's main activity is the distribution of electricity to end-users in East Denmark.

However, a closer look at the two companies revealed important overlaps that were central to the DCA's handling of the case. NESA was indirectly active on the wholesale market for electricity in East Denmark. With 36 per cent of the shares, NESA was the largest shareholder in ENERGI E2, which is the largest producer of wholesale electricity in East Denmark. This means that the merged entity will become the largest shareholder in ENERGI E2.

An ownership share of 36 per cent does not give Elsam formal control over ENERGI E2. But due to an agreement between NESA and ENERGI E2's second largest shareholder (the City of Copenhagen), Elsam will be entitled to nominate the chairman of ENERGI E2's board of directors. This implies that 36 per cent of the shares is likely to give Elsam a relatively high degree of control of ENERGI E2 and will make it possible for Elsam to influence ENERGI E2's commercial behaviour.

   As explained in the following subsection, East and West Denmark are (still) geographically distinct markets. However, there was a realistic expectation of an electrical connection of the two parts of the country in the foreseeable future.

A Brief View of the Danish Power Market

The structure of the electricity market in Denmark implies that both East Denmark and West Denmark often function as transit markets. When prices in Norway and Sweden are high, there is a flow of electricity from South to North. The flow turns when prices in Germany are high and Nordic prices low.

   The size of the cable connections from the neighbour price areas is crucial for how intensive competition from foreign countries can be. At the time of the handling of the merger larger cable capacities were expected, see Figure 11.1. Furthermore a cable connecting East and West Denmark was expected.

Figure 11.1 Cables in the present and the future

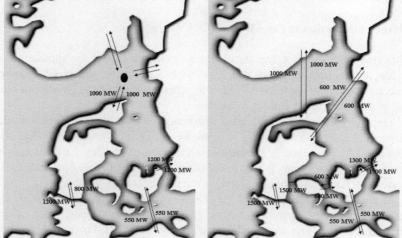

The trade of electricity in the Nordic region takes place either bilaterally or on Nord Pool – the Nordic Power Exchange.[4] Nord Pool operates a spot market for physical contracts in Norway, Sweden, Finland, and Denmark. In this market, each participant bids a price–quantity curve for each individual hour of the day. The price–quantity curve provides information on how much the participant wants to produce or consume at any given price level. Prices for sale and purchases are determined hourly throughout the day.

Nord Pool cumulates all buying and selling orders into one aggregate supply curve and one aggregate demand curve for each hour of the day. During periods with no cable congestion, the Nordic countries constitute one price area. In this single price area there is one common Nordic spot equilibrium price which is determined for each hour by the intersection of the demand and supply curves.

During periods with bottlenecks, Nord Pool splits the market into separate price areas with differing prices. When cables in the Nordic countries are congested the flow of power is directed towards the price areas with the highest prices.

At the time of the merger there was no cable connecting East and West Denmark. As long as there is no cable between East Denmark and West Denmark, a dominant producer in either West Denmark or East Denmark can exploit this transit role to increase prices and profits.

A dominant producer in a transit area such as the two Danish price areas has to a certain degree the opportunity to set its price somewhere in the interval of the price spread between the regions to the south and to the north and maintain a price on the home market at the high end of this spread. To analyse the effect of the merger the model has to allow for this conduct.

Merger Simulation in the Elsam–NESA Merger

Eltra (the TSO in West Denmark) has developed a model for simulation of prices, production, demand and flow in the cables in the Nordic power market. The model (MARS: MARket Simulation) include the Nord Pool area and an interface to the European market.

The DCA'a simulation model is differentiated from Eltra's MARS model in particular by: 1) assuming exogenous prices in Norway, Sweden and Germany; 2) the player's strategy is a question of the level of the supply curve and not the slope; 3) the model is far more simple; and 4) the model is a one shot model and not calculating merger effects hour by hour.

In the Elsam–NESA case the DCA put substantial effort into the development and specification of a merger simulation model. The model differed from the previous models applied by the DCA. The reason for this was that the characteristics of the power market were in favour of a Supply Function Equilibrium model.

To develop a model that mirrors the functioning of the market it is necessary to make some assumptions about the characteristics of the market including how present and potential new players behave. No different from other cases, the DCA's model of the power market applied in this merger case reflects a simplification of the market.

It is of course not possible to mirror the functioning of the market perfectly in a number of economic/mathematical equations of which the merger simulation model consists. However the model can after all, if not predict a precise effect, produce a hint of the merger effect.

At the time of the handling of the merger considerable changes in the future market structures were expected. The model reflects the fact of two different price areas in Denmark: a price area in West Denmark and a price area in East Denmark. In the model it was presupposed that the two price areas were connected by a 600 MW cable. Furthermore it was presupposed that the cables to Norway, Sweden and Germany were enlarged as reflected in Figure 11.1.

In the model a general assumption is that Elsam will gain control over ENERGI E2. Furthermore the model was specified in a way that took into account that in the medium run all combined heat and power plants will (contrary to the time when the merger took place) sell their power production on market conditions. These additional power plants will then potentially supply up to 20 per cent of total production in Denmark.[5]

In order to determine how each producer of electricity in equilibrium will supply electricity we estimated how these players historically had submitted supply curves to Nord Pool. In relation to this issue Elsam has contributed to the analysis by revealing its cost structure to the Danish Competition Authority. By combining the supply curves submitted to Nord Pool and the cost structure, we get an idea about the relation between the marginal cost curves and the supply curves. It turns out that historically the supply curves submitted are based on the marginal cost curves added a fixed mark-up. Based on these findings we use the following functional form for the mark-up to extract the supply curves for each producer of electricity:

$$P_i = \mu_i + MC_i(q_i) \tag{11.1}$$

where P is the price, $MC_i(q_i)$ is marginal costs for producer i at the production level q_i and μ_i is the mark-up set by producer i. With a simplified marginal cost function of the form $MC_i(q_i) = d_i + e_i * q_i$ we get the linear supply functions:

$$q_i = (P_i - \mu_i - a_i)/e_i \tag{11.2}$$

For each producer of electricity the supply is linear in the price, which is in accordance with the supply functions submitted to Nord Pool. Total domestic supply in each market is:

$$Q(P) = \sum_i (P - \mu_i - d_i)/e_i \tag{12.3}$$

As with the supply curves we assume the demand curves to be linear. Using this functional form gives a conservative estimate on the price effect of the merger compared to other functional forms.[6]

To determine the parameter values in the demand relation we use estimates from analysts that are engaged in this market. In the MARS model a price elasticity of −0.1 has been used for the Danish market. In an equivalent analysis the Norwegian consulting firm ECON uses price elasticities in the interval −0.3 to −0.2. Since in the model we use a linear demand curve the elasticity changes depending on the price. Based on this, we use a price elasticity of −0.1 for the representative market price with increasing elasticity at higher prices.

In order to determine total supply and total demand of electricity in the market it is necessary to take into account imports and exports in the model. In Nord Pool as in the DCA's merger simulation model imports (exports) are treated as additional supply (demand). When the price reaches the price in a neighbour price area the supply (demand) curve moves to the right, see Figure 11.2. The supply (demand) curve is moved corresponding to the capacity of the relevant cable.

Figure 11.2 Total supply and demand in each market

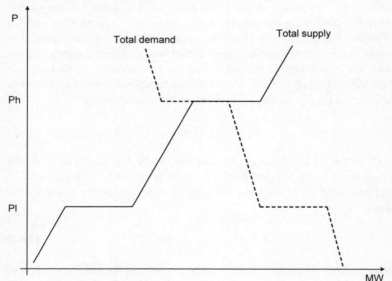

*Note:*The size of the additional supply at the point Pl (the lowest price of the neighbouring countries) and Ph (the highest price of the neighbouring countries) is given by the capacity for the pipeline connecting the two relevant markets.

Information on total supply and demand allows us to determine an analytical expression of the equilibrium price. With information on marginal costs, capacity constraints, total demand and prices in the neighbouring price areas the first order conditions can be derived and numerical equilibrium prices etc. can be calibrated.

We calculate the effects from the merger given different scenarios for marginal costs, demand and prices in neighbouring price areas and capacities. Subsequently we weight these scenarios in line with historical data in order to find the expected effects from the merger. To take account of seasonality, changes in precipitation, wind conditions and the like, the number of scenarios amounts to 108.

Based on these weighted scenarios we find that the average price of wholesale electricity will increase by 2–4 per cent if the merger is approved without further undertaking corresponding to a value of 200–300 mill. DKK.

Conclusion on the Merger Simulation in the Elsam–NESA Merger

It is important to stress that the results of the merger simulation were based on the assumption that Elsam was the majority owner of shares in ENERGI E2. The results of the merger simulation cannot enter uncritically into the assessment of the merger entirely on the basis of this assumption. Of course uncertainty is another relevant aspect of the merger simulation model results.

The DCA found that if the Elsam–NESA merger had been approved without remedies, a cable between West Denmark and East Denmark would not have led to more effective competition in Denmark. In particular, the DCA found it most likely that the fact that NESA holds 36 per cent of the shares in ENERGI E2 might impede Elsam and ENERGI E2 from competing against each other in the future. For more comprehensive considerations please see DCA (2004) or Pedersen, Smidt and Christiansen (2004).

In the end, the DCA had no doubt that Elsam's partial ownership of ENERGI E2 was anticompetitive but still it would clearly be fruitful with better quantitative measures of ownership control.

Taking into account among other things that Elsam became a minority shareholder in ENERGI E2 but was entitled to appoint two members of the board of directors – including the chairman – it was estimated based on the results from the merger simulation model that the merger would increase prices by 1–3 per cent.

The DCA approved the Elsam–NESA merger conditional upon a package of remedies negotiated with the parties (see Table 11.2).

Table 11.2 Most important remedies – the Elsam–NESA case

- Elsam shall sell off production capacity in the form of a number of small combined power and heat plants in West Denmark (230 MW)
- Elsam shall sell off virtual production capacity in West Denmark (600 MW)
- Elsam shall abstain from buying small combined power and heat plants in the future
- Elsam shall abstain from entering production agreements with small combined power and heat plants
- Elsam shall be responsible for constructing a cable between East Denmark and West Denmark

Source: DCA (2004), chapter 1.

An important remedy is that Elsam will sell production capacity in West Denmark.

In total, Elsam committed to sell a yearly capacity of 830 MW. In rough terms this amounts to 20 per cent of the average Danish demand for electricity (4,000 MW) and about 6 per cent of the total production capacity in Denmark (12,000 MW).

3. POTENTIAL APPLICATION OF SIMULATION MODELS

Based on the same principles as in a merger simulation model – which basically is to describe the market by economic theory and mathematical equations – it is possible to apply market simulation models to other fields within the competition area.

Examples of such potential fields could be: vertical mergers; horizontal and vertical agreements; market delineation; cartels.

A first obvious extension of the horizontal merger simulation models is to model vertical mergers. Such models can give the opportunity to consider the trade-off between elimination of double marginalization and incentives to margin squeeze/price discrimination.

From a very general point of view a merger is a way of influencing the conduct of other market participants. Another – not as final – way to influence the conduct of other market participants is to enter into an agreement with these parties. Modelling horizontal or vertical agreements can of course be too troublesome compared with the benefits.

The hypothetical monopolist test and the SSNIP are well known concepts when it comes to market delineation. Market simulation models can be applied to estimate the potential increase in price when another competitor is annexed into the hypothetical monopolist.

Evaluating the price effects of cartels is generally speaking the mirror of evaluating the price effects of mergers. Another way to put this is to say that the effect of splitting a cartel can be compared to the effect of splitting up a merger. This can be characterized as "backwards merger simulation".

The DCA has only in one case applied market simulation models to other purposes than merger simulation. In the Danish Crown–Steff-Houlberg merger a market simulation model was applied as a supplementary analysis for the delineation of the relevant market.

NOTES

1. Council Regulation (EC) No 139/2004 of 20 January 2004 on the control of concentrations between undertakings.
2. For a more thorough presentation see Pedersen, Smidt and Christiansen (2004).
3. The full report from the Danish Competition Authority from March 2004, "Fusionen mellem Elsam og NESA", can found at the DCA's website: www.ks.dk/publikationer/konkurrence/2004. In the following the report will occasionally be referred to as DCA (2004). More English information about the merger can be found on the homepage, www.ks.dk/english/competition/national/2004/elsam.
4. For more information about Nord Pool, see www.nordpool.com.
5. Please see "A powerful competition policy" by the Norwegian Competition Authority (2003).
6. See Mathiesen (2000).

12. On Simulation and Reality: A Swedish Example

Arvid Nilsson and Niklas Strand*

How accurate are the simulation models that are used to analyse the effects of mergers? In this chapter we try to address the issue by comparing the simulation results for a merger in the Swedish fresh bread market with the actual outcome after the merger. The simulations were performed as a part of the Swedish Competition Authority's investigation of the merger in February and March 2003. The merger was unconditionally cleared on March 18. Two years later we can look at what really happened after the merger was consummated.

1. THE SWEDISH BREAD MARKET

The two merging parties, Cerealia AB and Schulstad A/S were both active in the production of fresh bread. Cerealia was number two and Schulstad number four in the industry in terms of sales. The market leader in Sweden was Pågen, with the brands Pågen and Pååls. Other major competitors are Polarbröd and Fazer, but they are only strong in certain segments of the markets. The merger did not create or strengthen a dominant position in the segments for dark bread, flat bread, or speciality bread (for hot dogs, hamburgers etc.). The merging parties sold 60 per cent of the sweet rye bread (limpa), which was a possible cause for concern. This particular bread type is very popular in Sweden and Cerealia was the market leader with its brand Skogaholm even before the merger. The merging parties argued that the relevant market was the entire fresh bread market in Sweden and that the merger would not create a dominant position. The relevant geographical market was undisputedly Sweden. Table 12.1 shows the market shares for the different companies in the segments limpa and white bread. We can see that the merged firm has lost some market share to the rivals.

Table 12.1 Market share at time of merger (2002) and later development, (per cent)

	2002	2003	2004
Limpa, market size: SEK 0.8 billion			
Cerealia and Schulstad	60	58	57
Cerealia	44	39	52
Schulstad	16	19	5
Pågen/Pååls	17	17	26
Fazer	3	3	3
Others	20	21	14
White bread, market size: SEK 1.4 billion			
Cerealia and Schulstad	34	33	34
Cerealia	16	16	19
Schulstad	17	17	16
Pågen/Pååls	47	46	47
Others	19	22	19

Note: All data provided by AC Nielsen.

There have been some major changes in the brand management of both Cerealia and Pågen during the last two years. Cerealia has combined its product line with that of Schulstad and several products have been relabelled or discontinued. They have closed more than half of their production facilities since the merger and invested in one entirely new one. Pågen has relabelled most of the products with the brand Pååls in favour of the brand Pågen. They have also closed two production facilities and sold off two together with a couple of brand names.

2. THE SIMULATION

The simulations were done in-house at the Swedish Competition Authority during the 25-day-long phase one investigation using the Mathematica program SimMergerLite. The parties were very helpful in supplying the data and some marketing research studies they had conducted.

Model

We used a Logit demand model, assuming that consumers make discrete choices among the alternatives in the market or do not buy at all. By using the Logit demand we assume that a price rise on one product causes consumers to switch to the other products in relation to these products' markets shares (the independence of irrelevant alternatives assumption). If, for example, the price of Schulstad's white bread increases, most consumers would turn to Pågen and fewer to Cerealia. The assumption is reasonable on the bread market since products which sell a lot have more shelf space in the stores.

The US Department of Justice used a transformed Logit model called the Antitrust Logit Model (ALM) when simulating the merger between Interstate Bakeries and Continental Baking in 1995 (Werden 2000). An advantage with the ALM is that it may be used when there is incomplete information on the elasticities. The best way is generally to estimate every cross-price elasticity one by one. This would, however, be an impossible task in our case since the number of products is around 2000 according to AC Nielsen[1] which gives 4 000 000 cross-price elasticities. By choosing the ALM, we only need two elasticities, the market elasticity and a measure of the level of substitutability between the products in the market.

Data

The merger took place in the early spring of 2003 and the prices and quantities we use in the simulation are the averages from 2002. Ideally, we would have liked to use the prices at the time of the merger, but those were not available. We assumed further that the retailers would not change their margins as a result of the merger, which means that we can use retail prices instead of wholesale prices. Cerealia supplied us with scanner data gathered by AC Nielsen on nearly all fresh bread sold in Sweden. The prices are the actual prices, including discounts, which the consumers have paid at the computerized checkout in the stores. We constructed the yearly average price by dividing the total value by the total quantity to get the average price per kilo. We focused on the five major brands in each segment and aggregated the rest into one player. We further aggregated all the different breads sold under the same brand in the same segment, which means that we were down from 2000 products to 28. The post-merger data was provided by AC Nielsen directly and covers the same market segments.

Elasticities

Fresh bread has an inelastic demand; an increase in the price of all bread by 1 per cent results in a decrease in the quantity sold of less than 1 per cent. Bread is often used in the literature as an example of a market with low elasticity (Huang and Lin 2000). A recent figure of the total demand elasticity for fresh bread in Sweden is 0.4 (Dimaranan, McDougall and Hertel 2002). The data we have from AC Nielsen does not cover all fresh bread sold, however. Small shops (less than 100 m^2) are not covered and bread sold without EAN code is not covered. We adjust for this by simulating with a market elasticity of 1 to 1.5 when simulating different segments of the fresh bread market.

When it comes to the elasticity of certain products, it can be very high. The merging parties provided us with data from several discount campaigns with price reductions ranging from 7 to 41 per cent. An estimation of the own-price elasticity from this data yielded a figure of around nine. This figure clearly overstates the true price elasticity as it includes the intertemporal substitution effect. Since we are aggregating a lot of products in our simulations, we will use far lower elasticity figures. In the simulations we let the firms' own-price elasticities vary from two to five, approximately.

Calibration and Efficiencies

When calibrating the model we get the corresponding marginal costs from the first-order condition. These were in line with the ones we got from the merging parties. The merging parties claimed that there would be substantial efficiencies resulting from the merger, something that we did not take into account in our simulations. From the latest quarterly report from Cerealia (January–August 2004) we learn that the expected synergies have as yet not been realized as planned.

3. RESULTS

We analysed five different segments of the fresh bread market, but here we only report the most interesting segments, which are white bread and sweet rye bread (limpa). We started by simulating them separately, but information gathered from the merging parties and their competitors told us that that these two segments were close to each other, so we continued by simulating them as one market. For the sake of brevity, we report only the simulations for limpa and white bread taken together as the relevant market. Our simulations resulted in predicted price increases of 3 to 5 per cent for Cerealia, 4.5 to 8 per cent for Schulstad and 1.5 to 2.7 per cent for the market for white bread and limpa.

Figure 12.1 below shows our estimates compared to the actual outcome, where we assume that the entire effect of the merger is realised by 2003. For 2004 we assume that the prices follow the development of food in general, which in fact declined between 2003 and 2004. The thin lines show the upper and lower bound of our simulation results.

Figure 12.1 Predicted effects and actual outcomes

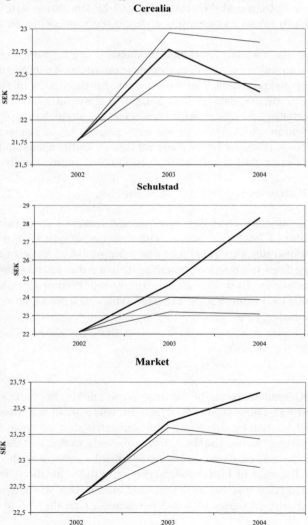

The results from the simulations compared to the actual outcome on the market reveal that our simulations underestimated the price rises. The market price increased by 3.3 per cent between 2002 and 2003 and an additional 1.2 per cent between 2003 and 2004, when food in general got cheaper. Since we used the Logit demand model, this is not altogether surprising. The Logit model gives conservative effects compared to, for example, the AIDS model. It is, however, quite striking how the price of fresh bread has increased considering that there was actually a small deflation in the overall price level on food and non-alcoholic beverages between 2003 and 2004. There may, of course, be other reasons for why the prices have risen. We have, however, not found any evidence that the costs of producing bread have risen more than the costs of producing other food or that the quality of the bread has increased considerably, so the merger remains a prime suspect.

The fact that Schulstad's prices continued to increase in 2004 while Cerealia's prices declined in combination with reciprocal shifts in the firms' market shares indicates that some of the lower-price brands of Schulstad have been relabelled Cerealia.

4.   CONCLUSIONS

The simulation model predicted moderate price rises, too moderate considering what happened in reality. It is too early to draw any definitive conclusions. But in order for the Logit demand model to predict average market price increases of the size observed in practice (>4.5 per cent) the market elasticity for the "white bread and limpa" market needs to be 0.45 with brand elasticities of 2.0 or less, which is clearly not reasonable for such a small part of the bread market. We claim that it is the small convexity of the Logit demand function that is to blame for the poor predictions; there are other demand specifications which may have performed better in the present case. We will extend this work further and analyse the merger simulations we did in this case more thoroughly in the future. We plan to re-do the simulations using other demand models which may prove useful for future merger investigations.

NOTES

*   Both at the Swedish Competition Authority, SE-103 85 Stockholm, Sweden, e-mail: arvid.nilsson@kkv.se, niklas.strand@kkv.se. The views expressed in this paper are those of the authors and do not necessarily correspond to the views of the Swedish Competition Authority.
1.   AC Nielsen is a private company who gathers scanner data from all food retailers.

13. What Merger Simulation is Not: Hessenatie–Noord Natie in Retrospect

Patrick Van Cayseele*

At the end of this book, it is my daunting task to explain what merger simulation is not. The reader by now has absorbed many wise dos and don'ts and pros and cons, but it is very instructive to see how inexperienced parties participating in the merger review process might be misguided regarding what merger simulation tries to accomplish, as the result of questionable Guidelines introduced by the EC (see European Commission 1997). It illustrates several points raised in the many contributions to this volume and indicates the pitfalls that surrogates for appropriate merger simulation techniques have.

Since the misunderstanding and shortcomings of merger simulation experienced in a practical setting are illustrated, by means of a particular case dealt with by the Belgian Antitrust Authority, it should be clear from the outset that neither the outcome of the merger review process ("the decision" taken by the Council), nor the arguments of a *particular* party involved are targeted.[1] It is argued that in the end, the proper decision was taken. This is done by showing in retrospect that a simple exercise in merger simulation would indeed show why some concerns could be raised (that is why a second phase investigation was opened) but that in the end, most concerns disappeared and the merger could be cleared.

Meanwhile, several parties used arguments and concepts that captured some ideas of merger simulation, but elaborated them in the perspective of market definition guidelines. Again, this is not to say that one party or another underperformed in representing their company or the Ministry of Economic Affairs. On the contrary, the merger case we investigate was one of the best prepared in the entire history of Belgian competition policy. A variety of studies so as to get a feel of potential price increases after the merger were surveyed. Figures showing the co-evolution of prices for handling cargo in several ports were compared, to show that all of these places were supplying services in the same market.

But at some point in time, the need to have a proper merger simulation was felt, and from several sides, ad hoc attempts were then made to shed light on the case by using surrogate approaches to merger simulation. This is dangerous for two reasons. First, it creates the impression that something is proven, but in fact, it isn't. Second, these surrogate exercises tend to keep the argumentation in the stage of determining the relevant market, and then focussing on market shares, rather than leaving the market structure dimension to focus on the post-merger performance of the industry.

To show these issues, this chapter is organized as follows. The next section introduces the case that is used to show what constitutes an inappropriate substitute to merger simulation. Then an exposition of an approach *similar* to one parties could have used is given.[2] Thereby, the key features of a proper merger simulation as proposed by Werden (2005) are taken up, not exhaustively, but at least those seriously violated in the previous exposition. In a third section, it is shown how without considerable effort, a proper merger simulation *could* have been done. This illustrates a further point raised by Werden (2005), namely that with limited effort, merger simulation quickly becomes very illustrative of what the post-merger trends will be. Of course, further research should refine the findings of this section, and a last and concluding section points this out. In terms of policy implications, it then becomes clear that in the end, the right conclusion was taken, but that at the same time, the surrogate could have led to a wrong decision in the worst case, and wasn't very helpful in the best case.

1. THE MERGER HESSENATIE–NOORD NATIE

On 21 April, 2001, Compagnie Maritime Belge/Hessenatie and Noord Natie entered a file to obtain approval for a merger. The companies that requested the clearing of the merger are both active in the handling of container traffic in the port of Antwerp. Based on statistical data regarding the handling of TEUs (Twenty foot Equivalent Units, i.e. a container of standard size), post-merger market concentration would have increased tremendously in the port of Antwerp. If the ports of Rotterdam, Bremen and Hamburg are included in the relevant market, the post-merger concentration ratio still would be high. At the same time, a competitor located in Rotterdam already had a market share exceeding the post-merger market share for Antwerp in the Antwerp–Hamburg range.

Clearly, based on prima facie evidence, this is a potentially very harmful merger, since two very close competitors merge. That Hessenatie and Noord Natie are close competitors is beyond any doubt. They are located in the same port, and can use the same pool of dockworkers, hinterland facilities, and so on. The discussion mainly focussed on the correct delineation of the market and in the end, the Belgian Antitrust Authority decided to open a second stage investigation.

The authority asked for an additional report on the appropriate economic delineation of the relevant market for transhipment container handling with inland destination (as well as container repair), and explicitly ordered to investigation of the impact of the merger on pricing (see Raad voor de Mededinging 2001a).

An elaborate report was proposed to the authority, in which all parties contributed to a better understanding of the competitive situation. At least three worthwhile research initiatives can be mentioned. Some can be classified as low-tech while others made an attempt at using more high-tech methods available, yet none arrived at a serious merger simulation.[3]

On the contrary, the more that was tried out regarding merger simulation, the more the reasoning went wrong, showing a poor understanding of what the technique of merger simulation is about. We first start with a discussion of some of the simpler arguments, then move on to the more sophisticated analysis. All of the arguments presented in this part are valid, and helpful for understanding the final decision. We then move on to what is a surrogate for merger simulation and show how this exercise is completely at odds with what a real merger simulation is (see Werden 2005).

Valid Empirical Techniques and Arguments

One of the first elements pointing to a sufficient degree of competition after the merger has taken place is the fact that there are few regions in the North-West of Europe where containers are exclusively shipped through one port. If one defines a captive region as one where only one port in the Le Havre–Hamburg range is used to ship containers, Hamburg and Bremen are most sheltered, with over 15 per cent of the regions they cater for not considering other ports to handle containers. This is explained by their location, in the north, where clients can hardly go south all the way to Rotterdam or Antwerp. They are followed by Le Havre and Rotterdam who have between 5 and 10 per cent of their traffic going to regions where no other port competes. Finally there is Antwerp which has just about 1 per cent of the regions it caters for that will not consider going elsewhere.

So clearly then even if Hessenatie and Noord Natie merge into one, they will probably not raise prices too much because regarding 99 per cent of its traffic, the Antwerp port competes with other ports. But of course, if competition is not vigorous in the non-captive segment, the post-merger price increases nonetheless might still be substantial.

A few studies exist that make an attempt at estimating the own price elasticity of demand for Antwerp, Bremen, Hamburg and Rotterdam. On average, the elasticities for Rotterdam are lower than those for Antwerp. So it seems that if there is one container handler (or port authority or any other operator) that can price somewhat independently, it would be Rotterdam. But of course, these figures are the result of the competitive interaction before the merger, where if Hessenatie increased its price, it was bound to lose traffic immediately to Noord Natie.

Finally, another argument showing that all ports are interdependent, is the strong co-movement of prices charged for handling a TEU. Referring to a study made by an independent consultant, over a period of seven years, it can be shown how tariffs move together between the ports of Antwerp, Bremen, Hamburg and Rotterdam.[4]

In the end then, a number of countervailing forces exist as to what the final result of the merger on prices for handling TEUs would have been. On the one hand, Hessenatie and Noord Natie are very close competitors. On the other hand, there seems to be effective competition from other ports in the Le Havre–Hamburg range with Antwerp as a location not being sheltered at all.

Since the nature of competition is Bertrand Competition in (geographically) differentiated goods, we know from the supermodularity of the game that post-merger prices will increase (see Deneckere and Davidson 1985; Vives 1990; or van Cayseele 2002). This will hold for both the prices charged by the combined entity in Antwerp, as well as ECT in Rotterdam, HHLA in Hamburg or Eurogate in Bremen. *The key question however is: by how much?*

Dangerous Substitutes to Proper Merger Simulation

The question raised at the end of the previous section lies at the heart of what merger review is about: assessing the unilateral effects of an operation in terms of predicting the post-merger increase in price. To answer the question, a percentage must be raised. This was done, claiming that without any doubt, the merged entity could act independently if it didn't exceed a price increase equal to this percentage.

In order to defend this percentage, an expert's opinion could be cited. The expert would be a market party making statements on the substitutability of ports. According to such an expert, the range of substitution would be limited to a strict subset of the Le Havre–Hamburg range. But as we know from Werden (2005): "Expert intuition on quantitative matters, such as likely price increases, is a black box."

This indeed also would have been the case here, for the percentage cannot be built upon any economic argument or model, only upon a personal appreciation of how port X could be circumvented by shipping containers to port Y, based upon the final destinations that needed to be reached.

Moreover, this could quickly lead to the reaction of another party, making the claim that the possibilities for substitution were unnecessarily limited by this expert, and hence that the likely price increases were overestimated. To show this, the concept of "a continuous chain of substitution" enters the discussion.

The concept is in the EC Guidelines publication on Market Definition of December 1997, indicating that a relevant market may contain products that are not direct substitutes for each other. It argues that A and C, although not in direct competition with each other, may be contained in the same relevant market. The reason is that they are both constrained in their pricing by B, who is in "the middle".

To illustrate the existence of the "continuous chain of substitution" in container handling, parties could draw graphs similar to the ones shown in Figures 13.1, 13.2, 13.3 and 13.4. These figures have been made for pedagogical reasons, to show why nothing compares to proper merger simulation. They represent the geographical area of the Le Havre–Hamburg range, showing both the UK and part of the European continent, as well as the five ports involved.

Around each port, a circle with a radius of approximately 300 kilometres is drawn. This corresponds to the so-called medium distance range for the hinterlands. It can be taken as a lower bound for the penetration of container traffic into the hinterland. Since, starting from Hamburg, the circle around it intersects with the one around Bremen, and even the ones around Antwerp and Rotterdam, there is competition between those ports, at least in the areas where their circles intersect. That is of course if the underlying assumptions of this graphical model hold true, and they are quite particular. In fact, this approach assumes that between 0 and 300 kilometre, transport costs are nil, whereas they are assumed to be prohibitively high once 300 kilometres are reached.

The same argumentation holds for Hamburg, Rotterdam, or any other port in the Le Havre–Hamburg range. As a matter of fact, Figure 13.1 shows how only in three areas, are importers restricted to using one harbour. In the north-east corner, this is Hamburg, in the south-west, Le Havre.[5] Figure 13.3 illustrates these regions by shading them in dark.

Hence, in this example the Le Havre–Hamburg range constitutes a "continuous chain of substitution", and a relevant product market is the entire area. The market shares that matter then are not those in Belgium or even the Benelux cluster, but those on the entire range. These are not so elevated and hence there should be much less fear for approving an anti-competitive merger.

Figure 13.1 Hinterland regions and number of ports competing before merger

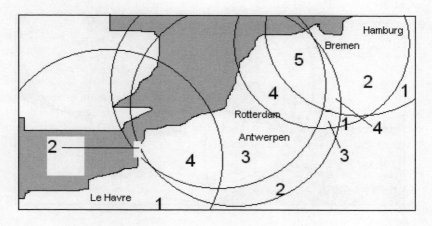

Figure 13.2 Hinterland regions and number of ports competing after merger

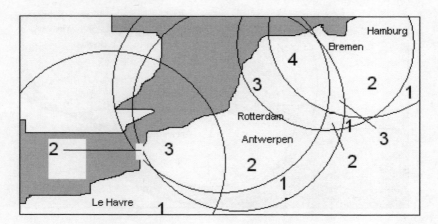

This line of reasoning is of course extremely dangerous for the merger to get approved, for it can easily be turned around. To see this, consider Figures 13.2 and 13.4. Figure 13.2 corresponds to Figure 13.1, except that the number of ports that compete after the merger are written down. Corresponding in Figure 13.4, another shaded area has been added since there is an additional region where now only one port is used to import containers. This time, the player is … the merged entity Hessenatie–Noord Natie, in Antwerp!

Figure 13.3 Hinterland regions served by only one port shaded dark, before merger

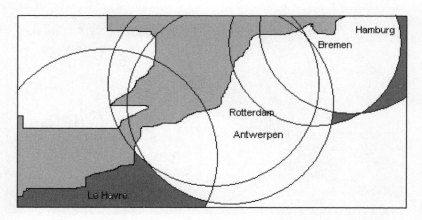

Figure 13.4 Hinterland regions served by only one port shaded dark, after merger

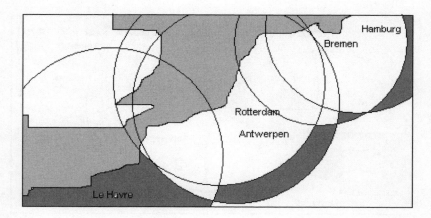

Now this "moon-shaped" region where Hessenatie–Noord Natie have a post-merger monopoly position is of considerable importance, not only because of its size, but also economically. To a very large extent it falls in the continental part of the so-called "blue banana", a region extending from London over the North of France, Benelux, the Rhine area to Switzerland and the north of Italy. And the blue banana is economically one of the most important areas of Europe. So it is to be expected that a lot of container traffic goes to this region and, hence, that the merged operator, contrary to the 1 per cent mentioned in section 2, would have an important captive market. If that is the case, the merged entity will raise the prices considerably in the post-merger equilibrium.

Fortunately for Hessenatie and Noord Natie, the argument is not correct, because the regions shaded in Figures 13.2 and 13.4 are not exclusively covered by a single container operator in one port. Market shares indicate how both Antwerp and Rotterdam compete all the way in the Le Havre and Hamburg "circles", as well as in the "critical moon-shaped region" mentioned above.

The practice of drawing circles of the same perimeter around the ports to argue in favour of a "continuous chain of substitution" therefore suffers from many shortcomings. Essentially, the approach is purely "mechanical", as opposed to what modern economics has tried to accomplish over half a century, through the use of noncooperative game theory and the Nash solution concept. As explained by Werden (2005), these insights have entered antitrust policy for a long time on the other side of the Atlantic: "The 1992 revision of the U.S. Horizontal Merger Guidelines introduced the term unilateral effects." And "One shot, non-cooperative oligopoly games give rise to unilateral merger effects." Also: "If non-merging firms operate on the same best-response function before and after a merger, the competitive effects of a merger are unilateral." Finally, "The U.S. enforcement agencies have challenged many mergers on the basis of unilateral effects, and the courts have accepted such theories."

By drawing circles, one is far from an oligopoly model that makes any sense. For one thing, the radius of all circles was set equal to 300 kilometres. But the range over which one port can ship containers precisely depends among other things on price, as well as on quality indicators. To show why such a mechanical approach is manifestly ridiculous, consider the post-merger increase in prices that merger authorities are afraid of. The result will be that the radius of the circles will change, because the merging parties increase their price, but also the outsiders. The relative magnitude of these increases will change the post merger equilibrium market shares. Hence, it is completely impossible to infer anything regarding the post-merger performance of an industry by such a mechanical approach.

On the contrary, the "continuous chain of substitution" concept, and the mechanical implementation of it leads to "market-share-based presumptions" (see Werden 2005).

Indeed, since we know from game theory that the post–merger price will increase, the question raised in section 2 was: by how much? All of the conflicting views held by parties have not contributed a single bit of information to answer this very essential question, although the answer can be reached in a way that is not all that difficult.

2. A BACK OF THE ENVELOPE MERGER SIMULATION FOR HESSENATIE–NOORD NATIE

In the final decision (see Raad voor de Mededinging 2001b), the Authority thus could not do anything else than conclude that: "regarding the impact of the concentration it has to be said that the research done could not come up with conclusive *scientific* evidence …".

In this section, it is shown that with a little effort and skill, scientific evidence could have been provided to the decision makers, in the form of an exercise in merger simulation.

Any academic economist who has studied oligopoly theory knows that a "continuous chain of substitution" always exists, since no matter what the model withheld is, the "N firms" compete with each other. Otherwise, there is no game-theoretic interaction, and the firms should not be included in the particular game of industry investigated. The EC guideline thus merely introduces an empty box.

Of course, any particular model will dictate a different degree of substitution between products. In the Bertrand and Cournot models, products are perfect substitutes, with an extreme impact on equilibrium pricing in the first model. In the Shubik model (Shubik and Levitan 1980), substitution is still kept symmetric, but becomes less than perfect. Still other models like "address" types impose asymmetry between the products involved, while limiting the degree of substitution. For a survey in the context of merger simulation, see Goppelsröder (2004) and Goppelsröder and Schinkel (2005).

Calibrating an Elementary Discrete Choice Model

In the present, as an initial approximation, we focus on a triopoly model, that merges into duopoly. The merging parties are located in the same geographical place, namely Antwerp. The competitor left over is ECT, located in Rotterdam. Besides a geographical difference, the ports differ according to a quality indicator which remains unobserved. While it is known that productivity and efficiency are very high in the port of Antwerp, a survey among German importers nonetheless reveals that Antwerp is handicapped by access. Indeed, Rotterdam is near the open sea while Antwerp needs to be approached over a waterway which is subject to tidal streams that, together with depth, render access less trivial.

This quality premium for Rotterdam is denoted by v, and assumed to be distributed uniformly over the interval $(0, k)$, with k a parameter that will be calibrated to pre-merger market shares. Therefore, if u denotes the utility that an importer obtains when he gets a container, he will choose to ship it through Rotterdam if

$$(u+v)-(p^R+tx)\geq u-(p^A+ty)$$

where p^R and p^A denote the prices charged by the container handlers in Rotterdam and Antwerp respectively, t is the cost for transporting a TEU one kilometre, and finally x and y denote the distance in kilometres from Rotterdam and Antwerp respectively, to the destination, i.e. the location of the importer.

Given the distributional assumption made, it is then easy to show that the market share for Rotterdam is given by

$$s^R=1-[p^R-p^A+t(x-y)]/k \qquad (10.1)$$

Before the merger, we assume that the two operators located in Antwerp compete in prices, and hence that the Bertrand outcome results,[6] or

$$p^A=c \qquad (10.2)$$

Where c denotes a constant average cost for handling a TEU.
    Profits for Rotterdam are maximized when

$$p^R=[k-t(x-y)+2c]/2 \qquad (10.3)$$

When solving for the Nash equilibrium in prices, we therefore obtain,

$$s^R=1/2-[t(x-y)]/2k \qquad (10.4)$$

and

$$s^A=1/2+[t(x-y)]/2k \qquad (10.5)$$

By taking the ratio of market shares of Rotterdam over Antwerp, and denoting it by g, k can be inferred by computing

$$k=t(x-y)[(1+g)/(1-g)] \qquad (10.6)$$

Data availability and time have restricted the scope of this exercise to seven observations. Data were collected from a variety of sources, like Vlaamse Havencommissie (2003). The year of observation is 1997. For two regions in Belgium and five in the Netherlands, we computed market shares of both ports. The distances x and y then where computed by taking the distance from Rotterdam and Antwerp respectively to the main city in that region, using www.mappy.com. The per TEU per kilometre transport cost was normalized to 1.

Using an OLS regression technique, we estimate that:

$$k = 89.05$$
$$(2.69)$$

where t statistics are in parenthesis. Also, on average, for the regions we focus on, the average distance from both ports is approximately nil, 0.3 kilometre to be precise. The pre-merger ratio of prices simulated by these findings is equal to 1.52 whereas in reality it was approximately 1.33.

An Initial Merger Simulation

The model together with its calibrated parameter can be used to illustrate how merger simulation would go. The ultimate goal of merger review is to assess whether or not the operation intended will increase post-merger prices with a small but significant nontransitory increase in prices, i.e. to do the SSNIP test.[7] Usually, 5 per cent is considered most of the time as the threshold, but this is completely arbitrary (see van Cayseele 1994). In the few practical applications that prevail in merger review, multiples of this percentage are used to draw firm policy conclusions, due to the sensitivity of the exercise or certain parameter estimates.

In the present model, t was normalized to 1 and hence in doing the SSNIP test, we have to take this into account. Formally, the SSNIP5 (where 5 denotes the threshold) test is passed when

$$(p^A - c)/c = (k + z)/3d < 5/100 \tag{10.7}$$

In order to understand equation (10.7), it is necessary to know that the post-merger price charged by Hessenatie and Noord Natie, is given by

$$p^A = k/3 + (tz)/3 + c \tag{10.8}$$

where z denotes the average difference in distances from the locations considered and the two ports. Also, equation (10.7) uses d, where $d = c/t$.

Precisely this ratio is critical for the outcome and at the same time depends on our estimates for the constant average cost of handling a TEU and the cost of transporting it one kilometre. For the first cost, a ramification by a transportation economist on the one hand, and the pre-merger price charges by the operators in Antwerp (which according to our Bertrand assumption should be equal to it) on the other hand, were compared. Both figures were very close to each other.

For the cost of transporting a TEU one kilometre inland, more variation was obtained. A lot depends on how the container can be transported to reach the final destination. If inland shipping can be done using a vessel (barge), the cost will be much lower than by railroad or truck. On average, it seems that a lot of container traffic goes inland by barge, but some destinations constitute an exception.

Therefore, anything within a range from $d = 200$ to $d = 300$ probably can be defended. As a tremendous and often overlooked advantage of merger simulation, one has the possibility to toy around with different values, and to "stretch" them to the limits of reason. Here, the range $d = 200$ to $d = 300$ still is well within reason. For the value $d = 300$, we predict a post-merger price increase between 5 and 10 per cent. For $d = 200$, the figure lies in the range of 10 to 15 per cent.

Clearly then, the merger indeed was potentially harmful and a second stage investigation required. But given the need to also stretch the threshold value for the SSNIP test, as well as other reasons we elaborate on next, the anti-competitive effects of the merger remain within bounds.

3. CLEARING THE MERGER BETWEEN HESSENATIE AND NOORD NATIE

Although limited, and subject to improvement (see also below), at least a quantitative assessment of the impact of the merger could be given, using merger simulation. Decision makers on 3 August, 2001, however, didn't have this information at their disposal. But still other factors were available that pointed towards clearing the case.

First of all, after the merger, one independent competitor remained, in Antwerp. Next, a party not captured by the operators but who also defended the interests of other parties such as transporters intervened to testify that competition would still remain after the merger within the port of Antwerp. And finally entry, potential in 2001 but realized meanwhile, constituted an important disciplinary force. More particularly, a new container terminal opened in Flushing, while Ostend start shipping containers (on a very small scale) from 2001 on.

The initial merger simulation exercise can still be improved in many respects. First of all, Antwerp not only competes with Rotterdam, but also with Le Havre, Bremen and Hamburg, and for many more regions than the seven located in Belgium and the Netherlands.

Besides extending the data collection process, other improvements are possible. For example, the quality indicator could be refined, using days of strike and other elements of the speed of cargo handling. The connection to inland waterways, tariffs charged by inland ports, tariffs charged by railroad companies, the possibility to replicate the handling of a container in Antwerp by shipping it to Rotterdam and putting it on a barge over the Scheld–Rhine canal ... all could be included. And in terms of the specification, the better known Antitrust Logit Model (see Werden 1997) or the Random Coefficients Model (see Berry 1994) could be used.

NOTES

*   Katholieke Universiteit Leuven and Universiteit van Amsterdam. Comments by H. Degryse, P. van Bergeijk and F. Verboven have been appreciated. All remaining errors are mine.

1.   Many parties are occupied by the Belgian merger review process. Government officials from the Ministry of Economic Affairs conduct an investigation to assess the impact of a merger that has to be cleared in advance. Only mergers exceeding a certain threshold need investigation (see van Cayseele et al. 2003) for the Belgian thresholds in an international perspective. Next, the merger review file enters into the legal environment because it is taken to a specialized court (administratief rechtscollege), the Council, by independent officials instructing the court (korps van verslaggevers). Neither the members of the Council nor the instructors can be considered to be parties involved in the merger review, since their task is to make a judgement on the admissibility of the merger.

During the hearings that may be held in order to reach a decision, a number of parties who are truly involved in the case are requested to develop their arguments. For the present case, these parties include:

1.   lawyers representing one of the merging companies or both companies
2.   managers of this company or both companies
3.   lawyers and managers of other companies affected, who ask to be heard, for instance shipping companies, importers, ...
4.   expert witnesses
5.   government officials of port authorities and the Ministry of Mobility and Transport and later on in the process
6.   Government officials of the Ministry of Economic Affairs who have to watch after the "general economic interest".

The author was a member of the Council when the decision on Hessenatie–Noord Natie was ruled.

2.   We again stress the words: *similar* and *could*, i.e. maybe not those actually used in the case.

3.   For a classification of low-tech and high-tech empirical methods in merger review, see Coscelli and van Reenan (2003).

4.   It should be remarked that parallelism cannot be claimed by pointing to a graph. One should investigate correlation or stationarity of the time series.

5.   Figures 13.1 and 13.2 thus read as follows: each number indicates the number of container handlers that meet in this particular region. For Figure 13.1, the numbers correspond to the

situation before the merger. North of Rotterdam, for example, one finds a region with a "4" in it. This says that here, Hessenatie (Antwerp), Noordnatie (Antwerp), ECT (Rotterdam) and Eurogate (Bremen) compete. The situation in reality is somewhat more complex, since the pre-merger situation in Antwerp with more than one container handler is by no means unique. Bremerhaven also hosts North Sea Terminals, Le Havre has Terminals de Normandie, GMP and CNMP, and so on. Even in Antwerp,there is a third player, although a smaller one, also remaining outside the merger. So in fact, the numbers should be higher.

6.   Unless:
1) Hessenatie and Noord Natie colluded before the merger in which case the merger doesn't change a thing;
2) capacity constraints exist, in which case the Cournot model would be relevant, see Kreps and Scheinkman (1983);
3) capacity constraints and First Refusal Contracts exist in which case the monopoly outcome would result, see van Cayseele and Furth (2001),
this is a valid assumption.

7.   To be entirely correct, an SSNIP test defines a merger operation for which the participants, behaving as a hypothetical monopolist, can increase post-merger prices by a certain percentage. Since the merger between Hessenatie and Noord Natie could already lead to a substantial price increase, it is not necessary to extend the operation by including ECT, Eurogate and so on to define a relevant antitrust market.

References

Autorità Garante della Concorrenza e del Mercato (1994), "Davide Campari Milano / Società italiane Koninklijke BolsWessanen", *Bollettino n. 50.*

Baker, J. (1999), "Econometric Analysis in in FTC v. Staples", *Journal of Public Policy and Marketing,* **18**, 11–21.

Baldick and Hogan (2002), "Capacity Constrained Supply Function Equilibrium Models of Electricity Markets: Stability, Non-decreasing Constraints, and Function Space Iterations", UCEI POWER Working Paper.

Baldick and Hogan (2004), "Polynomial Approximations and Supply Function Equilibrium Stability", Working paper, Center for Business and Government, John F. Kennedy School of Government, Harvard University.

Bartelsman, E.J. and M. Doms (2000), "Understanding Productivity: Lessons from Longitudinal Microdata", *Journal of Economic Literature,* **83**(3), 569–594.

Battalio, R., L. Samuelson, and J. van Huyck, (2001), "Optimization Incentives and Coordination Failure in Laboratory Stag Hunt Games", Econometrica, **69**(3), 749–764.

Bergeijk, P.A.G. van and R.C.G. Haffner (1996), *Privatization, Deregulation and the Macroeconomy: Measurement, Modelling and Policy,* UK and Brookfield, USA: Cheltenham.

Bergeijk, P.A.G. van, A. L. Bovenberg, E.E.C. van Damme and J. van Sinderen (eds.) (1997), *Economic Science and Practice: The Roles of Academic Economists and Policymakers,* Cheltenham, UK and Northampton, MA, USA: Edward Elgar.

Bergman, L. and B. Andersson (1995), "Market Structure and the Price of Electricity: An ex ante Analysis of the deregulated Swedish Electricity Market", *The Energy Journal,* **16**, 97–109.

Berry S. (1994), "Estimating Discrete-choice Models of Product Differentiation", *Rand Journal of Economics,* **25**, 242–262.

Berry, S., J. Levinsohn and A. Pakes (1995), "Automobile Prices in Market Equilibrium", *Econometrica,* **63**, 841–890.

Bertrand, Joseph L.F. (1883), "Review of 'Théorie Mathématique de la Richesse Sociale', and 'Recherches sur les Principes Mathématiques de la

Théorie de Richesse'", *Journal des Savants*, **67**, 499–508. A modern translation by James Friedman appears in Andrew F. Daughety (ed.) (1988), *Cournot Oligopoly*, Cambridge: Cambridge University Press, pp. 73–81.

Bishop, S. and M. Walker (2002), *The Economics of EC Competition Law*, 2nd edition, London: Sweet & Maxwell.

Boone, J. (2004a), "A new way to measure competition", TILEC Discussion Paper 2004–004.

Boone, J. (2004b), "Balance of power", TILEC Discussion Paper 2004–021.

Borenstein, S. and J. Bushnell (1999), "An Empirical Analysis of the Potential for Market Power in California's Electricity Industry", *Journal of Industrial Economics*, **47**, 285.

Bower, J. and D. Bunn (1999), "An Agent-Based Model Comparison of Pool and Bilateral Market Mechanisms for Electricity Trading in England and Wales", *Energy Modeling Forum 17*.

Brannman, L. and L. Froeb (2000), "Mergers, Cartels, Set-Asides, and Bidding Preferences in Asymmetric Oral Auctions", *Review of Economics and Statistics*, **82**, 283–290.

Cabral, L. (1995), "Conjectural Variations as a Reduced Form", *Economic Letters,* **49**(4), 397–402.

CAISO (2002), "Analysis of Trading and Scheduling Strategies Described in Enron Memos", available at www.caiso.com.

Capps, Oral Jr., Jeffrey Church, Alan Love (2001), *Specification Issues and Confidence Intervals in Unilateral Price Effects Analysis*, working paper, November.

Chamberlin, Edward H. (1933), *The Theory of Monopolistic Competition*, Cambridge, Mass.: Harvard University Press, 8th ed. 1962.

Coleman, M. and D. Scheffman (2005), "FTC Perspectives on the Use of Econometric Analyses in Antitrust Cases", forthcoming in: J. Harkrider (ed.), *The Use of Econometrics in Antitrust,* American Bar Association Section on Antitrust.

Coscelli A. and J. van Reenen (2003), "Empirical Assessment of Market Power: From Low Tech to High Tech", in: *The Use of Economics in EC Competition Law*, IBC, Brussels.

Cournot, Antoine Augustin (1838), *Researches into the Mathematical Principles of the Theory of Wealth*, translated by Nathaniel T. Bacon, New York: Augustus M. Kelley, 1971.

Court of First Instance (2002), Judgment in case T-342/99: Airtours/First Choice vs. European Commission.

Crooke, Philip, Luke Froeb, Steven Tschantz and Gregory J. Werden (1999), "The effects of assumed demand form on simulated post-merger equilibria", *Review of Industrial Organization*, **15**(3), 205–17.

Dalkir, S, Logan J. and R.T. Masson (2000), "Mergers in Symmetric and Asymmetric Non-cooperative Auction Markets: The Effects on Prices and Efficiency", *International Journal of Industrial Organisation*, **18**, 383–413.

Danish Competition Authority (DCA) (2004), "Fusionen mellem Elsam og NESA", March.

Davidson, C. and R. Deneckere (1984), "Horizontal Mergers and Collusive Behaviour", *International Journal of Industrial Organisation*, **2**, 117–132.

Day, C. and D. Bunn (2001), "Divestiture of Generation Assets in the Electricity Pool of England and Wales", *Journal of Regulatory Economics*, **19**, 123.

Day, C., B. Hobbs and J. Pang (2002), "Oligopolistic Competition in Power Networks: A Conjectured Supply Function Approach", to be published.

Deaton, A. and J. Muellbauer (1980), "Economics and consumer behavior", New York: Cambridge University Press.

Deloitte (2004), "Benutting vraagrespons in de geliberaliseerde elektriciteitsmarkt", Deloitte, Management & ICT Consultants, Amstelveen.

Delta (2004), "Sloecentrale", Press release Delta N.V., available at www.delta.nl.

Deneckere, Raymond and Carl Davidson (1985), "Incentives to form coalitions with Bertrand competition", *RAND Journal of Economics*, **16**(4), 473–486.

Dimaranan, B., R. McDougall and T. Hertel (2002), "V5 Documentation – Chapter 20: Behavioral Parameters", Center for Global Trade Analysis, Purdue University.

Dufwenberg, M. and U. Gneezy (2000), "Price competition and market concentration: an experimental study", *International Journal of Industrial Organization*, **18**, 7–22.

Duso, T., D.J. Neven and L.-H. Röller (2003), "The Political Economy of European Merger Control: Evidence using Stock Market Data," CEPR Discussion Paper DP3880.

Duso, T. and Lars-Henrdrik Röller (2003), "Endogenous Deregulation: Evidence from OECD Countries", *Economic Letters*, **81**(1), 67–71.

EC (2003), "Sydkraft/Graninge", European Commission Case No. COMP/M.3286.

ECN (1999), "Energie Verslag Nederland 1999", available at www.energie.nl.

EIM (2003), *Nulmeting administratieve lasten EZ regelgeving*, EIM Zoetermeer.

Electrabel (2004), "Electrabel investeert in Nederlandse stroomvoorziening", Press release Electrabel N.V., available at www.electrabel.nl.

Epstein, Roy J. and Daniel L. Rubinfeld (2002), "Merger Simulation: A Simplified Approach with New Applications", *Antitrust Law Journal*, **69**(3), 883–917,

Epstein, Roy J. and Daniel L. Rubinfeld (2003), *Merger Simulation with Brand-Level Margin Data: Extending PCAIDS with Nests,* working paper No. CPC03-40, Competition Policy Center, University of Berkeley, California, August.

Epstein, Roy J. and Daniel L. Rubinfeld (2004), "Merger Simulation with Brand-Level Margin Data: Extending PCAIDS with Nests", *Advances in Economic Analysis & Policy* (The B.E. Journals in Economic Analysis & Policy), **4**(1), March.

Euromonitor (2003), *The Market for Alcoholic Drinks in Italy.*

European Commission (1997), "Bekendmaking van de Commissie inzake de bepaling van de relevante markt voor het gemeenschappelijke mededingingsrecht", *Publicatieblad* C372/5 – C372/13.

European Commission (1999), Case no IV/M.1524: Airtours/First Choice.

European Commission (2004), *Council Regulation (EC) No 139/2004 of 20 January 2004 on the control of concentrations between undertakings*; OJ L 24, 29.01.2004, 1–22.

European Commission (2004), "Guidelines on the assessment of horizontal mergers under the Council Regulation on the control of concentrations between undertakings", *Official Journal of the European Union*, C 31/03.

Farrell, Joseph and Carl Shapiro (1990), "Horizontal Mergers: An Equilibrium Analysis", *American Economic Review*, **80**(1), 107–126.

Farrell J. and C. Shapiro (2001), "Scale Economies and Synergies in Horizontal Merger Analysis", *Antitrust Law Journal*, **68**, 685–710.

Fisher, F.M. (1987), "Horizontal Mergers: Triage and Treatment", *Journal of Economic Perspectives*, **1**, 23-40.

Fisher, Irving (1898), "Cournot and Mathematical Economics", *Quarterly Journal of Economics*, **12**(2), 119–138.

Forchheimer, Karl (1908), "Theoretishes zum unvollständigen monopole", *Jahrbuch für Gesetzgebung, Verwaltung und Volkswirtschaft*, **32**, 1–12.

Fridolfsson, S.-O. and J. Stennek (2005), "Why Mergers Reduce Profits and Raise Share Prices – A Theory of Preemptive Mergers", forthcoming in *International Journal of Industrial Organization*.

Froeb, L. and S. Tschantz (2002), "Mergers Among Bidders with Correlated Values", in D.J. Slottje (ed.), *Measuring Market Power*, Amsterdam: Elsevier.

Froeb, L., D. Hosken and J. Papalardo (2005), "Economics Research at the FTC: Information, Retrospections, and Retailing", forthcoming in the *Review of Industrial Organization*.

Frontier Economics (2003), "An initial assessment of the effect of the proposed takeover of Reliant by Nuon", report prepared for NMa.

Gent, C. van (1997), "New Dutch Competition Policy: A revolution without revolutionaries", in P.A.G. van Bergeijk, A.L. Bovenberg, E.E.C. van Damme and J. van Sinderen (eds), *Economic Science: Art or Asset? The case of The Netherlands*, Rotterdam: OCFEB, pp. 59–72.

Goppelsröder M. (2004), *Simulation Analysis in Merger Control, A Review of the Development and Application of Merger Simulation Techniques in the EU and US*, Den Haag: Nederlandse Mededingingsauthoriteit (NMa).

Goppelsröder M. an M. P. Schinkel (2005), "On the Use of Economic Modelling in European Merger Control", in P. van Bergeijk and E. Kloosterhuis, *Modelling European Mergers: Theory, Competition Policy and Case Studies*, Cheltenham, UK and Northampton, MA, USA: Edward Elgar.

Götte, L. and A. Schmutzler (2005), "Merger Policy: What can we learn from experiments?" discussion paper available at http://www.encore.nl.

Green, R. and D. Newbery (1992), "Competition in the British Electricity Spot Market", *Journal of Political Economy*, **100**(5), 929–953.

Griesmer, James H., Richard E. Levitan and M. Shubik (1967), "Toward a Study of Bidding Processes Part IV: Games with Unknown Costs". *Naval Research Logistics Quarterly*, **14**(4).

Haan, M.A., L. Schoonbeek, and B.M. Winkel (2005), "Experimental Results on Collusion. The role of information and communication", mimeo.

Hausman, Jerry A. and Gregory K. Leonard (1997), "Economic analysis of differentiated products mergers using real world data", *George Mason Law Review*, **5**(3), 321–346.

Hausman, J.A., G. Leonard and J.D. Zona (1994), "Competitive Analysis with Differentiated Products", *Annales D'Economie et de Statistique*, **34**, 159–180.

Hausman, J., G. Leonard and C. Vellturo (1996), "Market Definition under Price Discrimination", *Antitrust Law Journal*, **64**, 367–386.

Hobbs, B. (2001), "Linear Complementarity Models of Nash-Cournot Competition in Bilateral and POOLCO markets", *IEEE Transactions on Power Systems*, **16**(2), 194–202.

Holliday, A.J. and G.P. Hopper (1996), "Are there regimes of antitrust enforcement? An empirical analysis", Federal Reserve Bank of Philadelphia Working Paper 96-21, Philadelphia, October References.

Horn, H. and A. Wolinsky (1988), "Bilateral Monopolies and Incentive for Mergers", *The RAND Journal of Economics*, **19**, 408–419.

Huang, K.S. and B.-H. Lin (2000), "Estimation of Food Demand and Nutrient Elasticities from Household Survey Data", Technical Bulletin No. 1887, U.S. Department of Agriculture.

Huck, S., K.A. Konrad, W. Müller and H.T. Normann (2003), "Mergers and the perception of market power: The role of aspiration levels", mimeo.

Huck, S., H.T. Normann and J. Oechssler (2004), "Two are few and four are many: number effects in experimental oligopolies", *Journal of Economic Behavior and Organization*, **53**, 435–446.

Huyck, J.B. van, R.C. Battalio and R.O. Beil (1990), "Tacit Coordination Games, Strategic Uncertainty and Coordination Failure", American Economic Review, **80**, 234–248.

Inderst, R. and C. Wey (2003), "Bargaining, Mergers, and Technology Choice in Bilaterally Oligpolistic Industries", *The RAND Journal of Economics*, **34**(1), 1–19.

Inderst, R. and C. Wey (2004), "Buyer Power and Supplier Incentives", INSEAD working paper.

Ivaldi, M. and F. Verboven (2005), "Quantifying the Effects from Horizontal Mergers in European Competition Policy", forthcoming in *International Journal of Industrial Organization*.

Janssen, M.C.W., E. Dijkgraaf and E. Maasland (2004), *Literatuurstudie naar de kosten en baten van markttoezichthouders (review of literature on costs and benefits of market supervisors)*, Rotterdam: Erasmus University.

Joskow, P. and E. Kahn (2002), "A Quantitative Analysis of Pricing Behaviour in California's Wholesale Electricity Market During Summer 2000", *The Energy Journal*, **23**(4), 1–35.

Kehoe, T.J., T.N. Srinivasan and J. Whalley (2005), *Frontiers in Applied General Equilibrium Modeling*, Cambridge: Cambridge University Press.

Klemperer, Paul (2004), *Auctions: Theory and Practice*, Princeton: Princeton University Press.

Klemperer, Paul and M. Meyer (1989), "Supply Function Equilibria", *Econometrica*, **57**, 1243–1277.

Kolasky, W.J. and A.R. Dick (2003), "The Merger Guidelines and the Integration of Efficiencies into Antitrust Review of Horizontal Mergers", *Antitrust Law Journal*, **71**, 207–251.

Kreps, D.M. and J.A. Scheinkman (1983), "Quantity Pre-commitment and Bertrand Competition yield Cournot Outcomes", *The Bell Journal of Economics*, **14**, 326–337.

Lagerloef, J. and P. Heidhues (2005), "On the Desirability of an Efficiency Defense in Merger Control", forthcoming in *International Journal of Industrial Organization*.

Larson, N. and D. Salant (2003), "Equilibrium in Wholesale Electricity Markets", paper presented at Research Symposium on European Electricity Markets, The Hague.

Leonard, Robert J. (1994), "Reading Cournot, Reading Nash: the Creation and Stabilization of the Nash Equilibrium", *Economic Journal*, **104**(424),

492–511.

Lundval, K. (ed.) (2002), *The Pros and Cons of Merger Control: 10th Anniversary of the Swedish Competition Authority*, Stockholm: Swedish Competition Authority.

Lyons, B. and S. Davies (2003), *Efficiency Effects of a Global Merger in the Iron Ore Industry*, Final Report for DG Competition of the European Commission, 08.01.2003.

Martin, S. (1994), *Industrial Economics: Economic Analysis and Public Policy*, 2nd edition, Englewood Cliffs: Prentice Hall.

Maskin, E. (1992), "Auctions and privatization", in: H. Siebert (ed.), *Privatization: Symposium in Honor of Herbert Giersch*, Institut für Weltwirtschaft, University of Kiel, 115–136.

Mathiesen, Lars (2000), "Numerisk modellering av markeder med differensierte produkter", SNF report 11/00, Marts.

Milgrom, P. R. (1981), "Rational Expectations, Information Acquisition, and Competitive Bidding", *Econometrica*, **49**, 921–943.

Motta, M. (2004), *Competition Policy: Theory and Practice*, Cambridge: Cambridge University Press.

Nash, John (1950), "The Bargaining Problem", *Econometrica*, **18**(2), 155–162.

Nash, John (1951), "Non-cooperative games", *Annals of Mathematics*, **54**(2), 286–295, reprinted in Andrew F. Daughety (ed.), *Cournot Oligopoly*, Cambridge: Cambridge University Press, pp. 82–93, 1988.

Nash, John (1953), "Two-Person Cooperative Games", *Econometrica*, **21**(1), 128–140.

Neven, D. and L.-H. Röller (2002), "Discrepancies between Markets and Regulators: An Analysis of the First Ten Years of EU Merger Control", in Lundval (2002).

Neven, Damien J. and Lars-Hendrik Röller (2003), "On the Scope of Conflict in International, Merger Control", *Journal of Industry, Competition and Trade*, **3**(4), 235–249.

Neven D.J.and L.H. Röller (2005), "Consumer Surplus vs. Welfare Standard in a Political Economy Model of Merger Control", forthcoming in *International Journal of Industrial Organization*.

Nevo, Aviv (2000), "Mergers with Differentiated Products: The Case of the Ready-to-Eat Cereal Industry", *RAND Journal of Economics*, **31**(3), 395–421.

Nieuwenhuijsen and Nijkamp (2001), *Competition and Economic Performance*, EIM: Zoetermeer.

NMa (2003), "Besluit 3386/182 Nuon–Reliant Energy Europe", available at www.nmanet.nl.

NMa (2005), "Besluit 3386/407 Nuon–Reliant Energy Europe", available at www.nmanet.nl.

Nordic Competition Authorities (2003), "A Powerful Competition Policy".

OECD (2003), "Competition issues in the electricity sector", OECD document DAFFE/COMP 14.

Offerman, T.J.S. and J.J.M. Potters (2000), "Does Auctioning of Entry Licences Affect Consumers Prices? An Experimental Study", CentER Discussion Paper 2000–53.

Ortega Reichert, A. (1968), "Models for Competitive Bidding Under Uncertainty", Stanford University PhD thesis (and Technical Report No. 8, Department of Operations Research, Stanford University).

Osborne, Martin J. and Ariel Rubinstein (1990), *Bargaining and Markets*, San Diego: Academic Press.

Oxera (2004), *Costs and Benefits of Market Regulators. Part II Practical Application*, Oxford.

Patrick, R. and F. Wolak (2001), "The Impact of Market Rules and Market Structure on the Price Determination Process in the England and Wales Electricity Market", NBER Working Papers, 8248, National Bureau of Economic Research, Inc.

Pedersen, T., C. Smidt and P. Christiansen (2004), "Topics in Merger Control – Experiences from a recent merger in the Danish electricity sector", *World Competition Law and Economics Review*, 27(4), December.

Perry, M.K. and R.H. Porter (1985), "Oligopoly and the Incentive for Horizontal Merger", *American Economic Review*, 75(1), 219–227.

Peters, C. (2003), "Evaluating the Performance of Merger Simulation: Evidence from the U.S. Airline Industry", US DoJ working paper, January.

Pinkse, J. and M.S. Slade (2004), "Mergers, Brand Competition and the Price of a Pint", *European Economic Review*, 48, 617–643.

Pinkse, J., M.S. Slade and C. Brett (2002), "Spatial Price Competition: a Semiparametric Approach", *Econometrica*, 70(3), 1111–1153.

PwC, ABA (2003), "A Tax on Mergers? Surveying the Time and Costs to Business of Multi-jurisdictional Merger Reviews", *Business Law Journal*, 4, 3.

Raad voor de Mededinging (2001a), *Beslissing 2001-c/c-34*, Jaarverslag 2001, Bijlage, pp. 217–219.

Raad voor de Mededinging (2001b), *Beslissing 2001-c/c-41*, Jaarverslag 2001, Bijlage, pp. 246–249.

Röller, L.-H. and Pierre Buigues (2005), "The Office of the Chief Competition Economist at DG COMP", forthcoming.

Rubinstein, A. (1982), "Perfect Equilibria in a Bargaining Model", *Econometrica*, 50, 97–110.

Rudkevich, A. (1999), "Supply Function Equilibrium in Power Markets: Learning All the Way", TCA Technical Paper, 1299–1702.

Salant, S.W., S. Switzer and R.J. Reynolds (1983), "Losses from Horizontal Mergers: The Effects of an Exogenous Change in Industry Structure on Cournot-Nash Equilibrium", *Quarterly Journal of Economics*, **98**, 185–213.

Shubik M. and R. Levitan (1980), *Market Structure and Behavior*, Cambridge: Harvard University Press.

Stigler, G.J. (1964), "A theory of oligopoly", Journal of Political Economy, **72**, 44–61.

Stoft, S. (2002), "Power System Economics", Wiley: IEEE Press.

TenneT (2004), "TenneT en Statnett tekenen overeenkomst", Press release TenneT N.V., available at www.tennet.org.

Tirole, J. (1988), *The Theory of Industrial Organization*, Cambridge, Mass.: The MIT Press.

Tschantz, Steven, Philip Crooke and Luke Froeb (2000), "Mergers in Sealed Versus Oral Auctions", *International Journal of the Economics of Business*, **7**(2), 201–12.

US Department of Justice and US Federal Trade Commission (1992), *1992 Horizontal Merger Guidelines [with April 8, 1997, Revisions to Section 4 on Efficiencies]*.

Van Cayseele, P. (1994), *De Belgische Wet op de Mededinging: Concentraties in een Industrieel Economisch en Internationaal Juridisch Perspectief*, Antwerpen: Maklu.

Van Cayseele P. (2002), "The Bounds Approach to Antitrust", in A. Cucinotta, R. Pardolesi and R. van den Bergh (eds), *Post-Chicago Developments in Antitrust Law*, Cheltenham, UK and Northampton, MA, USA: Edward Elgar, pp. 87–107.

Van Cayseele P. and D. Furth (2001), "Two is not too Many for Monopoly", *Journal of Economics*, **74**(3), 231–258.

Van Cayseele P., J. Konings and J. De Loecker (2003), *Merger Review: How much of Industry is affected in an International Perspective?*, C.E.S. Discussion Paper Series 03.15, K.U. Leuven.

Vesterdorf, Bo (2004), "Standard of Proof in Merger Cases: Reflections in the Light of Recent Case Law of the Community Courts", Speech to the BIICL Third Annual Merger Control Conference.

Vickrey, William (1961), "Counterspeculation, Auctions, and Competitive Sealed Tenders", *Journal of Finance*, **16**(1), 8–37.

Vives, X. (1990), "Nash Equilibrium with Strategic Complements", *Journal of Mathematical Economics*, **19**(3), 305–321.

Vlaamse Havencommissie (2003), *Jaaroverzicht Vlaamse Havens*, SERV, Brussels, 136 p.

Walker, M. (2005), "The New Merger Regulation and Horizontal Guidelines: will they make a Difference?", in *Competition & Antitrust Review 2005*, 3rd edition, Colchester, UK: Euromoney Yearbook 2005.

Warzynski, F. (2003), "The Causes and Consequences of Sector-level Job Flows in Poland", *Economics of Transition*, **11**(2), 357–381.

Werden, Gregory J. (1996), "A Robust Test for Consumer Welfare Enhancing Mergers Among Sellers of Differentiated Products", *Journal of Industrial Economics*, **44**(4), 409–413.

Werden, Gregory J. (1997), "Simulating the Effects of Differentiated Products Mergers: a Practical Alternative to Structural Merger Policy", *George Mason Law Review*, **5**(3), 363–386.

Werden, G.J. (2000), "Expert Report in United States v. Interstate Bakeries Corp. and Continental Baking Co.", *International Journal of the Economics of Business*, **7**, 139–148.

Werden G. (2005), "Merger Simulation: Potentials and Pitfalls", in P. van Bergeijk and E. Kloosterhuis, *Modelling European Merger: Theory, Competition Policy and Case Studies*, Cheltenham, UK and Northampton, MA, USA: Edward Elgar.

Werden, Gregory J. and Luke M. Froeb (1994), "The Effects of Mergers in Differentiated Products Industries: Logit Demand and Merger Policy", *Journal of Law, Economics, & Organization*, **10**(2), 407–426.

Werden, Gregory J. and Luke M. Froeb (1996), "Simulation as an Alternative to Structural Merger Policy in Differentiated Products Industries", in Malcolm Coate and Andrew Kleit (eds), *The Economics of the Antitrust Process*, Boston: Kluwer Academic Publishers, pp. 65–88.

Werden, Gregory J. and Luke M. Froeb (1998), "The Entry-Inducing Effects of Horizontal Mergers", *Journal of Industrial Economics*, **46**(4), 525-543.

Werden, Gregory J. and Luke M. Froeb (2002), "Calibrated Economic Models Add Focus, Accuracy, and Persuasiveness to Merger Analysis", in Swedish Competition Authority (ed.), *The Pros and Cons of Merger Control*, pp. 63–82.

Werden, G.J. and L.M. Froeb (2005), "Unilateral Competitive Effects of Horizontal Mergers: Theory and Application Through Merger Simulation", forthcoming in P. Buccirossi (ed.), *Handbook of Antitrust Economics*, Cambridge, Mass.: MIT Press.

Werden, Gregory J. and George Rozanski (1994), "The Application of Section 7 to Differentiated Products Industries: the Market Delineation Dilemma', *Antitrust*, **8**(3), 40–43.

Werden, Gregory J., Luke M. Froeb and David T. Scheffman (2004), "A *Daubert* Discipline for Merger Simulation", *Antitrust*, **18**(3), 89–95.

Williams, E. and R. Rosen (1999), "A Better Approach to Market Power Analysis", Tellus Institute, Boston.

Williamson, O.E. (1968), "Economies as an Antitrust Defense: Welfare Tradeoffs", *The American Economic Review*, **58**(1), 18–36.

Wilson, R (1969), "Competitive Bidding with Disparate Information," *Management Science*, **15**, 446–448.

Wolfram, C. (1999), "Measuring Duopoly Power in the British Electricity Spot Market", *American Economic Review*, **89**(4), 805–826.

Index